Crime in Japan

Also by Dag Leonardsen

JAPAN AS A LOW-CRIME NATION

Crime in Japan

Paradise Lost?

Dag Leonardsen
Lillehammer University College, Norway

First published 2010 by
PALGRAVE MACMILLAN

Palgrave Macmillan in the UK is an imprint of Macmillan Publishers Limited, registered in England, company number 785998, of Houndmills, Basingstoke, Hampshire RG21 6XS.

Palgrave Macmillan in the US is a division of St Martin's Press LLC, 175 Fifth Avenue, New York, NY 10010.

Palgrave Macmillan is the global academic imprint of the above companies and has companies and representatives throughout the world.

Palgrave® and Macmillan® are registered trademarks in the United States, the United Kingdom, Europe and other countries.

ISBN: 978–0–230–23554–0 hardback

This book is printed on paper suitable for recycling and made from fully managed and sustained forest sources. Logging, pulping and manufacturing processes are expected to conform to the environmental regulations of the country of origin.

A catalogue record for this book is available from the British Library.

Library of Congress Cataloging-in-Publication Data

Leonardsen, Dag.
    Crime in Japan : paradise lost? / Dag Leonardsen.
      p. cm.
    Includes bibliographical references.
    ISBN 978–0–230–23554–0
      1. Crime – Japan. 2. Japan – Social conditions – 1989– I. Title.

HV7112.L46 2010
364.952—dc22
                                           2010002700

10 9 8 7 6 5 4 3 2 1
19 18 17 16 15 14 13 12 11 10

Printed and bound in Great Britain by
CPI Antony Rowe, Chippenham and Eastbourne

To Klang – for your inclusiveness

Contents

Illustrations

Tables

Figures

Preface and Acknowledgements

On my last trip to Japan in 2008, I was one evening sitting by the fire-place with my Japanese colleague and friend in his cottage. After a glass of *sake* he asked me about my impression of his country of today. I think I answered, perhaps in a culturally 'correct' way, that I held *ambiguous* feelings. Having read my Japanese newspapers (English version) daily for many years I was certainly aware of the blue moods that had entered this society over several years. Nevertheless, I was quite surprised by the grave tone in the voice of my colleague, when answering my return of the same question, by declaring: 'there is no optimism any more; there is no future to believe in'. After some further elaboration of his answer, I gradually decoded his message in a Durkheimian direction: it was a diagnosis of *anomie* (confusion about norms and confusion about aims) that my friend presented. Japan had reached a fork in the road. An era seemed to have reached its end. Something new had to come into being. In a situation of transition, I heard a message about a Japan that was run by a leadership without visions and without alternatives that people, especially among an increasing group of *outsiders*, could support. Japan was like a big tanker with no steering and with no competent politi-cians to take the lead. This had created a situation of disillusionment and a loss of hope for the future.

As will become clear throughout this book, I have reached much of the same conclusion as my colleague. Japan has, as Morishima (2000), an economic theorist, declares, come to a *deadlock,* and Morishima is depressingly clear in his judgement: Japan 'is unlikely to recover in the twenty-first century, and will instead gradually slide down into the depths'. Journalist McGregor (1996), who lived in Japan through the economic crisis in the early 1990s, adds to the above commentary by describing Japan as a 'creaky house of cards on the brink of collapse' (cover text). I am not in a position fully to validate these gloomy proph-ecies, but there are surprisingly many, strongly pessimistic, diagnoses about the state of this society. This goes for economic matters as well as for the broader cultural situation. When crime, suicide, and social retreatism (discussed in this book) seem to have increased for some years, I think these changes should be understood in this broader context.

In the present book I am not painting a very bright picture of the *trend* in how social conditions have developed in present-day Japan.

So this is not a very optimistic book, and it is definitely not a book about 'quick fixes'. Like quite a few other sociologists, I regard postmodern societies (like Japan) to be social constructions that have reached a point of development that call for deep reflexion, not primarily regarding *means,* but most of all regarding *measures.* A discussion about social prevention (*in casu* crime, suicide, and social retreatism) that does not reflect upon what Bauman (2004) designates 'the production of human waste' in modern society, and that does not open up a debate on *distributive justice,* is deemed to fall short of the fundamental challenges of our time. As long as exclusionary forces, so to speak, are built into the logic of modernisation, the production of social order in modern societies is facing some serious challenges. As will be documented in this book, Japan is no exception to this rule. However, with a cultural tradition that in many respects is different from Western societies, Japan is facing some distinctive problems which turn upon a special tension between traditionalism and modernism, cultural rooting and economic 'uprooting'. While complex social problems during times of neo-liberalism have increasingly been turned into criminal problems or eventually neglected, such a reaction is especially precarious in Japan. With a strong emphasis on consensus seeking and shame, problems of depression might evolve. It is against this broad background that I address my research topic: is Japan, usually known to be a low-crime and socially inclusive society, about to become a 'lost paradise', and what are the implications of the way present social problems are tackled?

While this book clearly deserves its place within the canon of what has been called 'the sociology of worry', I feel a strong urge to touch a more optimistic chord in this preface. Postmodern *societies* do not always offer the conditions that produce thoughtful consideration and care. Nevertheless, there are actually a lot of nice *human beings* out there! I have met quite a few of them, and *not least* in Japan. I am obviously not the only one. A common compliment about Japanese people is that their kindness and hospitality is 'spontaneous and springs from inherent goodwill and genuine concern for people' (De Mente, 1992: 32). After more than ten years of close contact with Japanese people it is tempting to make De Mente's judgement a 'datum'; this is how they are. However, don't let me be too grandiloquent in the opening of this book. My gratitude will be addressed to my own 'significant others'.

In preparing the present book I have been largely dependent on the data I have received from the Ministry of Justice and the National Police Agency/Police Policy Research Center/National Police Academy of Japan. First and foremost, I want to thank Kei Someda for organising meetings together with his colleagues (Shunko Watanabe, Taihei Mizukami, Yuichiro Tachi and Kiyofumi Koita) and supporting me with all the data I have requested. Questions I have had have been answered in written as well as in oral form. As (at that time) Senior Researcher at the Research Department, Research and Training Institute, the Ministry of Justice, Someda was very obliging and helpful. If the phrase, 'without whose help this book would never have appeared' ever had validity, it would be here. At the National Research Institute of Police Science, Yutaka Harada, Director and Takeshi Okabe, Researcher in Criminology were very supportive, as were Ko Shikata, Chief Police Superintendent at the National Police Agency and his colleagues from the National Research Institute of Police Science: Takayuki Miyadera, Senior Research Psychologist, and Taeko Wachi and Eriko Kuhara, both Research Psychologists. During this time I have also had the pleasure to meet the former Deputy Director at the Research and Training Institute, now Guest Professor, Takeshi Koyanagi. I greatly appreciate that he shared his insight into the criminological world of Japan with me. The same goes for Professor Setsuo Miyazawa, Professor Hiroshi Tsutomi (University of Shizuoka) and Dr Robert Yoder (Chuo University), with whom I had the pleasure to discuss my research topics. Professor Koichi Hamai (Ryukoku University) and Principal Lecturer Tom Ellis (University of Portsmouth) have been stimulating discussants when we have met at conferences and, as will be apparent when reading my book, their research on moral panics in Japan has contributed significantly to my own conception of crime in Japan.

From the very start of my Japan research I have had the advantage of getting closer to Japanese everyday life through my good friends, Professor Hiroshi Komuku and Professor Kazunori Matsumura. They have not only brought me into contact with a lot of exciting and knowledgeable people but they have also showed me a hospitality that I feel has given me a platform in Japan. Chie Asada, who in earlier years was a student at my college in Norway, has also been a good support for me while travelling in Japan.

In my own country I have received valuable comments from close, supportive, *and* critical voices in my own university, Lillehammer University College. Assistant Professors Bjarne Øvrelid, Hallgeir Brumoen, and Håkon Glommen Eriksen: I have a lot of good things to say about you! Also, an absolute necessity for getting this book finished was the economic support from my university. This, together with generous support from my colleagues at the Faculty of Health and Social Studies, has more than once made me stop and think: Yes, I can stay for some more years in academia.

Finally, the main handshake: Dr Monica Barry (the University of Strathclyde) was kind enough to do the proof reading that was absolutely necessary to bring my message outside Norway. But more important, with her keen eye for structure and logical consistency, she has helped me get this project through during a period when I could not see the wood for too many trees. Also, generously sharing her Japan contacts with me has been most helpful for my research. Thank you!

1
Japan – Quo Vadis?

In his introductory textbook on Japan, Duncan McCargo (2004: 1) declares that 'You are now entering contested territory. The nature of contemporary Japan is hotly debated by specialists and observers both inside and outside Japan'. It seems that no matter the topic, different scholars will most certainly end up with different perspectives and answers regarding Japanese society. The logical consequence for McCargo was to apply three alternative perspectives (mainstream, revisionist and culturalist) when presenting his overview of *Contemporary Japan*[1]. The interpretation of Japanese history, political economy, social structures and social policy, governing and political structures, socialisation and civil society and Japan's external relations – all these topics are presented with three different interpretations in the aforementioned book. In other words, the truth about Japanese society invites an answer that postmodernists will love. There is not one but many narratives to be told about Japan.

However, when it comes to the presentation of the crime situation in Japan the story has usually been less chaotic than what McCargo describes. To be sure, there are different versions regarding the interpretation of the crime picture in Japan, and, when it comes to explaining the remarkably *low* crime rates, some scholars will stress cultural explanations while others attach more importance to economic dimensions. Nevertheless, criminologists have been in surprising accord in proclaiming Japan as one of the *Nations not obsessed with crime* (Adler, 1983). When crime is reduced to simple quantitative indicators and we exclude certain crimes (see below), few will dispute the uniqueness of Japanese society, at least until the 1990s. Accordingly, Japan has become the favourite country for criminologists who are looking for odd cases.

The story I am presenting in this book is about social change in Japan since the early 1990s. It is a *sociologically* oriented book, primarily about crime (coined 'striking out'), but also about those who in times of depression choose to withdraw from society (coined 'striking in') or who even seek the final exit: suicide. Japan, for many years having held the reputation as a low-crime nation, might at the turn of the century seem to have lost some of its positive recognition in this regard. Furthermore, during a decennium of economic decay it seems that Japan has turned into a more exclusionary and a more punitive society. The implications of this can be registered in the statistics about social withdrawal.

Why should a Western criminologist be interested in these topics? The answer to this question is closely linked to research topics I raised in my former book about *Japan as a Low-Crime Nation* (Leonardsen, 2004), which basically was about learning from cross-cultural studies. In that book, the main aim was to find out the enigma of low crime rates in Japan. Here I gave an overview of the crime situation (excluding white-collar crime, domestic crime, organised crime and traffic offenses) in Japan during the period 1950–90. I came to the conclusion that Japanese society deserved its status of uniqueness. While registered crime in most Western countries skyrocketed in the 1960s, 1970s and 1980s, Japan could boast of stability; in some areas one could even refer to *decreasing* trends. I also pointed to what I described as the 'Western welfare paradox', namely that modern welfare problems (crime, drug addiction, divorce and suicide, i.e. types of alienation) seemed to increase in proportion to preventive interventions in this part of the world. Affluent countries with well-educated social scientists and planning experts at their disposal were obviously not capable of curbing crime[2]. However, in Japan, where social spending as a percentage of GDP at the end of the last century was at the average OECD level of the 1960s (Esping-Andersen, 1997; Gould, 1993), tourist information books would in unison proclaim that, when travelling in Japan, one does 'not have to worry about personal security' (De Mente, 1992: 66).

These two observations (little traditional crime in Japan and Western governments' failure to create security for their citizens) had made Japan an extraordinarily interesting society to study. How did Japan succeed in suspending the criminological law that rapid modernisation and urbanisation automatically meant more crime? And how could it be that generous Western welfare states (like the Nordic countries) were less successful in preventing some types of social problems (e.g. crime, drug addiction and divorce) than a very lean Japanese welfare state? These were the challenges I tried to look into.

My answer to the *first* of my research problems (little crime in Japan) turned out to be a support of the *cultural* explanation of low-crime Japan. I presented three perspectives to understand the Japanese paradox, which in condensed form were:

a. Little crime because of *social or organisational structures*. Despite rapid economic and technological change Japan has remained a society of primary groups. People are (for good or bad) always visible and reciprocally dependent on each other since they are constantly included in some type of small group and since they always are in some kind of dependency relation to other persons. This perspective implies a *structural* explanation to low crime, but where the structural elements are an expression of deeper cultural characteristics[3].

b. Little crime because of the *dominating values at the collective level*. Infused with Confucian, Buddhist and Shinto values Japanese people represent what I have called a defensive shame culture[4]. Principles of self-sacrifice are cultivated throughout society and it is very important to conform and adapt to the common stock of 'authorised', collective values. An individual Japanese will in all spheres of life be aware that she/he is always representing a broader 'we' that one is responsible for. This perspective implies that it is the totality of societal values – emitted from all significant social institutions – that contributes to the unique crime pattern.

c. Little crime because of *values transmitted through the socialisation process*. The collective normative regulation is supported at the micro level. In Japanese society there is a strong link between culture at large (society as a *sui generis* phenomenon) and ethical principles internalised in the personality of each individual (as 'conscience' or 'reason'). The personal codex of reserve is mirroring the collective codex of subjection and adaptation. The ways people are socialised in Japan make them little prepared to 'act out' (except when they leave their 'circles of obligation', Benedict, 1967). Japan is a typical representative of what Haley (1998) calls an 'apology and pardon culture' (cf. Hosoi and Nishimura (1999); Yoshida, 2000).

It was in the unique combination of these three perspectives (*plus* a stable and an inclusive economy) that I found the clue to understanding why Japan had become the 'darling of all criminologists'. Japan could be described as a low-crime society because the citizens were 'non-criminogen' (socialisation), and because the society as a macro structure (cultural values and organisation) was 'non-criminogen'. While Western societies have been described by the 'bowling alone' syndrome, i.e. people have become increasingly disconnected from each other, social structures have disintegrated and there is a serious loss of reciprocity, etc. (Putnam, 2001), Japan seemed to have preserved face-to-face relations through its unique group structure. While Western societies had reached a degree of pluralisation that had threatened predictability and consistency, I argued that Japan had preserved a more uniform base of values. While Western societies increasingly had given priority to individual freedom[5], socialisation in Japan was all about creating a group affinity through the sharing of common and strictly specified rules for conduct. At the micro level Japanese people were taught adaptation, patience and subjection to society at large, and they knew that they were always observed by *seken* (the others)[6]. When confronting characteristics of Japanese society with classical criminological theories about crime (Leonardsen, 2004), it became very plausible that low crime rates in Japan were more than a statistical illusion.

If these observations were to carry some credibility I simultaneously warned against simplistic conclusions. Despite the fact that a society 'functions' well regarding crime, one should not conclude that this is a 'good society'. Social integration, as measured by a simple crime index, does not really tell much about important qualities of this society. Japan has been ascribed a lot of negative labels, e.g. a 'Nanny State', a 'Suppressive State' or a 'Brezhnev State', and (in general) has been characterised as an authoritarian, hierarchical and patriarchal culture. If there has been broad agreement about describing Japan as a low-crime nation, there was certainly no corresponding agreement regarding what 'deeper' testimony this could give about the soundness of Japanese society. Little crime is not synonymous to social integration, it is not synonymous to freedom and open democracy and it is not synonymous to what Durkheim described as a morally integrated society. I made this statement explicit in my former book since a *description* of the low crime characteristics of a society could easily be interpreted as a normative *recommendation* to be copied. It should not. There is no scientific answer to the best recipe for the 'good society'. To Braithwaite (1989), Japan represents a communitarian example to learn from, while quite a few other authors (Dale, 1986; McCormack, 1996; McGregor, 1996; Sugimoto, 1997) have held far more critical views. Nevertheless, in times where Western societies have been keenly discussing remedies against an asserted 'loss of community', 'loss of social trust' and how social order could be reconstituted[7], and in times where 'social capital' has become one of the most popular concepts within Western sociology, I pointed out that we should allow ourselves to look at Japan as a *Lehrstück* (as Bertolt Brecht called it); not as a model to copy but (for good or bad) as an inspiration for imaginative thought.

My answer to the *second* research problem (why Western countries have failed to prevent crime) was primarily in the tradition of 'critical criminology'. My argument was that a low-crime society cannot be attained by way of delimited, ingenious social engineering interventions, but has to address society at large. In Young's (1999: 140) words, 'zero-tolerance of crime must mean zero-tolerance of inequality if it is to mean anything'. This perspective has its roots back to the founding fathers of sociology and implies that the abolition of crime, or at least, an essential reduction of crime, is possible only 'under certain social arrangements' (Taylor, Walton and Young, 1973: 281). These arrangements are first and foremost about curbing inequalities of wealth and power, about social inclusion and about creating a society based on solidarity and justice. Central to my argument was that governmental institutions in competitive market societies cannot create social harmony by way of *administrative* interventions unless one pays due attention to these basic sociological principles. In modern societies, social life is to a large extent subordinated under the imperative of the market[8] and this has implications for the crime situation (Currie (1998); Taylor, 1990). Community safety in this perspective is primarily a question of giving people a stake in society (Sennett, 2004) and thereby giving them recognition (Barry, 2006). If we are to address the question of crime prevention in more than a superficial way, my argument in *Japan as a low-crime society* was that we have to discuss harm rather than crime, social justice rather than criminal justice and discourses of rights rather than discipline and control (Scraton, 2002).

In sum, my interest for studying crime in Japan in my earlier book was twofold: an increasing discontentment with the *incapacity* of Western governments (even the egalitarian Nordic welfare states) to address the crime problem in an efficient way and, closely linked, an interest in a *cultural* interpretation of little crime in a highly modernised society. Having been critical of the New Right's attempts at redrawing moral lines as a reaction to increasing crime (i.e. 'blaming the victim'), Japan appeared to me to be a case where *cultural values* and a *group oriented social structure* have had a strong say regarding the crime situation. The logical question following this observation was to ask if there was a lesson to be learnt from Japan. I concluded that, yes, the recognition that 'individual freedom cannot be gained against society' (as Durkheim formulated it) was what Japan could remind individualistic Western countries about. Important to notice was that I 'extended' this message to include individual *rights* (rights to participate in productive as well as reproductive spheres) as well as *obligations* for the individual (implying values like altruism and other-directedness). However, from a Western point of view I characterised Japan ('ideal type') as a 'Hypernomia' (Dahrendorf, 1985) type of society (people being 'over-socialised'), with too little attention given to values like individual autonomy and individual rights. If Western societies (at the other extreme of the ideal type) approached an 'Anomia' ('normless') type of society, the challenge was defined as designing a compromise-like 'Synnomia' (Adler, 1983); a society that was able to include Durkheim's principle of social solidarity (where the individual recognises that dependence on society is a liberating dependency), as well as Young's (2007: 212) principle of 'a politics of diversity' (pluralism, hybridisation and crossover).

But then in the early 1990s 'shock waves' hit Japanese society. An economic setback (starting in 1990) together with some other incidents (more in Chapter 3), induced a 'new mood' in Japan. Towards the end of the twentieth century the Ministry of Justice had to admit that Japan could no longer adorn itself with the title 'The Safest Country in the World'. Not only was registered crime indubitably up, but a general uncertainty increasingly prevailed in society. A survey published in 2002 found that nearly twice as many Japanese felt their lives had got worse in the past five years as those who thought their lives had improved, and, by a 4-to-1 margin, Japanese expressed that when today's children come of age, life would be worse than at the present time. Only Guatemalans were gloomier in their expectations for the future (Zielenziger, 2002). A general (and steep) increase in the *fear* of crime was a part of this picture. This very *un*fortunate situation for Japanese society opened a very fortunate opportunity for criminologists, namely to analyse which impacts had seemingly had such a strong, negative impact on Japanese society. If Japan until 1990 had been an interesting case for studying characteristics of a typical low-crime society, one could now look at Japan as a country which could disclose 'significant variables' that apparently had changed the social web there. If the special type of Japanese 'Confucian Capitalism' had contributed to social stability during times of prosperity, then the challenge now was to find out why, under the new circumstances, this (again: *apparently*) was no longer the case. If public figures about crime, suicide and *hikikomori* (social withdrawal) were valid; what were the important changes in

Japanese society that had contributed to this development? These are the research questions that have led to the present book.

Against this background I shall in the next chapters look into the following interconnected topics:

Chapter 2: What are the main cultural characteristics of Japanese society (e.g. that are of an obvious *criminological* relevance)? When writing about processes of social change one has to know something about the country and the culture where these changes take place. Data about crime, suicide, etc. have to be interpreted in their relevant *cultural context*. The challenge represented by different types of social change will vary according to different types of 'meaning universes'. A suicide in Japan is not 'the same' as a suicide in Norway. Revolts among Japanese youth are registered with a different instrument and a different scale in Japan than in England. Different cultures have different 'sensibilities' and thereby varying ways of reacting to one and the same social impulse. While an earthquake in Japan will be registered at the same 'Richter scale' in Japan and Italy, and an equal impulse will give the same deflection in both countries, this is not the case with social problems. Accordingly, we need to know something about the *context* where change takes place. As we shall see, the concept of 'moral panic[9]' has to be interpreted in its cultural context to be correctly decoded. This is why in Chapter 2 I will give an elementary introduction to Japanese culture in order to better understand the soil that social changes percolate into. The main message is that, in spite of being a culture of endurance and serenity, minor contraventions of regulations (especially among the youth) and minor social disturbances in society are easily interpreted in ways that might be described as overdramatised. The 'instrument' used to register social changes is more sensitive than in most Western countries, and, accordingly, this should be kept in mind when evaluating the *extent* of change that has taken place. Also, one should notice that throughout history, Japanese society has been a culture where the 'mainstreaming' and the 'moulding' of its citizens into a compliant and consensus oriented group of people has been central. 'Obedience', 'endurance', 'adaptation' and 'discipline': these are important values that permeate Japanese society. As we shall see, this has huge implications for how people tackle adversity.

Chapter 3: What kind of social, economic and cultural changes have really taken place in Japan since the early 1990s? This book takes a broad perspective on crime and social problems. As a sociologist, I regard varieties of deviant behaviour as reports on the state of society (which does not exclude a *volitional* perspective on crime, e.g. regarding crime as an *action!*). Accordingly, to understand fully the 'crime picture' in one particular country one has to know not only some general cultural characteristics of this country, but also main empirical data regarding economic, socio-structural and cultural dimensions. Chapter 3 gives an overview of the most important changes in Japan relating to this. As already indicated, Japanese society has faced significant *economic* changes since 1990. Although there are no simple causal links between economic stagnation (e.g. unemployment) and crime, economic safety and predictability are definitely of huge relevance for a variety of social problems, including crime (Grover, 2008; Watts, 1996). Therefore, I give the essential background information for this topic. Social change is also about changes in *social structures and cultural values*. While there is little doubt that Japan has experienced turmoil in the sphere of the economy during the last 20 years, it is more complicated to interpret changes along the sociocultural dimension. Part of the contemporary discussion in Japan is linked to an assertion of a general moral decay, with increasing crime as a natural concomitant. Special attention has been paid to the younger generation, and politicians as well as media have joined in expressing a general worry about the situation. Typical accusations presented are that the family and the school have failed in how they raise children. Accordingly, in Chapter 3 I ask to what extent these allegations are valid. Have these important agents of socialisation changed regarding their social structure and regarding the values they have conveyed? Is the famous Japanese group structure about to deteriorate? Are Japanese citizens less bonded than before? A short version of my answer is that the way children in Japan are 'morally raised' can hardly explain the asserted change in crime patterns. However, one should not disregard the negative impact that increasing rates of divorce and unemployment in combination with meagre social benefits have had on children's social environment. Neither should one disregard the effect that increasing uncertainty and pessimism among adults have had on what could be called a general loss of 'commitment to society', among the young as well as among adults. This loss of optimism and commitment probably does represent one of the biggest challenges to Japanese society today, and this is perhaps what should be the focus rather than the present outcry about 'moral decay' among youth.

Chapter 4: 'Striking out': has there really been an increase in crime in Japan? Having looked into changes in the economic sphere and the sphere of socialisation (family and school) I then try to answer if Japan still deserves the label of being a low-crime nation? While in my former book I concluded that Japanese 'superstructure' to a large extent had been preserved until 1990, and that this (together with a steady-growth, inclusionary economy) could explain low crime rates, in Chapter 4 I look at the eventual repercussions of economic and sociocultural changes for crime. The chapter starts with a documentation of an extensive *fear of crime* that has raged in this country for some years. It then discusses what the 'real' crime situation looks like (based on public statistics). Could Japan still be described as a system of 'victimless capitalism' (McGregor, 1996: 36) or have 'modernity' and global economic turbulence finally left their impression on traditional Japan[10]? I have to go into quite a few details in this presentation, partly because I try to trace how (especially) economic turbulence has affected *different* types of crimes, and partly because the exact year for *when* eventual changes have taken place is important for discussing if the registered crime increase is *real* (which is disputed). My conclusion is that crime in Japan actually has gone up (even though not to the extent that the government gives the impression of), and that the economic recession during the 1990s represents a main triggering cause for these changes.

Chapter 5: What is the authoritative reaction to the new crime situation? Japan has by some scholars been described as a country focusing on reintegration rather than on retribution concerning reactions to deviancy; it has been described as a solidaric rather than an egoistic society when it comes to societal values. Others have refuted this picture as being basically flawed – that such a description at best applies to the front stage rather than to the back stage of this society. Anyhow, being lenient on crime is certainly easier when law and order prevails than during times of increasing lawlessness. Authoritative reactions to crime during the last 15 years can bring this dispute about what kind of society Japan 'really' is one step further. In this chapter I present three analytical approaches as the starting point for understanding crime. To what extent do Japanese authorities interpret crime as generated by economic forces (unemployment, inequality and poverty), to what extent do they interpret them as generated by sociocultural forces (moral decay, dissolution of primary groups) and, finally, to what extent do they interpret crime in a social constructivist perspective, i.e. as a result of labelling processes generated in the political-administrative system? I conclude that at the rhetorical level, a wide, social scientific perspective can be identified (i.e. economic as well as sociocultural perspectives). However, when it comes to the sphere of *Realpolitik*, it seems that more punitive reactions dominate. In conclusion, Japan does not deserve a reputation as being a society of 'nurturant acceptance'.

Chapter 6: 'Striking in': to what extent does the economic crisis generate social retreatism (hikikomori and suicide) in society? As pointed out in Chapter 2, Japanese culture promotes endurance and discipline, adaptation and consensus, as cherished values. The individual is not supposed to bother others with their private troubles or to fight for their own rights. Silent perseverance is appreciated. What implications does economic depression and turbulence have for people's well-being? To what extent do Japanese citizens confront increasing unemployment, economic inequalities and increasing poverty by blaming themselves? In this chapter I take a closer look at the 'meaning' of suicide and social withdrawal in a culture like Japan's. To me, it seems that Confucian vertical structures and principles of shaming and blaming might have had a positive effect on Japanese economy after the Second World War. However, in times of decay I think there is a real danger that the same principles will create extensive mental problems in this society. In a culture that invites silent suffering rather than outspoken criticism when problems occur there will be a short distance between stoic perseverance and stoic withdrawal, which, in turn, might pave the road to different types of mental suffering. For those unable to compete in a liberalised and increasingly competitive economy, withdrawal to the private sphere (youth isolating themselves in their rooms) and/or committing suicide might become the preferred solution.

Chapter 7: Japan – a caring and crime preventive society? Each of the research questions raised in the preceding chapters should be regarded as 'preparatory' topics for approaching the overarching challenge in this book: finding out to what extent and in which way Japanese culture has some 'built-in' qualities that are important to prevent crime and, eventually, which of these qualities might have deteriorated during the last few years. As underlined throughout this book, my criminological curiosity does not refer to how some kind of social engineering techniques might help inhibit some types of crimes in some types of situations. Rather I am interested in what has been defined as the 'root causes' of crime. To me, these root causes are partly related to how people are economically (labour market) and institutionally (primary groups) situated, i.e. that people really have a stake in society, and partly related to belongingness to a joint community of values. In the final chapter I try to pull together the loose strings from the preceding chapters, both related to the present status of Japanese society and regarding what lessons can be taught from having studied Japan through boom and bust. Is Japan most of all a care-taking, non-repressive culture that contradicts 'Darwinian-like' processes triggered by 'competitive forces' in society, or are other characteristics more appropriate? From a Western perspective, what are the main challenges Japanese society is facing today? While running a risk of being too pretentious I end this chapter by pointing out a few points of policy that I think Japan should be heeding in the coming years if low crime should be attained by 'acceptable' measures.

From what is said above it should be clear that my ambitions with the present book are quite broad and they clearly touch upon *policy*-related questions. To me, a crime prevention strategy that is worth its name cannot avoid being involved in discussions of value conflicts and power structures in society. At the same time, there is no scientific answer to what should be a 'suitable amount of crime' (Christie, 2004) in a given society. Since this is a question about finding a fair distribution of rights and obligations, about finding the trade off between safety and autonomy, between social control and individual freedom, finding adequate crime prevention strategies is unavoidably a question involving value judgements. Furthermore, the complexity of discussing this topic becomes obvious when studying 'foreign' cultures. Does not a *collectivistic* Japanese culture represent a total 'package' of values that has to be judged as an interconnected totality? To be honest, I find this a challenging question with no simple answers. I do want to underline the importance of avoiding ethnocentric evaluations of other cultures. The intention with Chapter 2 is exactly to give due space for the reader to understand the complex web of values that in sum represent 'Japanese culture'[11]. Cross-cultural analyses will always have to start with gaining deep insight into indigenous cultures. However, at the same time it is important to maintain the ability to keep an outsider's distanced view on the same culture. Since challenges like these are central to much of the discussions I address in this book, let me elaborate a bit further some of these value-related questions. In which way could sociology be in a position to make value judgements about a whole country?

Generally speaking, Japan is a culture of shame and subordination of the individual to a collective will. It might seem that this type of culture has protected well (but in a controversial way!) against crime in times of prosperity and progress. The heavy weight put on endurance, acceptance and deference (*enryo*) certainly creates a climate of consensus seeking that is of relevance to the total crime situation in society. In times of progress one can imagine that a stress on perseverance will *reinforce* good fortune. However, in times of hardship it is an open question to what extent such qualities will trigger reactions in the direction of passive acceptance and personal blaming or, rather, more aggressive behaviour.

When asking how well Japanese culture protects its citizens in times of economic decay I will not analyse the Japanese welfare regime (i.e. institutional arrangements). Rather, I am interested in finding out what the citizens' de facto behaviour can tell about how well 'Japanese values' and 'Japanese principles of social organisation' succeed in counteracting *crime, suicides* and *hikikomori* during economic setbacks. Has the image of Japan (until the 1990s) as a society of social harmony been nothing but an expression of a happy alloy of economic prosperity and strong discipline, or has it also been an expression of tolerance and inclusion? As has often been pointed out, it is in times of decay that the true quality of a society can be told. In that case, the moment of truth for Japanese society has come. In this book I involve myself in a normative evaluation of Japanese society in the way that I use empirical data about the three referred types of social problems to 'judge' how well Japan protects its citizens when economic problems occur.

If Dore (1986, 1987) is correct in arguing that the Japanese never have caught up with Adam Smith, and if it is true that trust relationships and altruistic attitudes are built into some type of holistic philosophy in the Japanese society, then these qualities should show to advantage when stagnation and pessimism occur. If Japan really represents a kind of communitarian and solidaric ideal, then we should expect to find this value foundation flourishing during recession. Accordingly, what has happened in Japanese society since the early 1990s should be of great empirical and theoretical interest. If Japanese culture was successful in inoculating against crime 1950–90, how 'strong' has the cultural dimension been when hardship occurs? Is Japan a society that protects the most vulnerable individuals during a slump? Is Japan a society where attachment and bonding persist when economic forces pull in exclusionary directions? Is Japan a society where the centrifugal forces in the sociocultural system neutralise the centripetal forces in the economic system? Does the *collectivistic* Japanese culture also function in a collectivistic way during hardship, or does it rather *privatise* problems that occur, considering each man an isolated island? When Bauman (2001) argues that 'we all need to gain control over the conditions under which we struggle with the challenges of life – but for most of us such control can be gained only *collectively*' (italics in original) – the challenging question is to what extent Japan offers *collective* and non-repressive solutions to individual misfortunes. These are basic questions I approach an answer to in the final chapter of this book.

From what I have presented above, it follows that I want to use Japan as a case for tracing some fundamental and classical challenges in social science and philosophy. At the most fundamental level these questions relate to how we balance between the *individual* and *society*; how we balance between *autonomy/freedom* and *social control*; how we give space to individual *agency* within a broader framework of communal *obligations*; and, finally, how we find the trade off between *pluralism* and a *common stock of values*. Or, to bring the challenge up to the present-day situation: how do we confront the *Vertigo of late modernity* (Young, 2007) without resorting to authoritarian and suppressive means? Apparently, the challenge implied in these questions has reached present-day Japan. Confronted with a continuous increase in registered crime a leader article in the *Japan Echo* 2004 (Iwao, 2004) went directly into this delicate dilemma by claiming: 'The mass media and the public must grasp the connection between their insistence on personal privacy and the deterioration in public safety, and people need to start shouldering some of the responsibility for maintaining law and order'. If people request safety they must recognise their communal obligations; this is what is announced here, and, I think, such a message has validity in Western countries as well.

Let me finally make a few statements about the concept of 'crime'. In *Japan as a low-crime nation* I was focusing on the so-called traditional, predatory types of crime. This is the crime that within classical criminology has been regarded as a symptom of social disorganisation. As mentioned, my main perspective in that book was to regard crime primarily as an expression of social and material exclusion, i.e. as a strike against the established society from people who (by definition) had loosened their bonds to society. The *low* crime rate in Japan was accordingly seen as an expression of a society with a tightly knit social web. Japan distinguished itself as an inclusive, but also (in some ways) as a *repressive*, society. In the first section of my present book I will stick to the same delimitation of what I mean by crime. White-collar crime and organised crime are too complex topics to be included in my discussion (see Leonardsen, 2004: 35–38, 46–49, for further arguments regarding this exclusion). I do recognise that both these 'fields' are central to drawing the full picture about 'criminal Japan', and, as I underlined in my former book, available research makes Japan's uniqueness concerning those crimes dubious. However, in the present book I will in addition to 'traditional crime' also make a few remarks on *domestic violence,* since this is of direct relevance for the way we interpret the statistics on violence in general in Japan. When registered offenses of violence have increased in the 1990s this is not unrelated to the increased inclination to report domestic violence to the police.

With these introductory words we should be ready for our visit, in the ensuing chapters, to Japanese culture; to find out what kind of economic and social changes took place in the 1990s; to trace how these changes affected registered crime and how citizens and authorities reacted; to see what effects the turbulence had on people's inclination to withdraw from society, or even to commit suicide, and, finally, to discuss the more general question about Japan as more or less an inclusionary society.

2
Reacting to and Tackling Social Problems: Moral Panic and Perseverance

The cultural repertoire

In this chapter I am interested in some characteristics of Japanese society that are of importance for understanding how processes of social change are *interpreted* within this culture[1]. I ask within what frame of reference the economic and social turbulence that entered this society from the early 1990s were absorbed or confronted by Japanese people and the Japanese authorities. More specifically, the topic I am addressing is about a paradoxical situation where a cultural codex stressing values like *perseverance* and *discipline* seems to go in tandem with tendencies towards what some might describe as *overreaction* and *hypersensitivity*. It is about a culture where a general attitude of celebrating patience and an ability to bear with strong demands is paralleled by reactions of fear due to strict norms regarding deviance. This binary situation represents an alloy that makes Japan a particularly interesting case regarding a general debate on social disruptions and ways of reacting to these disruptions.

When confronted with incidents of what are described as 'bizarre crimes' or, when confronted with rising unemployment and new uncertainties in the labour market, what kind of 'cultural repertoire' do Japanese citizens possess that will decide what they make of these phenomena? What kind of cultural 'state of preparedness' is present in this country? To what extent do people turn into processes of self-blaming when problems appear, and to what extent do they turn their attention towards society and towards collective responses? To what extent do people individualise and internalise problems that appear, and to what extent do they collectivise and externalise them? As for the public authorities, I ask to what extent social problems are coded as 'moral problems' that can be addressed by re-moralising strategies, and to what extent they are coded as symptoms of deeper contradictions and conflict in society. To be able to answer questions like these it is necessary to take a brief look at some characteristics of Japanese culture.

By stressing the importance of knowing the cultural context for understanding the impacts of given changes, I subscribe to the social constructivism that is most precisely expressed in the Thomas theorem: 'If men define situations as real, they are real in their consequences'. As we shall see, there is disagreement about the empirical realities regarding the development of crime in Japan. The 'true' realities will never be known: they can only be stated as probabilities. But it *is* an empirical reality that the government really thinks and acts *as if* the crime situation has got worse. This has important consequences in itself that should be heeded. The empirical realities regarding suicides seem to be less contested. To my best knowledge, no one has denied that suicide has been on the rise. But even this situation calls for a careful linking between empirical facts and what people *make out* of these facts. Unless we understand that a social phenomenon is not good or bad, shameful or honourable in itself – it is the way we *interpret* the phenomenon that decides its status – then we will not be able to reach its meaning. As we know, it is the full complexity of the context that decides if an action is defined as a horrible murder or a heroic act of emancipation. This observation is easy to make as a 'philosophical' statement, but should most of all be borne in mind when it comes to empirical analyses.

One line of my argument will maintain that some characteristics of Japanese culture pave the way for fear reactions that easily end up as moral panics (Tokuoka, 2003; Toyama-Bialke, 2003)[2]. This, in turn, invites authoritarian reactions towards increased punitiveness and decreasing tolerance. At the same time, people are expected to put up with strain and afflictions. When insecurity threatens Japanese citizens (for example, regarding the employment situation) this will lead more easily to self-blaming and personal shame than to 'cool resignation' or politicised action. The outcome will be an increase in retreatist and depressive reactions.

In other words, one of my trajectories is related to what I call a hypersensitive reaction to social turbulence. The other is related to a hypothesis about increasing stress and depression due to the demands of discipline and endurance. I will maintain that crime problems and some other social problems have worsened in Japan during the last ten years.

However, it could be argued that the *reactions* to these changes either are out of proportion to the seriousness of these problems or become stronger and more punitive than 'necessary'. The relationship between *actual* and *perceived* problems is always a tricky challenge for social science to deconstruct. This is, among other things, a question of who has power to define what is to be sold as the 'true reality'. In general, open, democratic, pluralist and egalitarian societies have more 'observation points' than societies with the opposite characteristics. Consequently, such societies have more channels for alternative or supplementary storytelling and will be more immune to moral panics. I think that some essential characteristics of Japanese society should be kept in mind when we (in Chapters 3, 4 and 5) enter the discussion of what 'real' social changes have taken place in Japan over the last few years. At the same time, I will alert readers to the danger within Japanese society of increasing mental depression due to a tendency to internalise rather than externalise social problems. When the aggregate of individual social problems increases to an amount that makes them turn into social issues (cf. Mills, 1970) there is a real danger of collective mental depression if these problems remain as private problems. This danger is present in Japan today.

The lesson from Erikson and Durkheim

The first part of my message (overreaction turning into punitiveness) has been tellingly conveyed in two classical illustrations from the sociological canon. In both cases there is a lesson to be learnt regarding the importance of doing *context-specific* analyses and, particularly, of relating our understanding of a social phenomenon to the cognitive processes of interpretation. What does the mental map look like for those who try to give meaning to new or changing social phenomena?

When Kai Erikson (1966) explains the sudden appearance of witches in New England in 1692 he links this incident to the reality conception among those who initiated this process. His important message is that the social construction of witches and the dreadful implications thereof can only be understood if we take into regard the religious belief and morality conception among the Puritans. In modern-day society it is difficult to sell the idea of witches threatening the moral constitution of society. This is hardly because we live more decent lives today than in the days of Puritanism, but because we do not have a frame of reference (conception of reality) that makes such interpretations and this type of labelling possible. People who act deviantly

(or we should rather say, who are *perceived* to act deviantly) are categorised into other types of linguistic and mental universes where witches
are cognitively ruled out. What Erikson does is to show us how the
witches become a reflection of the fears and the *handling* of these fears
among the Puritans[3].

During anomic periods the Puritans settled their own uneasiness by
identifying satanic forces within their own society as 'deviant' females.
In other words, the story told is that it is the mentality structures called
'Puritanism' that gave witches their manifest existence during this
period. In this case, the feeling of fear led to reactions of 'striking out'
or a kind of moral panic.

An illustration of hyper-sensitivity regarding reactions to deviance is
given by Durkheim (1982) when inviting us to imagine a community
of saints within an exemplary and perfect monastery. Of course, such
a society would be free of crime. However, 'faults that appear venial to
the ordinary person will arouse the same scandal as does normal crime
in ordinary consciences. If, therefore, that community has the power to
judge and punish, it will term such acts criminal and deal with them
as such' (p. 100). Durkheim then continues his argument in much the
same way as Erikson does, by pointing out with what strong severity an
honourable man will judge his own slightest moral failings. And like
the Puritans, this man will easily extend the sphere of 'jurisdiction'
to other members of society and judge them by the same standards.
Without pushing the argument, it takes little fantasy to imagine what
kind of punitiveness such a mentality easily will trigger.

To me, the bottom line of the above illustrations is that:

a. *cultures that cultivate purity, consensus and harmony (like in a monastery) will easily react out of proportion to small deviations to the 'normal'
and taken-for-granted reality of everyday life.*
b. *cultures that have established fixed, standardised, authorised and monolithic horizons of reality (like the Puritans) will easily adopt authoritarian, top down and punitive reactions to unconventional behaviour.*[4]

Japan represents a culture that has some affinities to the above characteristics (but with important reservations). Consequently, when we
come to discuss empirical data about crime and social problems in
Japan, we have to have the wings that surround these data in memory.
In a landscape where everything is white as snow and everything is in
tranquil harmony, even small aberrations will become obtrusively visible and threatening. So, let us turn to the description of the Japanese

landscape (i.e. that part of the landscape that is of relevance to our discussion)[5].

The legacy of Confucius and Buddha

In *The Flight From Ambiguity* Donald Levine (1985) gives an interesting introduction to an essential difference between Western and Asian cultures. While precise expressions, clarity, unambiguousness, etc. have been central values in the West since the age of science (Levine talks about 'the modern assault on ambiguity'), *ambiguity* has actually been celebrated in Asia. This ambiguity was tellingly disclosed by Ruth Benedict (1967) when she presented an analysis of Japanese culture to the Americans. This is a synopsis of her presentation:

> The Japanese are, to the highest degree, both aggressive and unaggressive, both militaristic and aesthetic, both insolent and polite, rigid and adaptable, submissive and resentful of being pushed around, loyal and treacherous, brave and timid, conservative and hospitable to new ways. They are terribly concerned about what other people will think of their behavior, and they are also overcome by guilt when other people know nothing of their misstep. Their soldiers are disciplined to the hilt but are also insubordinate. (p. 2)

The title of the present chapter illustrates some of the same 'schizophrenia'. In discussing how Japanese people interpret changes that have taken place during the last two decades, it has to be done in ambiguous terms. It is a story about moral panic (i.e. what, from a Western perspective, many would define as an overdramatisation of the situation), as well as a story about silent endurance (acceptance, adaptation and finding one's place under given circumstances).

In respect of belief systems, Japanese culture is historically based on three pillars: Shintoism (Japan's ancient religion), Buddhism and Confucianism. The impact of *Shintoism* in everyday life in Japan today is not very distinct but the importance of *purity* still has a strong hold. The prolongation of this set of values leads to a general attitude of *alertness* and *cautiousness*. Another element of Shintoism which still has a strong hold in Japan is the emphasising of *obedience* within an elaborate network of vertical relations.

The quest for caution is not only a virtue in Shintoism but is even more strongly underlined within *Buddhist* thinking (Goldman, 1994; Goodman, 2000, 2002). This is often expressed as a demand for *empathy* to be shown (Dale, 1986: 45) and the importance of being sensitive and *self-synchronising* (ibid.: 110) in relation to other people. *Harmony* and *consensus* are much more appreciated than self-promotion and agitation for individual interests. *Reciprocity* has consequently to be expected in communicative relations[6]. From these principles can be deduced another central value, namely the importance of *self-control* and *restraint*. Attentiveness to other people's feelings goes together with a strong awareness of never creating situations where someone might lose face. It is the common good and the harmony of the group that has preference.

Confucianism is not a religious tradition in itself but throughout history this belief system has had a fundamental impact on the behavioural values of Japanese society. According to Takahashi (1991: 6), Confucian philosophy 'regulates every aspect of social life' in Japan, with a main emphasis on unconditional *loyalty to the ruler*, *filial piety* and strict observance of *proper social etiquette*. Takahashi underlines how Confucianism in Japan (to a far lesser extent than in China) has been used as a tool by the rulers to control the populace and to justify the existing political and social order[7]. However, these values still have a strong hold in the Japan of today and can easily be identified in modern industrial-labour relationships. Until recently, these relationships have been strongly influenced by the (Confucian) idea of unquestioning obedience to authority. Self-suppressing labourers were an important factor in the Japanese 'miracle economy' after the Second World War. Socialisation in Japanese schools is based on the same philosophy, plainly expressed in the 'moral education' (or 'moral suasion' as Garon, 1997, calls it) of pupils. Japanese children have 'always' been taught the importance of *respect* for people ranked above them in the hierarchy, respect for traditions, for hard work, for modesty, for prudence, for diligence and thereby, for submission. As I shall come back to in Chapter 6, an awareness of this value basis is fundamental to understanding Japanese society's meeting with late modernity. If citizens over time have been socialised into adaptive rather than emancipatory roles, if they have been socialised into self-blaming rather than politicised roles and if they have been socialised in the direction of a 'low-expectations' rather than a 'highly demanding' role regarding public welfare support, then these citizens will not only easily accept suffering and misery, but they will take the blame for their destiny. However, this way of reacting does not exclude moral panics, especially if authoritarian leaders and a consensus-oriented media 'blow the whistle' and dramatise situations, subjected citizens might easily become scared.

In my earlier works (Leonardsen, 2002; 2004) I have condensed my description of Japanese society to the term a *shame based consensus culture*. All the characteristics of the Shinto, Buddhist and Confucian value system presented above interact to create this totality: a totality that makes Japanese society significantly different from an ideal type of Western, individualistic society. Let me first focus on why Japanese people have become so *disciplined* (compared to Westerners).

It is essential to understand present-day Japanese culture in an historical perspective. For some 700 years Japan was a feudal society run by strong regional families and warlords (*shoguns*). During this period social order was maintained through suppressive measures. Henshall (1999: 151) reports that 'this included peer pressures in the form of group accountability. If one member of a group stepped out of line (moreover a tightly prescribed line), the whole group risked severe punishment'. According to Henshall, a person who acted in a 'rude' way (defined as 'acting in an other-than-expected manner') could be executed on the spot. In other words, this was a society of extremely strong control where each person was responsible for the behaviour of all the other members of the relevant group. This principle of *collective responsibility* has, although in strongly modified versions, characterised Japanese society until modern times[8]. The overall perspective directing this attitude was what Suehiro (1998: 163) calls the ideology of 'unselfish devotion to the state'. According to Suehiro, individual citizens in Japan have historically been expected to contribute to the 'common' good; putting aside, or even sacrificing, their individual interests for the interests of the *kyōdōtai* (i.e. the 'community', be it in the form of the national community, the village community or the corporate community).

'Guidance', 'dependence' and 'form' – three fundamental principles

Guidance

A central concept that illustrates the importance of discipline is the term *shido*, which could be translated as a form of guidance, leadership, supervision or instruction (McVeigh, 2004: 99). As we shall see in Chapter 4 this principle pervades most of the Japanese thinking within criminal policy, not least concerning the control of juveniles. From early socialisation in the family, via kindergartens, the school system and later all through life (e.g. in public and economic life), *shido* has until today been a broadly accepted core value which is systematically built into the (hierarchical) structure of Japanese society. A Japanese citizen will always be a 'contextualised citizen', meaning that he or she will stand in a (vertical) relation to another significant person. Finding one's place as a more or less anonymous and accepting part of the mass has been an imperative value throughout history. Receiving and obeying orders and guidance from authority is a central element of the *shido* principle. To accept the principle of *shido* is in many ways a *sine qua non* if one wants to live a normal life as a Japanese citizen. Someone who, for whatever reason, might want to distance him- or herself from vertical relationships wherein a *sempai* (senior) supervises a *kohai* (junior), wherein an *oyabun* (parent) dictates to a *kobun* (child), etc. will soon end up as an *ippiki okami* (a lonely wolf) and be ostracised from the group. And once you are without membership in a group you will automatically become isolated from most social relations in Japan. Obviously, this contextual frame is not without relevance for understanding suicide in this culture.

As Nakane (1970: 29) has shown in her classical book on the verticality principle in Japan, ranking is 'the principle controlling factor of social relations in Japan'. When this society is known as the country where people police themselves, this is not least due to the omnipresence of the *shido* principle. These *structural* characteristics hold a firm grip on the individual, and this is further fortified in what Dale (1986: 45) designates as a 'sociolinguistic choreography' in this society where ways of greeting and ways of speaking are elaborated into the smallest detail, often with catastrophic consequences for those who might fail. 'To neglect the performance of formalised greetings in Japan is not only considered rude; it borders on an explicit challenge to immediate social order. Morality is expressed through manners. This is because hierarchy and in-group/out-group status are grammatically embedded in the Japanese language' (ibid.: 44). Structurally arranged verticality principles are in other words amplified by cultural norms ('sociolinguistic choreography') that make obedience and adaptation a matter of course that is hardly reflected upon[9].

The importance of accepting 'the principle of guidance' (which is highly relevant to understanding reactions to crime in this country) has been elaborated in the literature under the headline 'learning to become Japanese' (Hendry, 1986). This literature often gravitates around the discussion on a form of total planning or designing of a unitary pedagogical system. Even though Japanese society has a long economic history of capitalistic market expansion, it has an even longer cultural history where the focus is on state control and uniform concepts of what the cultural heritage is all about. It is hardly an exaggeration to define educational policy in Japan in the twentieth century as 'technocratic', meaning by this an almost omnipotent conception of what can be attained by way of state regulations and directives (including the guidance of offenders). The phrase 'the making of a people' (Ben-Ari, 1997: 148) gives a precise expression of a strongly paternalistic attitude among Japanese politicians. Like the patriarchal father has the total responsibility of raising the members of his household (including his wife) to a harmonious and compliant group, the state should be responsible for the implementation of this ideology on the macro level (Garon, 1997). Ambaras (2006: 192) gives a vivid summing up of how this ideology was implemented (up to the present day and still continuing) when declaring that after 1945, 'government officials, social reformers, religious groups, and local notables had constructed a regime of socialisation premised on the notion that every aspect of a young person's life should be rendered visible and subject to intensive guidance'.

Naturally, the educational system became the most important arena for carrying through the idea of 'daily life guidance' and 'soul-searching sessions' (Sugimoto, 1997: 124). Different reports on the moral education of schoolchildren confirm the impression of a system where teachers meticulously investigate eating, sleeping, dressing and spending habits among students. According to Sugimoto (ibid.: 125) 'rigidity, stringency, and regimentation have increasingly dominated Japanese education since schools increased teacher control of pupils in the 1970s and 1980s'. Toyama-Bialke (2003) reports on how most elementary and junior high schools use a 'life style diary' as an essential tool for building strong relations between teachers and pupils. In these diaries the children 'write down how many hours they have studied at home, special things they have done and problems that are bothering them' (ibid.: 24). This fine-meshed system of bonding and monitoring (or, to use its more embellished form, 'guiding') of children's behaviour is not only restricted to the classroom.

Not even during the holidays do teachers' responsibilities for their pupils come to an end. According to Toyama-Bialke (ibid.: 26) teachers regularly patrol local trouble spots (like stores and entertainment centres) during the school vacation. As LeTendre (2000: 103) illustrates:

> The responsibility of the teacher extends far beyond the bounds of the school. Furukawa teachers patrolled the city at intervals during the summer break to observe local hot spots...Teachers are supported

by local counselling centers and the police in these efforts, creating a highly effective prevention network, but one that demands long hours from teachers.

This omnipresent obligation to keep an eye on pupils has to be understood as an expression of the fact that it is not only 'student guidance' (*seito shido*) that is part of the 'jurisdiction' of the teacher, but that even 'life guidance' (*seikatsu shido*) belongs to their mandate.

The relevance of understanding the omnipresence of the principle of guiding for a discussion of crime has been illustrated by Foljanty-Jost and Metzler (2003) in their comparison of juvenile delinquency in Japan and Germany. While in both countries there are regulations referring to what in Western countries is called 'status offenses' (missing school, hanging around with improper friends, etc.), in Japan this control is extended to a variety of so-called 'bad behaviours', which has clear moralistic connotations. Also, these authors underline how norms for correct behaviour during school time are specified in much more detail in Japan.[10] And for those children who still do not succeed in falling into line, training schools and detention centres take over. As McGregor (1996: 114) describes the situation, 'from the moment they leave home to the time they return in the evenings, Japanese people are protected by the inescapable embrace of the Nanny State'.

A final illustration of the strong belief in the principle of guiding is what is called the 'intergenerational programmes' which have been implemented since the early 1990s. Actually, this is not a unique invention for Japan, but the context and the framing of these programmes fit neatly into the message conveyed above, namely as an endeavour to preserve older adults' role 'as providers of guidance and support for people of younger generations, while, at the same time, promoting positive development outcomes for young people' (Kaplan et al. 1998: 1–2). As the family institution has assuredly lost its capacity for guiding its offspring, new support arrangements are needed to take care of this exceedingly important task, and the intergenerational programmes are aimed at supplementing familial support systems and maintaining social cohesion. In Japan these programmes have to be interpreted in a context where a culture of adaptation and acceptance can be taken for granted.

Dependence

Another important aspect of these cultural norms that support compliance to authority is the basic socialising principle of *amae*. According to psychiatrist Takeo Doi (1976), who introduced this concept to Western readers in his famous book *The Anatomy of Dependence* (notice the title!), anyone who wants to understand not only the psyche of each individual, but the whole social structure in Japan has to take this concept as the starting point. While Westerners cultivate *independence* as a basic value to strive for, in Japan the situation is in many ways reversed. The verb *amaeru* carries a meaning of 'being the object of love from others' or 'a wish to behave like a spoiled child' (Kalland, 1986: 67), both with the implication of creating relations of *dependency*. Traditionally, Japanese children have been taught that the outside world is full of dangers and that their mother or (later on) membership of an in-group is the only means that the individual can be protected and provided with a safe life. In spite of an almost total emotional involvement on the part of the mother, it has been argued that, in reality, the child is implanted with a basic absence of confidence during the first years of life (Dale, 1986), which, in turn, generates a need to be accepted and included in a group or a dyadic relationship. From early childhood one learns to appreciate being taken care of by others and to adapt to hierarchical relations. While all human beings are in need of predictability, a sense of belonging and a feeling of basic safety, these needs are structurally embedded in Japanese society via the vertical relations in which every citizen is enrolled. In his classical book *The Enigma of Japanese Power* van Wolferen (1989) emphasises this perspective by arguing that Japanese people actually are *conditioned* to accept as natural the unequal tie to a social superior and that some of them even develop a psychological need for this dependency. Johnson (1996: 5) renders intelligible the importance of these general cultural characteristics for the criminal justice system:

> The feudal principles of hierarchical social order linger in the Japanese social psychology today: knowing one's place in the social scheme, fulfilling the Confucian obligations that the ruler be benevolent and the ruled be obedient, and holding the respect of others by maintaining social harmony, even at the expense of self-interest. Within that normative system, the law-breaker is expected to be repentant and to undertake self-correction.

Even though 'the obedience of contemporary Japanese towards their superiors is generally no longer blind or totally unconditional, yet the element of choice is in most cases still lacking' (Wolferen, 1990: 170). As I shall come back to, present-day reforms within the criminal justice system are still based on premises that take for granted an acceptance of guidance and willingness to repent.

For our discussion, the important message is that from early child-hood each individual is led in the direction of dependence on and compliance with people of authority (parents, teachers, bosses and team leaders, all the way up to the emperor). A more or less silent acceptance is in many ways a prerequisite for full membership in soci-ety. In this way the need for open coercion will be minimised. Social order is created in a subtle way, first through the *amae* ideology and next safeguarded by hierarchical structures that totally encapsulate the individual. As expressed in the words of Rohlen (1989), the situa-tion could be described with the concept of 'the empty centre', mean-ing that necessary guidelines for the individual are put forward more as unexpressed expectations from the group to which he or she belongs than as manifest directions for action. Social order may only be appre-ciated by understanding opaque and floating power structures, vague ideological hegemonies and an unproblematised culture of consensus and harmony.

Form

While the principles of *shido* and *amae* are relatively obvious mecha-nisms of discipline and compliance, the concepts of *kata/shikata* have a more subtle impact in the same direction. These concepts con-note something like 'form', 'model', or 'way of doing things', and De Mente (1992) maintains that 'all of the primary attributes for which the Japanese are known – their strengths as well as their weaknesses – have their genesis in the cultural moulds referred to as *kata*'. According to De Mente (1992) the *absence* of *shikata* is absolutely unthinkable in Japan[11], and 'doing things the right way was often more important than doing the right things'. From this, one can conclude that form is not only more important than content but form has actually become synonymous with content, or indeed, with morality. For the Japanese there exists an inner order (the heart of each individual) and an outer order (cosmos), and these two worlds are linked together through a demand for *kata*. Each individual must know her or his own true heart, and then learn how to practise the correct *kata* so that she or he is in harmony with society and with the cosmos. In all regards it is impor-tant that each individual adapts to a common harmony by doing things the right way. This refers to strict procedures for how to behave and how to present oneself. As elaborated by McVeigh (1997: 45) Japan is characterised by an 'ethnomorality of etiquette' where 'manners them-selves take on central significance, their performance denoting moral-ity itself'. The presentation of self in everyday life (Goffman, 1959) is particularly complex and complicated in Japan. In this country it is important to express empathy through the correct etiquette. This can readily be seen in Japanese schools where everything from acceptance of school uniforms and a meticulous enforcement of rules for correct behaviour to regimes of cleaning and strictly enforced rules for greetings, etc. expresses the importance of *kata*. The drilling of the Japanese system of signs (*kanji*) gives an important illustration of this *kata* culture. Japanese children have to learn how to write thousands of complicated signs, something which demands strong discipline and endurance[12]. When Kerr (2001) says that the Japanese have a tendency to go to excess in everything they do, one reference for this characterisation is the *kata* phenomenon. If anything, when travelling in Japan you can always be certain of having watchful (but friendly!) eyes around you, and, as a Westerner, you will most certainly commit a lot of blunders regarding form (or customs).

The principle of *kata*, like the principle of *shido*, is thus an important element in understanding how order is created in Japanese society. By implication, the essence of these cultural characteristics will become particularly noticeable if one *opposes* this script. *Kata* is much more important than the individual's free expression, and this results in 'the taming and forced withering of the individual personality' (Henshall, 1999: 153) and – as I shall come back to – for those who break out, the total exclusion from the group.

One important 'function' of being socialised into *amae* relations and accepting *shido* and *kata* as guiding principles for social life is that another central value in Japanese society, *wa* ('harmony') is thoroughly taken care of. The supposition is that through a heavy stress on form, obedience and dependency relations harmony will be maintained and that a healthy consensus will oil society. The choreography of everyday life will be so elaborate that people's actual behaviour is made quite predictable. Individual agency is reduced to a minimum which, in turn, points in the direction of acceptance and endurance. However, a heavy stress on perfection and harmony will easily invite exaggerated reactions (seen from a Western point of observation) to even small aberrations. As I shall come back to in Chapter 4, this way of dramatising fears and challenges (e.g. regarding the crime situation) might seem to be part of the story in Japan. To the extent that the outcry about a social collapse and a spreading moral decay in Japan over the last 20 years might seem somewhat out of proportion, the overriding role played by the principles of *kata* and *wa* gives one answer to why this happens.

Conclusion: Do not disturb the harmony of the group

The cultural wings that make up the background for the way people think and act in their everyday lives is dominated by strong sensitiveness and other-directedness. Obligations towards group values imply that each person should be willing to bear quite extensive renunciations and to take these without complaint. Endurance is expected and can be taken for granted. As long as the individual is subordinate to the group, and as long as 'group membership is the basis for individual identity' (Stevens, 1977: 16), each citizen has to relinquish what are regarded to be particularistic interests. One should put up with injustice rather than disturb the harmony of the group. At the same time, people have been socialised in a way that will relatively easily trigger uncertainty and fear. The situation has some points of resemblance to what Moss (1997: 179) reports on the Semai people of Malaysia, who regard themselves 'as individually helpless beings living in a world that is filled with dangers'. To the Semai people the outside world represents a constant threat that the individual can be protected against only through depending on the group. Consequently, this culture is essentially a fear culture with helpless individuals who must depend on others for aid and comfort. When danger appears (like for example, thunderstorms) adults as well as children react with anxiety and flee to the company of others for protection. As in Japan, it is not independence and self-reliance that make the most important constituents of the value system but rather values that easily invoke feelings of fear. While safety and predictability represent basic values of universal importance for human beings, this becomes particularly true in cultures like Semai – and Japan. Since belonging and dependency on others (rather than autonomy and independence) are implanted from early childhood, people are relatively easily prone to feelings of anxiety.

In short, Japanese society represents an integrated 'package' with a large degree of consistency, continuity and coherence. In present-day Japan it is obviously the Confucian dimension that has left its strongest fingerprint on the culture: 'it has formed the bedrock values or primary premises which prescribe the people's consciousness and behavior' (Takahashi, 1991: 5). Even though a process of pluralisation is taking place today, it is still the case that educational institutions like kindergartens and schools, as well as public welfare offices, operate as agents for managing the population[13]. The power of the state and the ability this state has to govern and guide its people is not disclosed in a crude or violent way but operates 'behind the back of the actors' (to use a phrase from Karl Marx).

With this brief introduction to some aspects of Japanese culture I hope to have brought to attention the 'soil' in which social change takes place. Where harmony and adaptation to a common and restricted standard are regarded as a *doxa*, even small aberrations will be noticed and commented on. This will most certainly create a 'double situation' where *suppression* in combination with *depression* might be the unlucky result.

In Chapter 5 I shall show in more detail how these general cultural characteristics are expressed within the system of criminal justice and, particularly, towards juveniles. But first I shall look more closely into the extent of economic and socio-cultural changes that have taken place in Japan during the last 15–20 years.

3
Economic, Social, and Cultural Changes 1990–2005

The impetus for change amplifies

Like all modern societies, Japan is changing as globalisation and technological innovation proceed. Increasing economic and cultural integration leaves the nation state exposed to strong impulses for change. However, societies are characterised by institutional *inertia*. Social change is usually about very gradual and slow processes. This is especially true regarding the cultural sphere. Marx was probably right in distinguishing the socio-cultural system by two concepts: *social lag* and *adaptation*. By applying these concepts he argued that the most important engine for social change (in capitalist societies) is economic competition in the marketplace which, in turn, generates continuous technological innovation. Social and cultural patterns have their own relative autonomy, but will in general be heavily influenced by material and economic processes. As a consequence, social and cultural life will to a large extent be dependent on (have to adapt to, but with a time lag) what happens in the economy. This creates a tension between two rationalities, where values like *flexibility* and *instrumental rationality* (within the economic system) will be confronted by contradictory values like *stability* and *tradition* (within the socio-cultural system).

As a general rule, it is the socio-cultural system that will have to adapt. However, as I pointed out in *Japan as a Low-Crime Nation* (Leonardsen, 2004), Japan is a country that in important regards illustrates a kind of diverging logic where economic rationality actually has been strongly influenced by the socio-cultural system (cf. the assertion that Japan has 'modernised without having westernised'). During almost 50 years of modernisation, Japan has succeeded to a large extent in preserving strong elements of traditionalism within a framework of technological and economic readjustment. This indicates that in Japan, cultural values have had a stronger autonomy and independence than we are used to in Western countries. Social and cultural change has taken place at a slower pace than in most Western countries and 'traditional' values have been preserved to a large extent.

At the beginning of the 1990s a complex interplay of economic, social and environmental problems appeared that shook Japanese society to its foundations. With a more open economy (Japan became a member of the World Trade Organization in 1995), Western influence took a stronger hold in Japan and the impetus for social change amplified. In 1997 the economic crisis worsened even further and the government faced increasing pressure (from the International Monetary Fund and the United States) to rationalise its economy (Stiglitz, cited in Roberts and LaFree, 2001). New measures of liberalisation (e.g. privatisation and permission to use temporary workers) were introduced, especially from 1999 on.

Due to the economic slump during the 1990s, unemployment figures rose to unknown heights, and the Japanese economy went into a tailspin with a lot of repercussions. Furthermore, in 1995 the city of Kobe was destroyed by a terrible earthquake – an incident that soon became a showcase for assertions about how Japanese authorities neglected the protection of the country's own citizens.[1] The people's loss of confidence in their authorities and a corresponding loss of legitimacy were only two of the effects of this terrible incident. In the same year a shocking sarin gas attack took place on the Tokyo subway, killing 12 people and severely injuring many more. This incident represented a serious strike against what Japanese citizens had taken for granted during the post-war period: their own social safety (Kisala and Mullins, 2001). As a consequence, a creeping anxiety found its way into the pores of Japanese society, and soon the country approached what could be described as a *legitimation crisis* (for the politicians and bureaucrats, Hirata, 2002: 5) and a *motivational crisis* (for the general public). Most books on Japan covering the period since the early 1990s include a section on the 'lost decade' and the loss of commitment for project 'Japan Inc.'. After some 50 years of well orchestrated modernisation, where everybody had found their place within a broader context of meaning, an incipient anomic situation could be registered. At home as well as abroad[2], Japanese leaders seemed to lose confidence and prestige. From the middle of the 1990s many observers argued that Japanese society was heading for the biggest and the most abrupt social upheaval since the war.

One could expect that events like this would have an impact on the crime situation. In Chapter 1, I presented three analytical dimensions of society of relevance to understanding low crime rates in Japan: *social/organisational structures* (group society), *dominating collective values* (Confucian, hierarchical society; *macro*-level values) and *values transmitted through the socialisation process* (dependency and shame; *micro* level values). In addition, I pointed to the relevance *a stable and inclusive economy* would have for preventing crime. This analytical approach is presented in Figure 3.1.

If crime has changed in Japan since the 1990s, it is logical to comment on these four dimensions. Has Japan over the last couple of decades changed in a way that has made crime/social problems a more likely alternative for action? Have societal conditions in Japan become more like those in Western countries? If the answer to these questions is in the affirmative, in what way can one suggest that economic, socio-structural and/or cultural changes have influenced the new situation? These questions are expressions of a general debate among criminologists, with varying focus on either 'economic' (Roberts and LaFree, 2001) or more commonly, 'cultural' explanations of crime rates in Japan.

From one point of view[3], one could argue that the most important question of criminological relevance is to what extent Japanese society

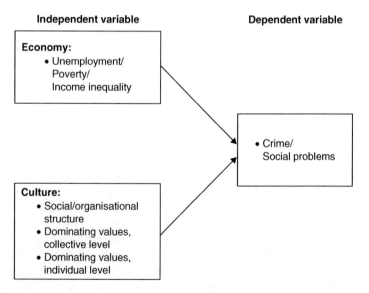

Figure 3.1   A causal model for crime/social problems

has become *more exclusionary* (regarding economic and social 'belonging') since the early 1990s[4]. In that case one has to ask if Japanese society has changed in ways that have made crime a more likely choice for different groups of people. Are more people today in a situation of being set free from different bonds than there were 20 years ago, which in turn may have created new social problems? To what extent are people differently situated – be it in the role as family members, wage earners, students, citizens, etc – than they were a couple of decades ago? And most important, to what extent has Japanese society experienced economic and structural changes that might be described as *criminologically relevant?*

From a less materialistic or a less structural point of view[5], one could maintain that *changing attitudes, changing 'mentalities'* and *changing moral values* represent an important approach to understanding crime. Like in Western countries, a lot of people (including politicians) in Japan turned to this type of explanation when crime figures started to climb toward the end of the 1990s (a lot of illustrations can be found in different editions of Japan Echo, more in Chapter 4). Warnings about a 'moral decay' (at the individual level), most typically taking place among the younger generation, have been common in public debate. Others have focused on 'mentality changes' (at the societal level), where attention is directed towards the collective parameters for manoeuvring (e.g. a general 'survival of the fittest' ideology). Instead of criticising the individual, this perspective scrutinises the school, the family (often with accusations about moral laxity and indulgence) or anonymous 'society' in general. In this case there is often an implication of disempowerment and impotence; we are all caught in a kind of collective trap where solutions at the individual level are hard to identify.

In this chapter I will explore these questions. First of all, I will give an overview of what I regard as the most significant changes in Japanese *economic* life since 1990. This section will focus on labour market relations, with special attention to the situation for younger people. Next, I will analyse the two primary institutions in charge of socialisation, namely the *family* and the *school*. While these institutions represent the most fundamental social *structures* that give youngsters a basic belonging and a collective identity, they also represent the main arenas for the transmission of cultural values. The question is: have the family institution and the school system in Japan changed in a significant way during the last 20 years? Have they gradually changed in ways that could be defined as worrying from a criminological point of view? Questions related to cultural values are complex and hard to grasp. In this chapter

I reduce my ambitions to analysing to what extent Japanese schools have become more 'relaxed' in their way of transferring the 'moral codex' to the coming generations. In Chapter 7 I will return to the descriptive question if there really is – as many contend – a youth crisis in Japan today and if a *lasting* change of formative values in this society has actually taken place.

When we try to answer the question about the *extent* of economic, social and cultural change in Japan, this can easily be read as a simple 'positivistic' question, i.e. a question of finding quantitative indicators along relevant dimensions. In this perspective 'social change' is a matter of *objective* facts. Of course, this is part of the story and this is the story that in the main will be told here. However, without entering the long-lasting debate about 'Japanese uniqueness', one should have Chapter 2 in mind when reading this one, i.e. the cultural soil within which the 'objective' changes take place. We know from communication theory that one and the same message is regularly decoded in different ways by different receivers. The same perspective holds for cultures. It is also reasonable to believe that relatively small and undramatic impulses of change will invite comparatively strong reactions in Japan.

The economy: Liberalisation and turbulence

> Among the intellectuals it is not hard to detect the New Pessimism; among the citizenry, the Same Old Apathy. In short, the topics on the minds of the nation today tend to concentrate on the ultra-personal – keeping one's head above water at the office, in the school, or around the neighbour-hood – and the ultra-practical – 'network or perish'. (*Japan Times*, November 26, 2000)

> Depression has become an increasingly serious malaise suffered by Japan's corporate warriors as they bear up to the stress caused by the prolonged economic slump and the spectre of job loss, or, for those not idled by a workforce reduction, an increased workload. The stress is further compounded as more and more Japanese firms shed their lifetime employment systems and adopt Western-style, merit-based employee assessments, where performance is key, specialist say. The soaring stress levels have now prompted Japanese firms to step up efforts to look after their employees' mental health, as they come to the realization that serious depression not only leads to suicide but also reduced corporate productivity. (*Japan Times*, December 20, 2001)

The period 1990–2000 is often described as 'the lost decade' by japanologists. At the start of the 1990s the debate in Japan changed from
explaining the economic miracle to understanding an extensive debacle
(Ikeda, cited in Vij, 2007: 160). For many years Japan was admired for its
sound economy. However, on October 6, 2005, *The Economist* had the
following merciless evaluation of the status of the Japanese economy:
'No country in modern history has moved so swiftly from worldwide
adulation to dismissal or even contempt as did Japan'.

What a change! In an evaluation of the Japanese welfare state
(until 1990), Esping-Andersen (1997) argued that Japan had avoided
many of the heavy social problems that other welfare states had experienced. Extremely rapid economic growth, full employment, an elaborate
educational system, a fairly even income distribution and little poverty, marginalisation and crime were the essence of the success history.
As many scholars argued at that time, Japanese society was so infused
with welfare that it did not need a Scandinavian type of welfare state
model. In spite of being an economic superpower based on a competitive market economy, the way Japanese society was organised seemed
to inoculate against modern social problems (like crime and divorce).
'The central message that emerges from Japan's success (in the post-war
era) is that there is more than one way to organize capitalism', professor
of political science, T.J. Pempel ascertained[6]. To many observers Japan
was the strange exception to the rule that heavy state intervention in a
world of open markets could survive for only a short period of time.

However, in 1990, *The Economist* and other critical voices seemed to
be proven right. The so-called bubble economy burst and the Japanese
economy plunged into a *lasting recession*. According to estimates made
by the OECD, the economic collapse caused a wealth-decline equal to
two years of GDP (Bigsten, 2004). During the following years and right
up until the present-day pessimism and stagnation have characterised
Japanese society. The extensive market reforms that Western societies embarked on from the late 1970s were gradually (some would say
too gradually!) copied in Japan. Today Japan's economy can no longer
be described as a 'viagra economy' (*EBSCOhost*, January 1, 2005),
'financial feudalism' (Zinsmeister, 1993), 'financial socialism' (*The
Economist*, October 6, 2005) or even 'the last socialist country on the
planet' (Taro, in Schoppa, 2006: 1). Even though reforms have moved
more slowly in Japan under Prime Minister Koizumi than was the case
in England under Margaret Thatcher[7], and even though Confucianism
still remains the essence of the cultural web in Japan, basic premises
in the economic system have been changed (see Nakagawa, 1999;
Vogel, 1999).

The main point to notice for *my* discussion is the *new uncertainty* that was expressed in a survey from 1998, where 68 per cent of respondents stated that they often felt worried or anxious (almost double the percentage in a comparable 1990 survey). The same survey revealed a similar increase in feelings of irritation and anger (Tipton, 2002: 217). The genesis of this nervous social climate could be sought in the annual reports produced by the major Japanese corporations. During the 1990s, these reports underlined more and more the importance of improving their employment practices in order to strengthen their market competitiveness. While avowed obligations to the welfare of the employees used to be a major task for employers, it was how to restructure and rationalise the companies that increasingly came to dominate the agenda. For those companies who found it difficult to fire loyal employees overnight, more subtle mechanisms were made use of: redundant workers received a status as 'window employees' where they were 'given a desk by a window with no work to do and ostracised by fellow workers in the hope of their voluntary resignation' (ibid.: 215). To the extent that crime and other social problems have to do with decreasing predictability, increasing material uncertainty and social exclusion, it should not come as a surprise if indications of social disruption appeared in Japan towards the end of the millennium.

In a study of *Migrant Labour in Japan,* Sellek (2001: 93) argues that since late 1991 Japanese corporations, in addition to dismissing surplus employees, have implemented cutbacks in overtime work, encouraged employees to take more holidays, reduced the number of part-time and temporary employees and stimulated voluntary retirement. The ratio of job offers to applicants suffered a marked drop from 1991 to 1992, but was still above 1 (one offer per applicant). However, in July 1999 the ratio was down to 0.46 (46 available jobs for every 100 applicants). In the same year 1.18 million workers left their jobs as a result of corporate insolvency/restructuring.

These structural changes in the Japanese economy gradually gave rise to a debate on *mounting inequalities* in Japan. Before the burst of the bubble economy, Japan used to be described as one big 'middle class society', but widening disparities in recent years have been the number one concern among Japanese people (according to a survey presented in the *Asahi Shimbun*, see Schad-Seifert, 2006). Books like Tachibanaki Toshiaki's *Nihon no Keizai (Japan's Economic Inequality,* 1998) and Sato Toshiki's *Fubyodi Shakai Nihon (Japan as an Unequal Society,* 2000) became bestsellers, as did Takuro Morinaga's book in 2003–2004 on how to survive on low wages (*The Economist,* October 6, 2005). This literature is mirroring a new situation where 'the image of an affluent and equal Japanese society has now been replaced by an image of overt economic inequality in people's mind' (Ishida, 2006: 7). Actually, Japan's Gini coefficient has been on an increase since the early 1980s. According to Tachibanaki (2005: 4) this index (measuring inequalities of income distribution) reached a top score in 2002, which he characterises as a 'large increase in inequality' (p. 5). When comparing Japan with other OECD countries Tachibanaki concludes that 'Japan's income inequality is currently among the highest of the advanced and industrialized countries' (p. 5). However, it is only during the last five to six years that this topic has become a public concern.

According to the Ministry of Internal Affairs and Communications the unemployment rate in Japan fluctuated between 1.5 and 2.5 per cent in the 1970s and 1980s but then started increasing from 1992, with an especially sharp jump between 1997 and 2002 (more than 5 per cent)[8]. The official numbers confirm the 1990s as a period of slump – for women as well as for men. In a cross-national perspective the unemployment rate is not very dramatic, but from a Japanese point of view the changes were regarded as exceptional. The frame of reference was full employment and strong job security over many years. This could no longer be taken for granted, which implied that *trust* in the government's ability to handle the economy crumbled. Against this background one could argue that the 1990s inaugurated a change in the 'mental climate' in Japan (to which I will return below).

Traditionally, *women* have had a transient and auxiliary role in the Japanese labour market. Their primary obligation has been the care of the family, while paid work has been temporary (before marriage) and part-time (after some years of care giving). When companies had to restructure due to the recession it was workers with part-time or temporary status (i.e. *women*) who first lost their jobs, but these groups are actually not included in the unemployment statistics (Tipton, 2002: 214–15)[9]. On the other hand, the total number of workers holding contingent jobs almost exploded during the 1990s, which implies that the structure of opportunities for women also showed some 'positive' elements. This, together with an exodus of young Japanese women from corporations to work as temporaries, might explain the relatively low female unemployment rate since 1999.

In 2001, *Social Science Japan Journal* (vol. 4 no. 2) devoted full attention to a debate on 'atypical' and 'irregular' labour in contemporary Japan. According to the Editor-in-Chief, Suehiro Akira (2004: 159), the Japanese labour market underwent changes during the 1990s in the direction of diversification of the terms on which people worked. By this he meant a rapid increase in various forms of employment *outside* the regular labour market, i.e. atypical or irregular labour contracts. Today this group is labelled the new 'precariat' of Japan, combining the word 'precarious' (insecurity in the labour market) with 'proletariat' (Ueno, 2007). These new forms include contract work where people are hired on a short-term basis and are paid by the hour. Helped by changes to the employment law, increased flexibility was attained for employers while employees experienced increased uncertainty and lower wages (part-time workers and others on temporary contracts are paid far less than regular workers). Irregular workers made up 18.8 per cent of the labour force in 1990, while in 2005 this figure had increased to 30 per cent (i.e. 20 million people, predominantly women, young people and the fairly low-skilled, *The Economist,* October 6, 2005). During the period 1990–2000, the number in non-standard employment rose by 44 per cent, while the number of people in standard employment rose by just 4 per cent (Sato, 2001). In 2005, 70 per cent of the employed at the famous electronics firm *Canon* were hired on irregular terms. Ten years earlier the figure was only 10 per cent. To what extent this change is a reflection of autonomous choices made by workers themselves, and/or to what extent it is a result of public and corporate policy changes is an ongoing debate in Japan today, to which I will return below (Honda, 2006; Osawa, 2004; Sato et al. 2004).

Accompanying the changes in the labour market was a public debate on the concepts of *kachigumi* (winners) and *makegumi* (losers). According to Yamada (2005: 9), those who had been lucky enough to get jobs as regular employees at reputable companies ('core workers') belonged to the first group, while part-timers and others on temporary contracts ('non-regular workers') belonged to the second group. The new economic split that appeared in Japanese society towards the end of the century was not only a question of *economic* disparities, but even more importantly, it was about *status* differences and differences related to expectations for the future. It was this *qualitative* dimension regarding 'the social psychology of hope' (Nesse, 1999) that Yamada (2005) was especially worried about: 'Society, in short, is splitting into two classes: a higher one consisting of people with hope, and a lower one consisting of those without. I have dubbed this the "expectation gap"' (p. 10). Independent of how much money people with an unstable link to the labour market could succeed in earning, they would nevertheless be permanently trapped in a situation where it would be hard to accumulate know-how, win recognition for their work, have a feeling of basic security, plan for the future and (in the case of men) to be considered as a potential marriage partner.

To the extent that unemployment and material uncertainty are triggering crime and other social problems, one should – *ceteris paribus* – expect climbing rates of crime and other social problems in Japan towards the end of the century. However, we have to be more specific in this complicated discussion, so let me take a closer look at the labour market situation among *youth*. Since most crimes (relatively) are committed by young people it is of special interest to analyse how this group has been affected by the recession. The period of youth has been defined as a *liminal* stage (Barry, 2006), characterised by transition, ambiguity, openness and indeterminacy. To the extent that our understanding of crime is contingent on our understanding of social control (formal and informal), it should be of interest to analyse how the economic crisis from the early 1990s affected young people, materially and mentally.

From a sociological point of view, the situation for an increasing number of young people in present-day Japan is close to one aspect of Durkheim's concept of *anomie,* namely a strong feeling of *purposelessness.* The implications are, according to Yamada (2005: 13), predictable: 'When young people's efforts go unrewarded in society, we can also expect to see an increase in the number who withdraw from that society'. The manifestations of this withdrawal (following Yamada) could be children who refuse to go to school, people who seclude themselves at home (*hikikomori*, see chapter 6), thrill-seeking people and an increase in promiscuous behaviour, drug use and crime. An expression of this growing worry about a group of excluded youth could be found in *Japan Echo* (2005: 1). The first edition from that year was titled 'Japan's New Misfits', where the link between exclusion and crime was drawn explicitly in the editorial:

In November 2004, two shocking and remarkably similar murders took place in Ibaraki, a prefecture not far north of Tokyo. In both cases, a youth out of school, unemployed, and living at home, killed his parents and other family members. In both cases, the reported cause of the carnage was the frustration and hopelessness of a young man secluded in his home and unable to find a place in society, who vented his emotions on his family.

According to the editor, 'there is no question that conditions are harsh for young adults trying to get a foothold in today's society'. While Japanese society only a few years earlier had offered straightforward expectations and straightforward career paths for the younger genera-tion, this was no longer the case. The author of books like *Wither the modern family*, *The Era of Parasite Singles* and *Expectation-Gap Society* (all three titles published in Japanese), Masahiro Yamada (2005), described the new situation for young people by emphasising a sharp division between those whose efforts were rewarded and those whose efforts were not. The result, as Yamada saw it, was a society where hopes for the future were extinguished for a significant group of youth.

A broad documentation of the work environment for young peo-ple during the 1990s was given in Genda Yuji's (2005) prize-winning book *A Nagging Sense of Job Insecurity: The New Reality Facing Japanese Youth* (published in Japan in 2001). The main message in Yuji's book is that this group has more and more been deprived of job and training opportunities, 'which in turn has given rise to young people who move from one part-time or contract job to another. Reduced to the status of social underdogs, Japanese young people have had no alternative but to become economically dependent on their parents' (p. xi). While Japan's aggregate unemployment rate reached 5 per cent in 2001, Yuji documents that the steep increase in unemployment was mainly due to a rise in *youth* unemployment, which in 2001 reached 12.4 per cent. According to this scholar it is not moral explanations, like a change in the work ethic among youth that lies behind young people's job flip-ping, but quite simply the recession and the protectionist policy (in favour of the middle-aged and older workers) the government has run.

The discussion on these changing conditions regarding the *labour market* has for some 10–15 years been linked to two concepts: *freet-ers* and *NEETs*. The term *freeter* (which, in contradiction to *NEETs*, is a purely Japanese word) is a contraction of the English words *free time* and the German words *Frei Arbeiter*. The word was originally coined a couple of years *before* the economic crash of 1990, and, at that time, referred to young people (between 15 and 34 years of age, excluding housewives and students) who deliberately chose to be serial part-time workers (or *job hoppers* as Honda, 2006: 5, calls them). As long as the economy was booming, being a *freeter* could have some positive connotations. Instead of dying from *karoshi* (overwork), as some 30,000 Japanese people do every year (Takahashi, 1991), quite a few young people preferred a com-bination of freedom/material scarcity to little freedom/affluence. To some people the *freeters* were characterised as independent individu-als who pursued their own dreams and tried to live life to the full-est (Chiavacci, 2005; Sato et al. 2004). However, when the *freeter* role, as a consequence of economic contraction, changed from being an idiosyncratic choice to becoming an involuntary trap, the 'glamour' that once was associated with this role faded[10].

It is not easy to give exact numbers regarding the group of *freeters*, but estimates made by the Japan Institute of Labour indicate that the total number increased from 1 million in 1992 to approximately 2 million in 2000[11]. This institute differentiates between the *moratorium* type of *freeters*, the *dream pursuing* type and the *no alternative* type. While the first two of these groups are characterised by people who deliberately choose not to join the regular, full-time labour market, the 'no alternative' group are people who cannot find employment after leaving school or university (cf. the distinction between 'winning *freeters*' and 'losing *freeters*', Yamada, 2005: 9).

The phenomenon called *NEETs* is an abbreviation for Not in Education, Employment or Training, and applies to a growing number of young Japanese (aged 18–35 years) who do not hold any type of job (regular or temporary) and who do not even try to get one. Originally this concept was coined in Britain, but was introduced in Japan in 2004 by Tamaki Saito (cf. *Japan Echo,* 2005). Today, almost half a million young Japanese people belong to this group, which represents a smouldering headache for the government. In a society that very much preaches a version of the biblical idea that 'in the sweat of your face you shall eat your bread', young people who apparently just 'give in' and seclude themselves from society, represent a practical as well as an ideological challenge. Traditional Japanese culture stresses the importance of finding one's place in society, adapting to the established norms and doing what one is expected to do. It is within such a perspective one has to interpret the fact that in the fiscal year April 2005 to March 2006 the Ministry of Health, Labor and Welfare spent some 100 billion yen on improving young people's life skills and fostering their independence and willingness to take on challenges (Saito and Genda, 2005: 15). To the extent that the younger generation chooses *exit* rather than *voice* as its modus operandi, the core values of society are defied.

Another topic of significance for young people's relation to the labour market refers to recent changes in the Japanese system of transition from school to work. Due to what is called the 'periodical blanket recruitment system', nearly all school-leavers and university graduates in Japan have (since the 1960s) found their future jobs *before* graduation (blue collars as well as white collars). Japanese schools have for a long time had an important screening function, which means that the educational system has 'exerted a profound influence on the student's destination after graduation' (Honda, 2004: 104)[12]. In a society of order and predictability this system has created a smooth transition from education to work. Accordingly, Japan has attracted positive attention from foreign countries due to the efficiency of this system. In combination with a rapidly expanding labour market (1960–90), the liminal phase for young people has obviously been eased a lot because of this well-established relationship between schools and employers (cf. Japan as a safety-seeking culture).

Since the early 1990s this has changed, and it has changed due to a significant decline in the number of new job openings. This has especially affected the situation for high school students and university graduates (Honda, 2004, 2006; Chiavacci, 2005). The total number of job openings offered was at a peak in 1992 (1,676,000). From that year the numbers fell to 935,000 in 1994, to 535,000 in 1996 and stopped at 240,000 in 2002. The proportion of new high school graduates securing employment decreased from 35 per cent in 1990 to only 17 per cent in 2005 (Eades et al. 2005: 13; Honda, 2006: 4). The demand for university graduates more than halved in the middle of the 1990s (compared to the late 1980s) and today fluctuates at about 1.3 job offers per graduate, compared to 2.5 or even nearly 3 job openings in around 1990 (Chiavacci, 2005). Even though remnants of the old 'periodical blanket recruitment' system still exist, today this will apply only to a small minority of students. Accordingly, the economic bust, in combination with the government's belief in the principle of flexibility and less intervention in the economy, has had a significant effect on the transition from school to work. As documented by Honda (2006: 113), Japan is now facing a grim reality regarding the youth labour market, and the traditional stability and security of the Japanese transition system has vanished. The present system benefits only a group of advantaged youth, while those most at risk are stigmatised and excluded. Today, scholars as well as public authorities are in consensus that young people are facing a considerably tougher future when trying to get admittance to secure employment[13]. It goes without saying that these problems with finding jobs hit even harder among discharged prisoners. While in 1995 51 per cent of discharged inmates found a job, this percentage had decreased to 32 in 2004 (White Paper on Crime: 2005: 337). According to Herbert (2005: 149) 80 per cent of novice *yakuza* (members of organised crime groups) did not complete high school in the late 1980s (compared to 2 per cent of the population as a whole), and the very difficult labour market situation for youth does certainly exacerbate the situation.

At this point of my analysis I will draw no firm conclusions regarding economic recession and crime (or other social problems). This is a topic implying complex methodological considerations. Pointing out some possible interrelationships between, for example, unemployment and crime is a risky business. If crime increases when unemployment rises, this is only a statistical, not necessarily a causal, relationship. The same, of course, is true if crime should happen to decline during a period of rising unemployment. Both variables ('crime' and 'unemployment') are too complex to be suitable for that type of conclusion. Nevertheless, I have included this presentation exactly because I have as a basic premise that how people are materially situated will (as a general rule) affect the statistical probability of rule breaking behaviour (for a broad discussion of this topic, see Grover, 2008). A life situation characterised by marginality and exclusion is (*ceteris paribus*) more likely to be associated with crime and other social problems than a life of inclusion. A society that offers pessimism for an increasing part of the younger generation will (*ceteris paribus*) potentially be more problematic than a society offering optimism for the future. In the case of Japan, Tamura (2004: 4) has made the connection between a looser attachment to the labour market and social control explicit:

> Along with this rising unemployment, the economic downturn has brought about changes in the relationship between individuals and companies. Strong economic growth allowed companies to provide lifetime employment and seniority-based salary systems with regular raises, but today workers can no longer expect these perks. As a result, more and more young people have lost the sense of attachment to their companies – and the controls those private enterprises once had over individuals' behavior have also decreased. *This has brought a decline in order and other crime-related factors to the surface* (italics added).

Of course, this type of argument is more assertive than documentary. I return to a more detailed analysis in Chapter 4. Before ending this (what we might call) 'indicative analysis', let me connect the present chapter on socio-economic changes to the next chapter (about crime) by giving the final word to the Research and Training Institute of the Ministry of Justice. In the White Paper on Crime for 2003 the situation for marginalised youth was discussed in detail and the following observation was made:

> Another problem is that a number of juveniles do not go to school or fail to adapt themselves to school and not a few of them leave

or drop out of school. Due to [a] high unemployment rate among juveniles because of recessions, difficulties in finding jobs not only among high school dropouts but also among junior high school/ high school graduates, and the decline in motivation for working among juveniles, the number of unemployed juveniles has been increasing. Juveniles tend to worry about what their friends think of them while lacking a sense of belonging to society or sympathy for the weak, and show tendency of justifying violence or irresponsible or apathetic attitude toward society. Such changes in the attitudes of juveniles should not be disregarded.

These results imply the existence of a mechanism in which juveniles, who have left families or schools and found no place in society, suffer desolation of mind, and while hanging around late at night, they commit robbery for the purpose of obtaining money or articles quickly, without any sense of guilt but merely under the influence of friends, and finally damage victims by their violent acts. (p. 475)

In short, the *economic* climate in Japan during the last 15 years has changed in a way that has made many people, not least young people, more insecure. After many years of stable economic growth, with a school-to-work system that made the transition short and predictable, with a comparatively high job security at least for male employees, huge transformations took place. Declarations about Japan as a form of 'victimless capitalism' (McGregor, 1996), will now have to be made with precautions. The 'grim reality of the youth labour market' (Honda, 2004: 113) and the 'nagging sense of job insecurity' (Genda Yuji, 2005) become especially threatening for a traditionally safety-seeking population with a comparatively weak state-supported welfare system. The splitting of society into winning and losing strata that has appeared during the last decade represents a challenge to the trust relationship between government and citizens. The worst negative effect of the 'New Economy' is probably the loss of hope among the younger generation. As Yamada (2005: 13) rhetorically asks, 'if hard work and long-term efforts are unlikely to pay off, why not dispense with them and live for the pleasure of the moment?' To the extent that Braithwaite (1991: 40) is right when arguing that, 'powerlessness and poverty increase the chances that needs are so little satisfied that crime is an irresistible temptation to actors alienated from the social order and that punishment is non-credible to actors who have nothing to lose', it is equally reasonable to assume that crime has increased in Japan during the last ten years.

From this description of changes in economic parameters, the next step is to look into socio-structural and cultural changes. Has anything of criminological relevance taken place in Japanese society when it comes to the *family* and the *educational* institution?

Primary and secondary socialisation: Weakened prerequisites for social inclusion?

> Middle school students have changed greatly over the past 10 years. Remaining nervously in their own shells, they have become more selfish and stubborn. It has been impossible to predict what they do when. Much of the blame rests with parents who treat their offsets like pets. Schools, formerly respected as 'sacred ground', have been target of serious vandalism. And violent behaviour is on the rise; even children who appear well behaved can attack at the drop of a hat. (Kawakami, 1998)

My starting point in this section is the basic lesson that an important prerequisite for the feeling of individual belonging is the existence of social structures that safeguard automatic membership in a primary group ('the nursery of human nature' as Cooley, 1983, called them). To the extent that a society gives a more or less *automatic* (i.e. *ascribed* more than attained) membership to all its citizens in some type of primary group, one important premise for social integration is established. Within the primary group one can assume a reciprocal understanding and a reciprocal sentiment that give everybody a feeling of togetherness and belonging (what Gøran Rosenberg described as the 'warm circle', see Bauman, 2001: 10[14]). The primary group is the primary site for safeguarding the ontological security for each individual. The family institution is of course the archetype of this basic social organisation, but more generally sociologists include in this concept all kinds of face-to-face, small groups that are non-specialised and relatively long-lasting.

In *Japan as a Low-Crime Nation* I concluded that Japanese 'groupism' created a network for the individual that obviously had an important criminological relevance: 'The omnipresence of groupism creates a tight society (with its own price!) that functions preventively regarding crime' (Leonardsen, 2004: 127)[15]. The importance of belongingness is in Japan closely linked to the positive celebration of *dependence* (Doi, 1976). It is not only the family institution that links Japanese citizens to a social network. Cultural values that underline the importance of submission to a mythologised 'common good' and the harmony of the group[16] are matched by structural arrangements in schools and places of work that encapsulate nearly every citizen. MacIntyre (1984) talks about 'the situated self' to describe individuals located in such a group where moral thinking is formed in reference to significant others. Being outside of a group in Japan is synonymous to being a non-citizen (*hikokumin*, Ezawa, 1990; Nakane, 1970). Until recently, relatively few people have had such a status in Japan (see Stevens, 1997). As Bellah (2003) elaborates in historical detail, the group ideology is omnipresent in Japan and has been so since the beginning of historic time. The idea of the superior status of the group and the community has a sacred quality, and the implications are ubiquitous: 'Science, ethics, philosophy, and virtually all aspects of culture are valuable only insofar as they contribute to the realization of value in the group, not as ends in themselves. Ethics consist mainly in acting as one should in one's group – there is no universal ethic' (p. 185).

In *Order by Accident: The Origins and Consequences of Conformity in Contemporary Japan,* Miller and Kanazawa (2000) argue how this ubiquitous group structure has through the years laid the foundation for social order in this society. Rather than cultural values (like Confucianism) they maintain that group monitoring and sanctioning (in the family, work group, clubs and so on) are what keep people in line. While the explicit purpose of this structuring of social life is to maintain control over the member's behaviour, the unintended consequence is order for the entire society ('how small-group interactions have macro-level consequences', p. 133). Unfortunately, these authors are very brief about how recent turbulence has affected the striking conformity in this society. So what can be said about this? Let me first comment on the *primary* primary group, the family institution.

The family in transition

The family is no longer a place where one feels security. If children thought of the family in this way they would not commit suicide. The family has become a place where there is no more communication among its members. The individual homes in the local district have no contact with each other any more. Therefore the morals, the habits, and the common sense of the local community can no longer be transmitted to the children through the home. The children feel no pressure from the local society and walk along the streets proudly smoking cigarettes, gather in front of convenience stores until late at night, or calmly put on makeup on the train. Children who do not feel the gaze of other people have lost their sense of morality'. (Ogi, a well-known commentator on educational matters, quoted in Ackermann, 2004: 70)

Today, the family institution has become a more fragile social group to more Japanese people than it used to be. This represents a special challenge in a culture where *dependence* on significant others and *predictability* in one's lives have been taken for granted. Kaplan et al. (1998) argue that Japan had traditionally been known for its enduring and resilient family structure, which provided support for people of all ages. Japan could for many years boast of having one of the lowest divorce rates in the modern world. When Fukuyama (2000) uses the Scandinavian countries as a negative case regarding quality of life for children (due to high divorce rates and high rates of female labour force participation), he recommends the socially conservative culture of Japan as a better alternative. This apparently empirically based argument is no longer valid. In spite of strong cultural[17], economic and legal barriers[18] to getting a divorce, the socially conservative, collective culture of Japanese society is no longer preventing this country's people from adopting the individualistic and emancipated Western attitude regarding divorce. Since the late 1980s divorce rates have shown an upward trend (a slight increase even from the 1960s), reaching a peak of 290,000 in 2002, declining to 255,000 in 2007 (Statistical Handbook of Japan[19]). This gives a divorce rate of 2.02 (compared to 2.30 in 2002), which places the Japanese divorce rate around the middle of European countries (the US level is double that of Japan, while Italy and Greece have less than half the rate of Japan (Curtin, 2002)[20]. Social change has obviously reached the family institution in Japan.

These changes are actually very disturbing because they take place in a culture where the welfare support for single-parent families is less adequate than in the Scandinavian countries[21]. As we shall see, a divorce in Japan is more likely to be accompanied by economic hardship than in many Western countries. Also, the rising divorce rates are especially disturbing against a cultural background where harmony, loyalty and long-term commitment are cherished values. This means that a decision to divorce has to be made against strong countervailing forces and with a lot of shame built into the process[22]. As Ono (2006: 8) points out, 'the stigma attached to divorce is therefore likely to be greater in Japan, because divorce is not just a private affair – a breakup of the couples – but a breakup involving the extended family'. For Japanese people, marriage is between family and family.

Divorce in Japan implies in the vast majority of cases (80–90 per cent according to Struck and Sakamaki, 2003) not only that the mother retains custody of the children, but also that the non-custodial parent has little or no contact with the children after the split (Caranci, 2007)[23]. 'It is as if the child loses a parent in an accident, as if that parent just dies' (Tokyo divorce lawyer Hiroshi Shibuya, in Caranci, 2007)[24]. There is little enforcement of child support orders in Japan, and upon divorce, the typical solution is that the father pays nothing for the child's support. This drastic implication is a consequence of the strong division of responsibility between husband and wife in the post-war period, in which children belonged to their mothers[25] ('good wife, wise mother-ideology') and the husbands belonged to their employers (according to McCargo, 2004, a common Japanese saying states that 'a good husband is healthy and absent'). Also, family experts say, divorce carries such a strong stigma that former spouses avoid seeing each other (Struck and Sakamaki, 2003). Until April 2007, divorced women faced tremendous economic challenges since all assets belonging to the husband remained his alone. Also in relation to the pension system, divorced women have been left with very scarce resources. Even though some public relief for divorced women exists, the waiting list of applicants is long and the cash benefits are meagre (Tanikawa, 2002). Certainly Japanese women's traditionally high dependence on their husbands has made them financially very vulnerable in the event of divorce. Roberts (2002: 69) refers to a survey by the Ministry of Health and Welfare showing that only one third of all divorced women had received a share of property or any form of compensation after the break up, and 'child support or a decent pension cannot always be counted on'. Furthermore, for those who return to the work force, it is part-time work and poorly paid jobs that are waiting.

There is reason to argue that psychological as well as economic stress related to a divorce is more pressing in Japan than in many Western countries. For social scientists who ask general questions about the social impacts of divorce, Japan (like other collectivistic cultures) reminds us that the answer has to be contingent, i.e. that it depends on the culture within which that divorce takes place. The growing debate on children living in poverty could illustrate this point.

According to Curtin (2003a), an alarming rise in the number of poor Japanese children gives reason for deep worry. Most of these children live in mother-headed households and 'many psychologists blame the excessive economic hardships faced by single-parent families as an important factor behind the worrying rise in lone-mother suicides'

(Curtin, 2003a). The gravity is underlined in the Citizen's Basic Living Survey, published in August 2002. When comparing the economic conditions for married couples versus single-mother households, this survey reports that the latter group had an average annual income which was only one third of a two-parent household. Keiji Hirano reports (*Japan Times*, March 12, 2009) that the economic slump has severely hit single-mother households because many of these women work as irregular employees. According to the director of 'Single Mothers' Forum', deregulation and privatisation has led schools to outsource catering and this has made the labour situation for single mothers less stable. The further implication of this is that the average single-parent family actually lived below the poverty line (i.e. with a household income falling below half that of the national average). While 59.4 per cent of married couples with children described their economic situation as 'difficult', 81.6 per cent of lone mothers reported that they experienced 'extreme hardship' (all figures reported in Curtin, 2003a). The relative poverty rate of single-mother households in 2004 was 66 per cent, compared to 11 per cent of households with both parents, and compared to other OECD countries Japan holds the third highest poverty rate for children in single-mother households (Fukue, 2009). In present-day Japan many women within this group could be described as 'working poor' (amounting to some 5.5 million people in 2005, according to Shimizu and Nakamura, 2007). While 86 per cent of these lone mothers are working, their average income is usually extremely low and their rights regarding sick pay, etc. are poor[26]. According to a survey, 33 per cent of single mothers go to work even when they feel sick (*Japan Times*, March 12, 2009). In the 'New Labour Market' that has appeared in Japan's liberalised economy over the last decade, irregular workers' (mostly women) wages are low and legal rights are few[27]. As most Japanese fathers fail to pay child support and social welfare benefits are very inadequate (and have been cut), one can imagine the stress this situation triggers[28]. At the start of the millennium the government even worsened the situation by restricting eligibility to various lone-mother welfare entitlements[29]. However, since April 2007, divorced women have become entitled to up to half of the benefits from their ex-husband's Employees' Pension (Caranci, 2007) which implies that at least *one* economic barrier for divorce is removed.

It has been pointed out that being a 'proper mother' is generally very demanding in Japan. This is even truer for divorced mothers, and Japanese culture adds further burdens to this status. Goodman (2002: 148) points to how the combined effect of an absent father[30], little support from an extended family or the community, 'the myth of motherhood' (i.e. women are naturally programmed to be good and caring mothers) and not least the idea that women have the full responsibility for their children's success can explain the broad existence of childrearing neurosis among mothers. For *divorced* mothers one can imagine what this means. A government survey published in 2005 disclosed that the vast majority of children in fatherless households were living 'far below the poverty line, creating a rapidly expanding underclass of impoverished families' (Curtin, 2005). Alarming reports have been presented in the media about low-income families where mothers and children have been dying from malnutrition[31], and (as I will return to) the rise in suicides among adults with monetary problems and among lone mothers is so steep that a non-profit group (*Ashinaga*) has recently been established that gives financial help to children who have lost their parents due to suicide (*Japan Times*, March 13, 2003). According to Curtin (2003a), suicides for financial reasons among lone mothers 'have shot up in the last five years with local and national newspapers carrying daily reports of tragedies'. While people facing economic hardship in earlier days could usually count on an extended family network for help, due to weakened family ties this can no longer be taken for granted.

In sum: a significant increase in the number of divorces, inadequate and shrinking welfare benefits for lone mothers, an almost complete absence of the father (in economic as well as social terms) when divorce occurs and a culture where divorce still carries a strong burden of shame have made the Japanese family institution less secure for both children and their parents. In a country where the family has traditionally been regarded as the primary site for cultivating *amae* (dependence) relations[32], the changes in divorce rates are serious. This conclusion should not be interpreted as homage to the traditional family institution in Japan. Those who have argued that there were too *few* divorces in Japan in the 1960s and 1970s had strong arguments as for the repressive elements of the Japanese *ie* (household) institution. Nevertheless, the basic social structure that surrounds the individual from birth to death is less predictable and less secure today than a couple of decades ago. Kingston (2004: 259), describes status for the family institution in Japan today by saying that it is:

> being buffeted from all sides by rapid changes and growing strains in the social fabric that highlight the unrealistically high demands and expectations imposed by the government, employers, and the

prevailing ideology. These pressures are taking a toll that falls most heavily on women and their children. The prevalence of domestic violence, divorce, juvenile delinquency, suicide, and alienation are some of the disturbing signs of the times.

From a perspective of social integration, Japan has undoubtedly become a more fragile institution. This is further accentuated when paying attention to the change in the *ie* institution that has taken place during the last few decades. As Stevenson et al. (1986) argue, the wider household institution that was earlier the basic unit in Japanese society has gradually crumbled and turned Japanese families into what Kotani (2004: 41) describes as 'empty nests'. This has left each child more vulnerable than before. 'The concept of the child as a member of the general community has thus ceased to function, while loosening relationships within the *ie* system itself have confined the child to the individual family and to the biological parent-child relationship' Kotani (2004: 34). When this shrunken primary group (reproduction rate of 1.21, one of the lowest in the modern world) then breaks down there is really not much else to lean on. It is not only the case that many children are without a father present, they are also without brothers and sisters and to many children siblings are more a concept than a reality in everyday life. (For a further discussion on the social implications of the shrinking family, see Morioka, 1986: 69–70.)

One should not make a simple leap from divorces to anomie (crime, suicides and social problems in general). To the extent that flatteringly low indicators of social disruption (until the 1990s) have been maintained due to a culture of 'friendly authoritarianism' (Sugimoto, 1997), one has to remember that social stability is not synonymous with social harmony. Statistics are nothing more than social *indicators*, but these indicators tell precious little unless they are interpreted within a wider context of values and meanings[33]. However, a short summary of international research on the effects of divorce on children leaves little doubt about the conclusion. Clarke-Stewart and Brentano (2006: 121) sum up research within this field by saying that:

a variety of studies in which odd ratios are available show that children from divorced families are twice to three times as likely as children from intact families to have problems. In studies of nationally representative samples, children from divorced families are twice as likely to receive psychological help, to skip school or get suspended, to get in trouble with the police, to drop out of high school, to get pregnant as a teenager, to be out of work in their later teens and early twenties, to see their own marriages end in divorce, and to experience clinically significant psychological distress and depression in childhood and adulthood.

Clarke-Stewart is careful not to dramatise the negative aspects of the data. Even though the message is clear ('children see no benefit in divorce'), he reminds us not to forget that many – in fact most – divorce 'victims' are functioning well[34]. In the case of Japan, I find it important to keep in mind this 'sober' perspective, since the debate on this topic in Japan is quite heated and morally 'infected'. However, I also have to add that there are strong reasons to believe that stress symptoms connected to a divorce probably are stronger in Japan than in many Western countries. Even though the causal relationships between economic and social turbulence are complicated, and even though modern market societies (like Japan) also imply new opportunities, one has to disregard essential sociological theories as well as a lot of empirical data to wipe out the criminological relevance of the dramatic changes that have taken place in Japan in the last 20 years.

The school: More 'moral education' than ever

In the Japanese family the child is unique and can be spoiled, while outside the family it is all about adapting to universal standards, adapting to other people and acquiring an ability to serve rather than being served. Moving from being absolutely unique and strongly indulged by the mother to being one among many others is a big challenge for the youngsters[35]. Groups *outside* the family institution are the most important hotbed of collective thinking in Japan[36].

Since 'group pressure' is a main argument when explaining low crime rates in Japan, I shall first give some more details about *how* the transferring of group values traditionally takes place in Japan and *what* these values are all about. Next, the pertinent question will be if anything has changed in this regard during the last 20–30 years that can eventually explain increasing crime rates in the 1990s. In short, has the school system failed in its moral education, in 'building character'?

Starting in pre-school and school, group values are systematically and painstakingly drummed into each individual via a complicated network of controls, rules and regulations. At the age of three (the typical age for entering kindergarten), children have to replace a nepotistic familial socialisation with a universalistic and collectivistic ideology. From this age on it is a primary aim for teachers to get the children used to a future life where individualistic values are banned. Consequently, much time is devoted to peer-interaction and cooperation within the group, and this is regarded as the most effective way of curbing selfishness and narcissism. To the youngsters this means a painful break with an overly protective mother (who, until then, has created a 'cocoon of security', as Hendry, 1986: 56, denotes it).

Since *harmony* (i.e. within the group) is a superior value in Japan, and since the cultivation of this value probably functions as an important crime preventive mechanism (see Leonardsen, 2004), it has been essential to teach the child to be compliant and to find her or his place within a broader context. As a consequence, central government has a strong influence on values transmitted in Japanese pre-schools, even though the organisational structure is less rigid. Variations exist within this system (Holloway, 2000), but compared to Western countries the content of Japanese pre-school education is still relatively uniform[37]. Ben-Ari (1997: 21) brings strong testimony to this argument when describing a heavy bureaucratic intervention in the lives of Japanese children with what he calls an 'official design of the lives of youngsters and their families' (cf. Chapter 2) through a plethora of mechanisms: 'talks and lectures to parents, home visits, phone calls or personal meetings with teachers, documentation (like personal message books or class letters) sent home, the use of message boards at pre-schools, and the participation of parents in PTAs, parents' days and various parties and ceremonies'. At the end of his field study Ben-Ari had accumulated no less than three full kilos of records and documents with all kinds of information, mirroring the extensive flow of information and applications to the children's homes. The superior ideology in all these documents is defined in advance and taken for granted; the challenge is only how to implement this given value structure. Ambaras (2006) uses the phrase 'the moulding of a people' when describing state run socialisation of its inhabitants, and Japanese pre-school education gives a pregnant illustration of this concept.

As long as we focus only on the pre-schools, it may be that authors like Ben-Ari and Hendry are exaggerating the extent of uniformity and group pressure in the system. As Holloway (2000) points out, only 42 per cent of pre-schools are public; the rest are operated by private educational organisations (47 per cent), by religious organisations (5 per cent) and by individuals (6 per cent). Actually, there is considerable variation across the country and across different types of institutions. Strict discipline and structured curriculums may dominate at some places while free play and more permissive teachers may dominate at other places. This observation makes Holloway conclude that assertions about an excessive group-orientation among Japanese children represent a one-dimensional portrait. Nevertheless (and as Holloway herself underlines), Japanese pre-schools are regarded as core institutions that enable young children to learn about the basic values that Japanese society is built on. Central among these values are obedience, loyalty and adaptation – values that all contribute to prepare children to become a *shakaijin* (a member of society). The Ministry of Education reasserted this in its White Paper from 1994, called *New Directions in School Education: Fostering Strength for Life*. Here the task was defined as 'the pursuit of values that remain constant across the generations. The basic approaches to this task are character formation, including the development of knowledge, morals, and physical health....' (cited in Hood, 2001: 81). The principle of 'sweetness and harshness' (*ame to muchi*) is probably the best condensation of the dominating pedagogical philosophy in Japanese pre-schools, where the whip is held in readiness if the candy does not work.

For *my* discussion the important message is that *one* element contributing to making Japan a low-crime society is its extraordinarily strong focus on group membership and the moral demands that follow from this. Compliance, obedience, duty and development of a collective identity – such ideals are deeply embedded in Japanese society. However, there are also other elements in this ideology, namely the stressing of qualities like harmonious interaction with others, unselfish cooperation with others, taking one's turn, the ability to apologise, the importance of friendship, equality within the group and a fair distribution of duties. The relevance of all this in an analysis of crime is that, to the extent that committing crime takes agency, and that crime requires the ability to withdraw from informal social control (exercised by the group), Japanese citizens have traditionally been socialised in a culture with stronger crime prevention mechanisms than is the case in many Western societies. With a deeply embedded consciousness that the individual is always a representative of one or more groups, each citizen is continuously subordinated to a strong informal social control. The effect of this group ideology is further strengthened by the Buddhist and Confucian value structure that permeates everyday life in a group. As Ives (2005) emphasises, Zen Buddhism (which dominates in Japan) generates a behavioural attitude that is characterised by conflict avoidance and seeking of peace at any price. The most important idea according to this view is *not* to seek what is true, *not* to cherish opinions, *not* to stick your head forward and *not* to fight for your interests.

The accompanying message for those who accept this ideology is to know their rightful station in life. As I pointed out in Chapter 2, diligence, perseverance, humility, deference, obedience and penitent self-criticism are all regarded as important qualities for a well functioning group member.

While loyal obedience to the group is impressed from an early start in pre-school, this ideology is also carried on in the rest of the school system. This is especially apparent in the important role of the *han* groups in Japanese schools. These are relatively small groups which are systematically built into the school system, and whose members are changed or rotated after some time. The *han* group serves as a study group, a laboratory group and also a task team for cleaning, serving school lunch and performing other tasks during the day. According to Ishikida (2005: 59), this group structure contributes to building a feeling of solidarity among its participants, and the ideology that was first learnt in pre-school is further developed within the *han* setting.[38]

Based on the above descriptive presentation, several questions emerge regarding group structure and group ideology in Japanese schools during the last 20–30 years. Has Japan become less of a group-based society in terms of how the early formalised socialisation takes place? Is there less stress on the idea that it is by adapting to others and by obeying the group that the individual becomes a full member of society? Have children become more released from collective bondings than they used to be? Has anything of the Buddhist and Confucian value structure that dominated in the 1960s and 1970s been diluted since the economy collapsed?

As a matter of fact, the Japanese school system faced different educational reforms in the 1980s and 1990s (for details see Beauchamp, 1991; Ben-Ari, 1997; Hood, 2001; Ishikida, 2005; Okano and Tsuchiya, 1999). While Japan's system of schooling for many years had been celebrated for being efficient and for providing a high level of education for the whole population (Okano and Tsuchiya, 1999: 194), more and more critical voices reached the public sphere in the early 1980s. Life in kindergartens and nursery schools was said to be too regimented with too strong intervention from teachers. In primary and secondary school the critics pointed out that the system gave priority to rote learning with the accompanying 'examination hell' as a natural consequence. This, it was said, made Japanese children servile objects that were easy to manipulate, rather than preparing them to become independent and creative subjects. Furthermore, what Ueda (2000) called 'the collapse of human relationships' became a recurrent complaint directed towards youth. Among the worries that caught attention were assertions about a steep increase in registered cases of bullying (*ijime*). Numbers of cases reached a peak in 1986, and then another wave appeared in 1994; in both situations there was an intense media debate about children who had committed suicide as a consequence of harassment (for details, see Foljanty-Jost, ed., 2003). Also, an increase in the registered number of school refusals (especially in middle schools), peaking in 1994, was another sign of worry that triggered the need for school reforms. In short, from the early 1980s (i.e. *before* the economic crisis) and on there was a mounting public outcry about what was happening to the moral fabric of Japanese youth and what role the school system played in this regard.

What really came to trigger the perceived demand for educational reform were the murder of some vagrants executed by schoolchildren and the beating of a teacher by eight lower secondary school students (in 1983). Together with an asserted general growth of school violence and juvenile delinquency, this demand made the newly elected (1982) Prime Minister Nakasone present a 'declaration of war' against problem children. Reform of the educational system was the most important strategy for fulfilling this task, because, as Hood (2001) comments, educational reform would be a stepping-stone to a broader social reform of society. Nakasone's way of understanding the genesis of increasing social unrest in Japan was made explicit in his address to the Diet in 1983:

> I cannot believe that the problem of drugs, crime, violence, and other phenomena that corrode our youth are unrelated to the decline of the home as the basic unit of society and the lack of education for our young people in such basic and essential social patterns as courtesy, responsibility, honesty, brotherly love, neighbourly kindness, and the spirit of service. (Hood, 2001: 80)

Against this background Nakasone's Cabinet established in 1984 an Ad Hoc Council of Education (*Rinkyōshin*), which during a period of three years submitted four reports. One important implication of this reform process was *the implementation of a further reinforcement of moral education* (McVeigh, 2000: 89).

The initiatives for fortifying the moral aspects of the Japanese education system should perhaps be interpreted as a reaction to *conceived social problems among children* rather than as a reaction to preceding liberal reforms within the educational system. Even though changes had appeared regarding diversification and increased focus on creativity, this had not had any effect on the basic principles upon which primary and secondary education were based. The group ideology and the structural arrangements that this ideology was proclaimed through were present in Japanese schools in the 1970s and 1980s as much as they were in the 1950s and 1960s. This argument, regarding cause and effect, has to be stressed: while some discussants seem to take the (asserted) increase in social problems among youngsters as an expression of a more liberalised, or even Westernised, Japanese school system[39], I find it hard to trace any documentation supporting such a viewpoint. Rather, it seems that alertness towards the substantiation of moral education, teaching of good manners and discipline and implanting the principle of self-restraint (cf. Yoneyama's (1999) concept 'the structure of silence') has been present in Japanese schools all through this period, and if anything, *these values have been strengthened rather than weakened through the 1980s and 1990s* ('a refocusing on traditional past values', as Okano and Tsuchiya, 1999: 49, express it for this period). Both LeTendre (2000) and Yoneyama (1999) support such a conclusion by showing how 'The New Course of Study' (implemented in 1993) demanded that teachers gave grades for students' attitudes, motivations, cooperation, responsibility and willingness to participate in various school activities. Around the turn of the century this focus on moral education was further reinforced. In August 2000 the Education Ministry's National Institute for Educational Research and the Welfare Ministry's Institute of Public Health started a joint research project (including psychiatrists) 'to issue a report by the end of the next year with recommendations for parents on raising children and for teachers on coping with students' (*Asahi Shimbun*, August 24, 2000). And then, in 2008, drafts were unveiled by the Education Ministry (to become effective in 2011) which strongly emphasised moral education and, for the first time in 30 years, called for increased class hours and teaching content. According to the *Japan Times* (March 2, 2008), these reforms marked 'a major departure from the "more relaxed education" embodied in the current courses of study'. Since this is a salient point for my discussion in the next chapters, let me state my argument very explicitly:

Neither regarding ideological content, nor regarding organising principles does it seem appropriate to argue that social problems among youth could be linked to less attention to principles for proper behaviour in Japanese schools.

On the contrary, 'the state, along with corporate interests, has so successfully instilled orthodoxy about capitalism and Japanese identity that it is very hard for many to conceive of alternatives. Thus, the implementation of fundamental change becomes exceedingly difficult' (McVeigh, 2000: 89). Also, one has to remember that a basic principle for socialising children in Japan is the idea of 'whole-person-education' (*zenjin kyōiku*). While many will associate the Japanese school system with a formalised and disciplined cramming system, one easily forgets the other side of the coin, namely the importance within this ideology of developing the spirit (*kokoro*) and what is called 'education of the heart'. The country has for centuries cultivated Buddhist and Confucian values and this cultural heritage is not easily given up. The Education Ministry has always had a firm grip on the content of the Japanese curriculum and it has traditionally given little space for experimenting or alternative projects[40]. Moral education is so central in creating diligent workers who are aware of what it means to 'be a Japanese' that it would be unthinkable to yield at this point. Any assertions of moral decay in Japan should hardly be shouldered by the educational system[41].

In Japan in general, the *group* (rather than the individual) is still the main unit that decides priorities and navigating principles in society. Numerous guidelines for correct behaviour in organisations and institutions are in operation today as much as they were a long time ago. These guidelines (for example, as manuals for schoolteachers), 'begin with a definition of what it means to be human. To be human, we read, is to live within a social network, outside which the individual cannot exist; one's duty is the maintenance of this network so as to enable others to lead a wholly human life' (Ackermann, 2004: 69). In spite of economic turbulence, Japan should still be described as a consistent group society, and the *moral values* that follow from this *social structure* are imposed like before.

The above argument is not to say that the guiding values among the younger generation (*or* adults) have remained the same during the last decades. In Chapter 6, I shall look further into the present debate regarding assertions of a deep 'youth crisis' in Japan. Not only the media, but social researchers as well, have conveyed a story about 'the new breed' (Mathews and White, 2004: 5) disclosing attitudes and behaviour that challenge traditional Japanese values. However, in this chapter my main intention has been to discuss to what extent the primary agents of socialisation have 'diluted' the traditional value basis and thereby contributed to a moral decay in society. Even though there is no 'exact scientific' answer to this question, I find it hard to blame changes in educational guidelines for growing concerns about youth. If anything, discipline and demands for adaptation to the group seem to have been strengthened in step with reports on social unrest among schoolchildren. Furthermore, one should warn against taking the recurring cry about wayward youths at face value. Research done by Foljanty-Jost (ed.) (2003) gives reason to remind us about the dangers of 'moral panics' related to misbehaviour among youth. Even though problem behaviour obviously exists, and even though there are clear indications that there really was an increase in school violence at junior high schools in the mid-1990s, the general conclusion for these authors is that these problems are 'highly overestimated within Japanese public opinion' (Foljanty-Jost, ed., 2003: vii) and that 'there is no empirical research available concerning the decline of conformity among school children' (Foljanty-Jost and Metzler, 2003: 3).

Yoder (2004: 166) points to another important perspective in the debate on the asserted youth crisis, namely that what he describes as 'the escalation of adult social controls' in education has important implications from a *social class* perspective. It is the lower and lower-middle working class students who, according to this scholar, have become the target of increased supervision. Increasing apathy towards education among this group (an apathy that according to Yoder borders on contempt) has been confronted with control rather than structural changes. The new national educational reforms implemented in 2002, focusing the need for a resocialisation of adolescents at home, in the community and at school and stressing the importance of instilling traditional values in the youth, will according to Yoder only serve to make the situation worse than it already is. In other words, from this perspective, an eventual lack of morality among the coming generation may as easily be interpreted as an expression of too *much*, rather than too *little*, focus on morality.

In spite of the conclusion above, it remains to ask if there has been a more general change of values in Japanese society during the last 20 years. How have the economic crisis, the Aum attack, the Kobe earth-quake and the escalating environmental problems affected the way of thinking, the commitment people feel for 'project Japan' or for their general hopes for the future? Let me conclude this chapter by saying a few words about what Kingston (2004: xv) calls the 'loss of reassuring familiarity' that, according to him, is percolating through Japanese society and transforming it.

Japanese value structure under reconstruction?

I have argued that the dominant values at the collective level in Japan represent *one* of the explanations for the traditional low crime rate in this country. This is a story about a relatively homogenous society based on 'traditional' values (cf. Japan as a *collective shame culture*). Has Japanese society changed regarding this?

My answer is: 'Yes, to a certain extent'. Japan has, during the last couple of decades, become a more pluralistic society. In brief, in the 1945–90 period Japanese society was relatively autonomous economically[42] and the citizens were all, and to a remarkable extent, united in the common task of building the nation. Since that time, Japan has become more and more dependent on the global society[43], and thereby also more economically vulnerable, while its citizens have become less committed to 'Project Japan Inc.'. In a Mertonian perspective the situation could be expressed like this. Until the 1980s the Japanese (literally, *all* of them) were culturally as well as economically/structurally integrated in society. The aim for the future was set, it was culturally adopted by everyone and each citizen could expect to be included in the project. This changed in the 1990s, and the challenge now was not only related to the economic and structural exclusion (unemployment, divorces) of many people, but also to the fact that the cultural goals became more uncertain and even controversial. People started asking what they were striving for and where Japan was heading. While literally every Japanese citizen for some 40 years had been committed to a common goal, this could no longer be taken for granted.

The economic system in Japan could until recently be described as a 'hybrid'. At the outset, it was based on a classical capitalistic market ideology, but strong interventionist and Confucian principles made Japan an extraordinary case which caught an enormous interest and curiosity. Ronald Dore's (1986) concept of *'Flexible Rigidities'* grasps the essence of this perspective: A growing economy has to be based on more than competitive and efficient producers. It has to be based on a common purpose, commitment, social solidarity, trust relationships, or, in short, what Harvey Liebenstein (quoted in Dore: 1986) defined as the 'X-efficiency variable'. In 1987, Berger asked to what extent East Asian countries (like Japan) would in the future be able to continue their (until then) successful resistance to Western individualism. He concluded that 'the cross-national evidence on individuating modernity is strong enough to make one very sceptical about the ability of these societies to continue on their merry course of happy "groupism"' (p. 170). Berger foretold a future development where the traditional values would most likely have to yield in confrontation with advancing market competition. In many regards Berger's prophecy was right. In spite of an intensification of 'moral education' in schools (cf. above) the collective mentality structure in Japan has been under continuous strain. Due to the turbulence in the early 1990s, Japanese citizens have met with challenges that have changed their parameters for acting. A collectivistic culture based on principles like endurance, benevolence and collectivism has gradually lost some of its credence among many citizens, not the least among the youth. This 'quiet transformation' (as Kingston: 2004, calls it) is perhaps more profound than many realise.

First of all, the change of political ideology in the direction of more unfettered market liberalism (but see note 7 in this chapter) has undermined traditional, paternalistic values which, after all, contributed to a feeling of safety among citizens. The general *amae* ideology (being dependent on others), together with the senior-junior principle, ensured that one could always count on support from the group one belonged to, at least as long as one adapted to society's expectations. This has changed. Even though the picture is complex and Japan still is a far cry from a pure market society, given the traditional cultural setting people are used to in this country the Japanese actually experienced a 'culture shock' during the 1990s. Being used to a kind of 'victimless capitalism', Japanese citizens have been forced to accept more of a 'sink or swim' ideology. Economic reforms, particularly those initiated by the Koizumi government, have moved Japanese society away from principles of communal solidarity, since loss of economic and social safety has not been replaced by welfare benefits for the needy. In a culture where people traditionally could depend on and presume upon other people's benevolence, and where 'helplessness' (for those who were inside a group) has not carried the same negative stigma as in the West, the new impulses have certainly disturbed many people[44].

Next, empirical research supports the conclusion that essential value changes *have* taken place in Japan. Möhwald (2005) presents interesting survey data that indicate increasing differentiation, pluralisation and fragmentation of the Japanese value universe. What is interesting in Möhwald's data is that significant changes in values and attitudes had already occurred during the boom in the 1980s. According to this author, rapid economic growth in this period generated a new mentality where 'permissiveness' increased significantly, together with more pluralised lifestyles. To an increasing extent, consumerism became the major vehicle for self-expression, while, at the same time, a high degree of social control still persisted in society. With the burst of the bubble economy in 1990, values changed new direction. Optimism was replaced by pessimism, extravagance was replaced by modesty and consumerism was replaced by tendencies to withdraw from the market. It

is important to note that Möhwald complicates the argument by saying that a more self-expressive way of life went in tandem with strong
social control, at least until the 1990s. This confirms my argument
about ambiguity. 'Social change' represents an incredibly vague category, and, at this level, there is no problem finding arguments supporting stability as well as radical change[45]. However, it seems safe to argue
that Japanese society has become less monolithic in its value structure
than it used to be. While the official Japan has intensified the importance of traditional values in school programmes and in advisory campaigns towards parents on how to raise children in late modernity, new
mentalities have developed 'behind the curtain'. Increasing influence
from the internet, commercials and movies, and increasing exposure to
Western values, have all played a role in affecting traditional Japanese
values. The breakdown in the economy represents another engine for
value change in Japan. According to Möhwald the economic decline
has first and foremost affected males under 30 years, with lower educational levels and with employment in production and clerical jobs.
Möhwald (ibid.: 66–67) reports about this group:

> Their general value orientations are marked by a strong sense of self-
> interest and a tendency toward individualistic values that border on
> egoism. They show disregard for duties towards the family and tend
> to push for their own rights without regard for others. They display
> a strong orientation toward the hedonistic values of pleasure, amuse-
> ment, and consumption, and a relatively strong orientation toward
> acquisitive materialism and social advancement. They also tend
> toward instant gratification.

When Möhwald analyses his data at what he calls the 'psychological
level', he finds that the group of young men show a low degree of satisfaction with life, they harbour a great deal of insecurity, unhappiness
and anxiety and have weak integration with their social environment.
They have low self-esteem and self-reliance and they display tendencies
of anomie and mistrust. As regards work, they are described as avoiding responsibility and strenuous work. In conclusion, they 'are not well
adapted to the challenges now taking place' (p. 67) and, in consequence,
'this could lead to an increased disposition towards violence, some of it
linked to xenophobia or discrimination' (p. 74).

Scholars like Kingston (2004) and Hirata (2002) emphasise many of
the same characteristics as Möhwald. Kingston points to the recent concern in Japan about deteriorating public ethics, moral values and social

order. He uses an interesting glimpse of mentality change when observing that subway signs these days warn the passengers against punching train company employees, groping women, smashing ticket machines and chatting on their mobile phones. Not long ago, the only signs to be seen were the reminders suggesting that passengers offered their seats to elderly or pregnant women. Furthermore, Kingston uses reports on bullying, truancy, breakdown of classroom order, increasing divorce rates, child abuse and new forms of prostitution (or 'compensated dating' as it is called) as indications of an era of contention and change. Adding to this fading job security and declining respect for the elderly, Kingston represents a distinct voice among those arguing in the direction of 'abrupt and major shifts in national ideology' (p. 35). He sums it all up by arguing that 'the traditional face of Japan is fast becoming unrecognizable. The social relationships, assumptions, and norms characteristic of post-war Japan began to unravel with stunning speed in the 1990s' (p. 29).

Hirata (2002) stresses how a global pressure to open up Japanese markets has had spreading consequences on Japanese society at large. 'Indeed, the impacts of globalization have gone beyond changing lifestyles or "McDonaldization", but have affected people's belief systems, and normative orientations' (p. 27). Hirata has his main focus (when explaining change) on the international economy and the new communications technology. This technology gives people admission to new norms and ways of thinking and opens up new global networks (e.g. through non-governmental organisations). The effects of these global processes are, according to Hirata, a weakening of traditional values and belief systems. He is, for example, very explicit when arguing that 'Confucian cultural values of social hierarchy and conformity are losing their grip on increasing numbers of globally influenced, independent-minded people in Japan' (p. 28), a conclusion that in the main is echoed by Sakurai (2004: 28), arguing that 'a new culture is being created by the children of the countercultural generation of the 1960s'.

How does the above presentation compare to what I have written earlier about an intensified moral education in schools through the years? Obviously, conflicting processes are at work. From a superior societal perspective, Japan has gradually, and outside the control of political decisions, become more 'Westernised', more pluralist, less homogenous as for people's aspirations and less committed regarding 'Project Japan'. This might certainly be described as a significant 'change of values'. From the perspective of 'voluntaristic policy', cherished values have been implemented more steadfastly than ever.[46] What could be described as a from-the-outside, but very subtle, 'attack' on a traditional Japanese value structure, has been confronted with a moral rearmament from 'inside'.

However, I do think that especially Kingston (2004) (as well as Japanese politicians and media in general) is making a classical methodological mistake when drawing conclusions on the state of morality among youth from juvenile deviancy. It is problematic to use *behaviour* as an expression of *values*. If crime, drug use, bullying, divorce, etc. could be regarded as a kind of operationalised expression of moral preferences, then I could accept this way of arguing. But this is not sustainable. People's actions may or may not be an expression of their true intentions or their basic values. In general, criminology has taught us to be careful about inducing belief systems from manifest actions. It is often astonishing to register the conformist, traditional and established values criminal people express (which, in the case of Japanese youth, will be supported in Chapter 4). Consequently, we should warn against using the amount and character of social problems as an expression of which values these people cherish.

As we shall see in Chapter 4, the assertion about an egoistic and hedonistic turn in people's values has been echoed in the White Papers on Crime for some years, illustrated by data showing that crimes committed with the motive of 'obtaining entertainment expenses/extra spending money' have increased. To a large extent, this story also overlaps with the message sent by established society, the media and not the least politicians.

Negatively loaded descriptions like these, especially focusing the younger generation, do not represent anything new in Japan. As I shall show in Chapter 5, this 'youth labelling' is a cyclical phenomenon (like in the West). However, a critical stance to such presentations should not lead to a comparably simplistic rejection: 'things are as they were'. Probably, they are not. But *descriptions* are not the same as *causes*, and this is often where the cards get mixed. When crime is taken as an expression of a moral flaw (which, in a certain sense, could be sustainable) this does not permit a conclusion that moral values have decayed in society. If situational parameters have made crime a more likely alternative, then general morality could even have improved.

If we at this point link the survey data I have presented above with what I have written about *freeters*, *NEETs* and *single parasites*, there are clear indications that a certain transformation of some 'traditional' values has taken place in Japan during the last 20 years. The re-moralisation within primary education could probably be described as a kind of

compensatory reaction from the authorities to what they regard as a serious challenge to the established value hegemony. Economic decline
together with an intensified liberalistic agenda has been decoded by
adults and young people in ways that have made the future more uncertain and unpredictable: 'Most Japanese, are confused as to what goals
to set for themselves and how to go about achieving them', Genda Yuji
(2005) maintains; a quite common comment among japanologists
these days.

The supreme message that should be stated from this discussion
is the lesson from what is known as 'the social psychology of hope'
(Nesse, 1999). Human beings can survive a lot of suffering and pain as
long as they can put their faith in the future. Almost every citizen of
Japan found themselves in a terrible situation in 1945. Of course, they
were materially as well as mentally in an extremely depressed situation.
However, even though the future was not very bright, it would have
to be brighter than the present situation. For many people in Japan,
the present situation, characterised by material affluence, but with
gloomy prospects, is diametrically opposite to the after-war situation.
For the first time since the war, young people of today have reasons
to expect lower standards of living than their parents (Mathews and
White, 2004). As I read the 'sociological climate' in Japan today, this is
what gives reason for worry, and this represents the important cultural
change for Japan. Japanese people, young as well as adults, do not represent an active engine where they have deliberately changed or replaced
traditional values with alternative values. People (in general) have not
called the traditional Japanese value structure to account; they have not
declared this value structure dead and gone, and pointed to a new and
better alternative. On the contrary, much of the frustration in Japan
today is, if anything, linked to a sadness due to a feeling of 'community lost' rather than a happy feeling of 'freedom gained'. This implies
that my line of argument reverses the classical way of reasoning among
conservatives. Instead of maintaining that moral decay and new mentalities have produced a generation of disengaged citizens, the causal
link goes the other way around. The apparently new cultural values are
most of all (but not only!) an expression of a socio-economic structure
where people are facing little hope and have few expectations of collective solutions. The consequence is increasing individualism, for some
expressed as 'hedonistic and materialistic values of ego-centeredness'
(Möhwald, 2005: 62), and for some as a more resigned retreatism (see
Chapter 5). Single parasites, freeters and NEETs are more an expression
of a generation left with few alternative options than an expression of

a generation that has been contaminated with new values (Genda Yuji, 2005). The same conclusion is drawn in Mathews and White's book on *Japan's Changing Generations: Are Young People Creating a New Society?* As maintained by different authors in this anthology it is a paradox that, confronted with the new, gloomy economic realities, the younger generation seems to prefer 'exit' rather than 'voice'. The group of so-called *furiitaas* (young people who do not take regular career-track employment) 'are unwitting victims of the decline of the post-war Japanese economic order rather than conscious agents of its transformation' (Mathews, 2004: 133). They have, in Merton's (1968) terminology become 'retreatists' rather than 'rebels', i.e. they have abandoned both the goals and means of the established society.

Conclusion: Economic insecurity and continuing mainstreaming

To me, the most important element in understanding recent social change in Japan is to look at how people are *materially situated*. Since this perspective is essential for my understanding of social problems in Japan, it should be explicitly stated that a combination of *real* economic changes (job cuts, etc.) and (through a heated media debate) a *perceived* feeling of turbulence, can justify an argument that significant changes have taken place during the relevant period. These changes are not only exaggerated storytelling by overly safety-seeking and fragile Japanese citizens. They make lasting impression as 'bodily experiences', not just on lone mothers, ill-educated youths or poor day labourers, but on large segments of the population who share the same challenges – a low budget welfare state that has little but a tiny safety net to offer and a shame culture that makes failure (especially for bread-winning husbands) in economic life an unbearable burden. Speaking in Marxist terms, it seems safe to conclude that Japan's economic *base* is significantly changed due to more than 15 years of recession, with accompanying economic reforms. Even though economists with different ideological sympathies could wish for stronger measures to be taken, for a conservative and statist nation as Japan, the changes are notable. When it comes to *the superstructure*, one could say that a series of new public endeavours to 'mainstream' the population indicates continuation rather than any sharp rupture. While Japan until 1990 was a showcase regarding how to modernise the economy without modernising the culture, it seems that such a conclusion is still valid regarding the content of formalised education. Both in kindergartens and in schools, 'Japanese culture' is conveyed to no less an extent than before. In spite of reforms that have brought values supporting individualism and self-expression to the forefront, the focus is still on implanting traditional values. In addition, present-day reforms aiming to instil 'community service' as an obligatory part of the curriculum and giving credit to participation in voluntary organisations, etc. for entrance to high school are an indication that 'collectivistic obligations' are taken heed of. Furthermore, even though a ubiquitous consumerism has certainly contributed to a strengthening of privatised values, this is, as Bellah (2003) underlines, not synonymous to saying that individualism has replaced the traditional groupism. 'In many ways the individual is as dependent on the group as ever but group power is exerted through conformist pressure from peers more than through hierarchical authority' (Bellah, 2003: 205). Bellah concludes that the typical structure of Japanese life is by no means broken, and that 'Japan continues to be Asian but not Asian, Western but not Western, and in the very paradoxicality of its situation, acutely self-conscious' (p. 207). My own conclusion will emphasise that to what extent Japan has changed cannot be reduced to formulations like 'to some extent' or 'to a large extent'. It all depends on...But I *do* think that changes in the 1990s have made Japan a less crime resistant society, as will be argued in the next chapter.

4
Crime in Japan 1990–Mid-2000s

Overview

In the present chapter I start with a topic on which there is broad unanimity, namely the escalating *fear of crime* that entered Japanese society during the 1990s. I then give a relatively detailed presentation of *changes in reported crimes* in the last 15–20 years and ask if the fear of crime that people feel is based on 'hard realities' or if it is rather (as some maintain) an expression of 'moral panic'. After presenting the debate on this topic, I conclude that crime actually *has* increased, even though the situation has been dramatised and exaggerated, especially in relation to youth. Also, I discuss what role *domestic violence* may have played in relation to an increase in registered violent crime in Japan.

On the basis of this presentation and the documentation in Chapter 3 concerning economic and socio-cultural changes in Japan, I then conclude that the 'traditional' Confucian value structure of Japan could still be described as a 'crime prevention mechanism' (Japan is still a low-crime nation), but that with the implementation of more economic liberalism in combination with a welfare state that is not too generous, and with a more fragmented family institution than earlier, it seems that since the early 1990s Japan has turned into a less caring society. This topic will be further discussed in the final chapter.

I base this book on the empirical premise that social problems (in general) and crime (in particular) exist as given *facts* that can be meaningfully and statistically registered, counted and compared, year by year and country by country. Such a statement, of course, invites critical comments. From Durkheim's positivistic approach, where social life was to be considered as 'things' (*comme des choses*, Durkheim, 1982: 60), to phenomenological or postmodernist approaches, where crime as well

as crime statistics become 'social constructions', there are huge ontological and epistemological divergences. I deliberately put this debate aside,
both because I discussed this topic in my previous book on Japan, and
also because this is a well traded topic in criminology. Consequently,
I delimit myself to saying that *if* we are to discuss crime, crime prevention and criminal policy at all, and *if* comparative learning is not
defined away as an impossibility, we have no other choice but to combine our best critical judgement with whatever available empirical data
we can come across[1]. We know that official crime statistics are the tip of
an iceberg, and we know that registered crime very much mirrors definitions, priorities and resources on the control side. This is particularly
important to keep in mind when studying crime in Japan, where a very
wide concept of 'status offenses' and a sensitive stethoscope regarding
disorderly behaviour move the crime radar towards a state of readiness
and volatility. This said, I nevertheless invite the reader to join me in
an attempt to find out, not the final and complete story about crime in
Japan 1990–2007, but which one of the different reality descriptions
existing in today's Japan comes closest to what we never will succeed in
documenting: the definitively true story.

I started this book by referring to McCargo's (2004) description of
'Japanology' as 'contested territory'. No matter what the topic, different scholars hold diverging opinions about what contemporary Japan
is like. I continued by saying that when it comes to the presentation
of Japan as a low-crime nation (until the early 1990s) there have been
surprisingly few dissertations. However, diverging opinions have once
again entered the field of criminological debate when discussing the
crime situation during the last 15–20 years. On one side, the National
Police Agency/the National Police Academy of Japan and the Ministry
of Justice report increasing crime rates. On the other side, equally trust-
worthy sources have come up with correcting information which in
conclusion raises doubts about this 'official' interpretation.

The scholarly disagreement that exists about whether Japan still
deserves its unique status as a low-crime nation makes it necessary to
present more statistical details than I did in my former book. My interest
in crime in Japan is really not about empirical details but rather about
broad analytical and ideological questions (crime in collectivistic versus
individualistic cultures, to make it simple); it is about the influence of cultural, socio-structural and economic dimensions on social disintegration.
However, since the official version about a dramatic crime increase has
been contested, it is essential to take a closer look at the (exceptionally)
broad amount of data that exists. Is it only a 'chimera' we are discussing

(as Hamai and Ellis, 2008b, indicate), or is Japan really about to leave its role as a criminological rarity? To answer these questions, both the *type of crime* and at *what time* changes occur is of special interest. Consequently, the answer to some of my queries lies in the detail.

Furthermore, a closer look at statistical details is necessary to approach an answer regarding crime-triggering causes. What is the relevance of a *nervous economy*, of changes in *social structures* and of *moral attitudes* to the actual crime situation? I have struggled with deciding, from a very broad array of data, *what* information should be selected and presented in this chapter. It is in search of the following two research questions I have prioritised my sample of data:

- *Do public statistics about rapidly increasing crime tell the true story?*
- *If the answer to the first question is in the positive, to what extent does the economic decay play an important explanatory role, and to what extent do other factors influence the crime situation?*

Even though these research questions are put in a relatively precise way, it is difficult to give a comparatively precise, 'scientific' answer. Different ideological and methodological frameworks and tools will necessarily bring us diverging conclusions. This is how it has to be as long as we work in the business of *social* (and not natural) science. This should not be interpreted as a tribute to a postmodern declaration ('no reality exists') but rather as a humble acknowledgement of what a critical social science is all about. The intention is to give *my* interpretation of how crime has developed in Japan since the early 1990s and to give *my* interpretation of how asserted changes could be understood.

Increasing fear of crime

No matter what the *real* crime situation might look like, there is a general consensus that the *fear*[2] of crime in Japan increased palpably during the last years of the century. If crime ever was a topic of discussion before the mid-1990s it was primarily on a positive note, referring to Japan as the safest country in the world. However, towards the end of the century this picture changed significantly. According to the Public Relations Office of the Japanese Cabinet those who supported the statement, 'the crime situation is getting worse', increased from 19 per cent in 1998 to almost 50 per cent in 2005 (Hamai and Ellis, 2006: 158). A survey by the 'Japan Institute of Life Insurance' in 2002 showed that 79.8 per cent of the citizens 'strongly felt' on 'a daily basis' there had been an increase in crimes. The same year some 94 per cent of police officers answered 'I strongly feel so' (58.8 per cent) or 'I feel so' (35.3 per cent) when asked, 'Do you feel that crimes have increased from 10 years ago' (both surveys quoted in WP 2003: 285). Goto (2004: 24) refers to an opinion poll in 2004 revealing that, regarding recent crime trends, 29 per cent defined increasing brutality as the most disturbing change, 23 per cent replied 'the young age of offenders' and 17 per cent referred to 'the impulsive nature of many offenses', while 14 per cent answered the crimes' 'indiscriminateness'. Seventy-eight per cent of the respondents were 'worried/somewhat worried' about becoming a victim. Goto then refers to the conclusion in the *Asahi Shimbun* (which presented the poll), saying that 'recent crime trends were casting a shadow over people's lives and that fraud, burglary, and kidnappings were no longer felt to be misfortunes that befell "other people"' (op. cit.: 24). A survey from March 2004 disclosed that 94 per cent of eligible voters believed 'public safety had deteriorated in recent years' (*The Daily Yomiuri,* quoted in Johnson, 2006: 73). In the 2004 International Crime Victimisation Study (ICVS) people were asked questions like 'how safe do you feel when you walk alone after dark in the area where you live?', and 'how safe do you feel when you are alone at home after dark?' (van Dijk et al. 2007; cf. WP 2004: 204). Compared to the answers given to these questions in 2000 there was an increasing worry in Japan about becoming a crime victim (even though these data could not be described as very dramatic). Sixty-one per cent of the respondents in the ICVS study in 2004 indicated that public safety was bad (22.2 per cent 'neither good nor bad', 13.2 per cent 'good' and 3.6 per cent 'don't know'). It appeared from a 'Public Opinion Poll on Safety and Security' in 2004 that housebreaking was ranked as the number one fear, followed by pick-pocketing/snatching and violent offenses, while heinous offenses like homicide and robbery were ranked at the bottom (WP 2006: 260–61). In a separate poll on children's security (2006), three out of four respondents reported that they had some anxiety about the possibility that 'children around them might be involved in some kind of offense'. The ministry drew the conclusion that 'people have come to feel stronger worries about the environment surrounding children' (op. cit.: 315). Finally, in a 'Public Opinion Poll on Social Awareness' undertaken in 2006, in which respondents were asked to select the top eight fields they regarded as being on a deteriorating trend (multiple answers allowed), 'public safety' ranked top with 38.3 per cent, some 5 per cent ahead of 'national finances', 10 per cent more than 'employment/labour conditions' and almost 20 per cent ahead of 'business conditions'.

In short, these data indicate a change in the direction of an increasing fear of crime in Japan. According to the government, the public safety levels had entered what was described as 'a danger zone'. This worry was regularly commented on and interpreted in the White Papers on Crime, with expressions like:

> ...the number of people with concerns...seems to be mounting (WP 2002: preface);
>
> ...people have come to feel a real sense of crisis in the increase of crimes (WP 2003: preface);
>
> ...juvenile delinquency in recent years, along with the public's waning sense of security, is one of the major causes of heightened anxiety among the general public (WP 2005: preface);
>
> Japan's criminal situations have been rather serious and the general public has had deep-seated anxiety over public safety. (op. cit.: 242)

In particular, the White Paper on Crime from 2006 had a strong focus on the new public awareness on crime. The special analysis in this White Paper was entitled 'New Trends of Criminal Policy'. The continuous dramatisation of the crime situation in this edition is interesting reading since, at that time, registered crime had actually been *de*creasing for some three consecutive years[3]. Nevertheless, not only could the Ministry inform about a continuing growth in people's fear of crime, but the Ministry itself supported the worrisome attitude by proclaiming that 'the situation does not at all allow optimism' (op. cit.: preface). What is cause and what is effect in the public's deepening anxiety about crimes is not easy to tell.

No doubt, in Japan the Ministry of Justice has a very sensitive stethoscope on the crime situation and the way people feel about it. On the back of a very proud history, with exceptionally low crime figures, the new crime situation (as defined by the Ministry) obviously represented a huge challenge. It is hardly an exaggeration to talk about a kind of legitimation crisis for those who were in charge of this field. In a culture where shame and reputation are kept on account, crime policy and new strategies to prevent crime naturally came top of the agenda. The result was the compilation of an *Action Plan to Create A Crime-Resistant Society* (2003) with the telling subtitle *To Re-establish Japan as 'The Safest Country in the World'*. This story about alertness regarding crime is not only about a political-administrative system facing a devalued reputation and a loss of honour. It is also a story about a population that is easily upset due to a traditional culture of regimentation, predictability and safety seeking (cf. Chapter 2). In such a context relatively small disturbances can give comparatively strong amplifications on the 'fear-ometer'.

The expressed *feeling* of change, from Japan as 'a heaven for a cop' (1991) to a Japan with mounting anxiety among its citizens[4], was mirrored and arguably amplified by the media. Ota (2004: 20) commented on the situation in this way:

> We hear a lot of talk these days about the increase in crime and the resulting deterioration in public safety. Day after day, the media delivers a seemingly endless stream of stories about the occurrence of major crimes and developments in the investigations and trials of earlier incidents. Commentators rue the worsening of the situation, complain of the inadequacy of the authorities' response, and call for rigorous countermeasures.

In 2002 the *Yomiuri Shimbun* newspaper carried a long series of articles entitled 'Safety Meltdown', which in 2003 was continued by another series entitled 'Recovery of Safety'. Focus in these articles was on the asserted worsening public order and calls for prompt government measures (Tamura, 2004: 7). Statistics showing a quantitative increase in crime were broadcast to the general public with fear-creating *qualitative* details about 'bizarre' and 'atrocious' crimes. Minors killing minors, gangsters shooting other gangsters (even in the public sphere), adults and young people running amok in public places killing occasional passers by (even during the day time) and frightening reports about juveniles committing gruesome crimes, where *'their motives were hard to understand'* (WP 2005: 215, italics added) all contributed to a new public anxiety atmosphere. It was especially these 'hard-to-understand' and 'hard-to-protect-against' crimes that scared people the most. When ordinary citizens are given a feeling that *anything* can happen to *anybody,* a former taken-for-granted security no longer can be counted on and adults as well as children are given the impression that not even their private home or their classroom is safe, then an indefinable fear can creep in (Best, 1999). Crimes for gain committed by people who are in some kind of need might be frightening enough for citizens not accustomed to crime, but such crimes could at least be said to be intelligible (even though unacceptable). The White Paper of 2002 reports how young people who have never been involved in offenses are now becoming offenders (what criminologists designate 'the generalisation of juvenile delinquency', Yonekawa, 2003: 115). This feeling of fear related to seemingly unpredictable crimes, committed in unpredictable ways, in unpredictable places and by unpredictable people is further amplified by the authorities when asserting that 'there still exists concern over the frequent occurrence of offenses committed by foreign nationals visiting Japan, which has come to have a significant influence on public security in Japan' (op. cit.: 273).

Let me give but one concrete illustration of how the general public has been disturbed by a shocking murder case. On the morning on June 8, 2001, 'a knife-wielding man stormed an elementary school in Ikeda, Osaka Prefecture, and fatally stabbed eight children and wounded several others before he was subdued' (*Japan Times*, June 9, 2001). The perpetrator, who immediately admitted his guilt, reported he wanted to be hanged, but he referred to family and money problems as the triggering cause for his actions. According to Akane (2002: 3) this case 'caused a great shock to the general public and ordinary citizens in Japan began to concern themselves about the safety of public schools, streets, and their local community as a whole'. One thing that especially triggered the fear of crime in relation to this case was the fact that the perpetrator had committed a serious crime three years earlier (allegedly having put tranquilisers into a pot filled with drinking water for his colleagues) but walked free due to a psychiatric diagnosis after only one month of treatment. If people suffering from criminal insanity could be released on their own or their family's wishes (as Akane argues) then this case (it was argued) demonstrated the need for improving the general security for ordinary citizens. For groups fighting to improve the interests of victims, this event represented an important show case in the later debate on crime prevention in Japan. Quite a few 'spectacular' and bizarre crime episodes, from the Aum attack on the Tokyo subway in 1995 (killing 12 and injuring 5500) to a killing spree in June 2008 by a man fatally injuring seven people at a crowded intersection by running down four of them with his truck and then stabbing three more in the street, sent shock waves across Japan.

There are reasons to believe that the media has played an independent and not insignificant role in creating a climate of uneasiness and increasing punitiveness in Japan[5]. This link between more or less sensational media reports on this subject and an asserted crime wave has been pointed out by several scholars (Hamai and Ellis, 2006, 2008b; Fenwick, 2005; Miyazawa, 2008). Miyazawa (2008) uses the database of *Nihon Keizai Shimbun/Nikkei* (defined by Miyazawa as the least sensationalist among the four national dailies in Japan) and the *Asahi* (defined as the most liberal newspaper) to show how an increasing punitiveness prevails in public discourse in contemporary Japan. From the start of the century articles with the word *genbatsuka* (increasing the severity of punishment) proliferated at a pace disproportionate to crime statistics, according to Miyazawa. In my own archive (covering four Japanese dailies), I have a huge number of articles reporting escalating crime waves, atrocious and bizarre crimes, and so on, that have most probably induced a mounting fear of crime among Japanese citizens. However, the problem with the way spectacular crime incidents were reported was (according to Hamai and Ellis, 2008b: 1) that 'the Japanese press, inaccurately, associated the overall recorded crime with a rise in more serious crimes'. A general public informed about a steep increase of crime and media reports about some terrifying and seemingly 'irrational' cases are seemingly what have led to the new crime awareness in Japan.

Other indications of the increasing fear of crime in Japan are the sales of *security items,* such as locks and alarms; endeavours to *improve safety for children*, through better school/home/police communication, safety equipment for school children and crime prevention classes and the forming of *neighbourhood watch groups*, which patrol and inform local areas (for further details, see Leonardsen, 2006). These initiatives represent only a small illustration of the measures that have been taken by the Japanese government to reverse the asserted crime wave. However, they hopefully mediate a picture of a culture that takes crime seriously. If the 'Thomas theorem' has some validity (cf. Chapter 2) then we can already at this point of our discussion declare that Japan is struggling with a serious crime problem. This conclusion is (as mentioned above) clearly confirmed in the International Crime Victimisation Surveys, and the paradox is this: while Japan in the ICVS survey from 2004/2005 is still regarded as a low-crime nation, the citizens of this country appear to be among the most fearful of all participating countries (van Dijk et al. 2007: 127). So before we enter the empirical world of crime statistics we can conclude that, at the *existential* level, Japan has entered a new mood regarding crime[6].

If a state of increasing fear seems to be a 'given fact', this situation becomes more blurred when it comes to the 'real' crime situation. Is the new interest for crime in media, among politicians and in the general public audience mirroring a corresponding change of realities? Or, alternatively, has Japanese society, towards the end of the century, become a classical illustration of what Stanley Cohen (1967) coined as 'moral panic' (see Chapter 1, note 9)? Since much of the present debate turns upon this question – is the asserted crime increase real or is it rather mirroring *time-specific* incidents (around 1999–2000) on the control side? – we have to look into more details. I venture to do this only with a huge portion of humility and uncertainty[7]. Since native Japanese scholars, with an intimate knowledge about crime patterns and crime variations, interpret 'realities' quite differently, it is highly relevant to ask what kind of contribution a 'foreign gaze' can bring to this debate. Chances for misinterpretations are legion. But this is exactly how an academic debate should function; hopefully my contribution will help understand the bigger picture about crime in Japan.

The point of departure for coming to grips with the *real* crime situation will primarily be the White Papers on Crime (1999–2007), which are published annually by the *Research and Training Institute of the Ministry of Justice*. Each of these documents consists of some 300–500 pages of detailed statistical documentation on crimes, offenders, comparisons with other countries, treatment of offenders, victims and (each year) a special report on a chosen topic (e.g. special analyses on new trends in criminal policy, on juvenile delinquency, on treatment of offenders, on heinous/violent offenses and on economic offenses). In short, the Japanese White Papers on Crime represent a reservoir of data that leaves few of the empirically oriented questions unanswered. Actually, the amount of survey and statistical data about crimes, criminals, victims, treatment of offenders and countermeasures is so extensive that it takes deep concentration and trenchant reasoning to make the most of these data. In this regard there is no doubt that the Ministry of Justice, in its endeavours to prevent crime, is a true carrier of 'scientism'. The belief in naked data as the (nearly exclusive) source for intelligent, strategic action and policy-making, is striking. Ministerial optimism regarding finding the answer to the crime enigma in empirical data seems overstated to me. I think this comes at the price of too little attention to questions related to policy and interest conflicts that have, unavoidably, to be answered if the so-called root causes of crime are to be addressed.

Has crime increased?

A general overview

The 2006 White Paper on Crime gives a good overview of changes in reported crimes in Japan for the full postwar period (1946–2005). In Figure 4.1 traffic penal code offenses are excluded, and the presentation is split between thefts and non-traffic penal code offenses *excluding theft*. Thefts account for approximately three-quarters of all non-traffic

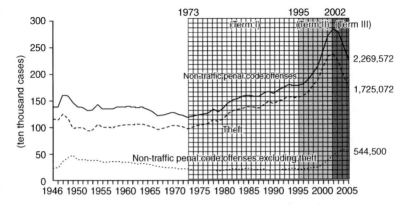

Figure 4.1 Number of reported cases for non-traffic penal code offenses, theft and non-traffic penal code offenses excluding theft (1946–2005)

Source: White Paper on Crime, 2006: 244

penal code offenses. By breaking down the figures in this way it is easier to identify the important distinction between 'mass crimes' (theft) and 'other crimes'.

The rough story about the crime situation (e.g. the crime rate for non-traffic penal code offenses) in Japan since Second World War is one of a surprisingly long period of stability of some 30 years – especially if we exclude theft. To be sure, for the period 1973–95 reported cases increased by nearly 0.59 million, but (as can be read from Figure 4.1) this change was entirely due to the increase in *thefts* (up by nearly 0.6 million cases in the same period). Other offenses remained almost at a constant level. While crime (also other than thefts) in other modernised countries skyrocketed from the 1960s and 1970s, figures from Japan confirm what tourist information books used to impart: Japan has for a long period been an exceptionally safe society regarding 'traditional' crime. However, from around 1995 (depending on types of crime) things started changing. For seven consecutive years registered crime increased rapidly and observers, abroad as well as in Japan, found themselves in a situation of bewilderment. What had been taken for granted through decades no longer seemed to be in line with reality. What was particularly disturbing was the statistical fact that not only thefts but other, more *violent* offenses, too, seemed to be on the increase. While the total amount of reported cases for non-traffic penal code offenses increased by 1.07 million, thefts accounted for 'only'

75 per cent of these cases. In other words, Japan seemed to experience not only a quantitative but also a *qualitative* change in crime. This was commented on in the 'Special Article' on 'the changing nature of heinous offenses' (WP 2003). After pointing to the general deteriorating circumstances of crime that had taken place during the recent years, the Ministry declared: 'People are feeling "insecure" instead of "safe" about public peace' (op. cit.: 283).

When countermeasures to the new crime situation were to be made, it was on the undisputable premise that crime was *really* and *significantly* up. Figures for reported crimes together with many surveys of people's opinions about the crime situation seemed to exclude any doubts regarding *facts*. All that needed to be discussed was how to take 'appropriate measures against the rapidly deteriorating circumstances of crime' (op. cit.: 283). To the extent that the Ministry of Justice regarded the total crime picture as a mirror of changes in the social environment, there was a strong conviction that Japanese society was in a process of negative transformation. Another worry for the Government was the problem of increasing numbers (absolute figures) of cleared offenders, which, in turn, led to a pressure on prison capacity. Together with extended terms of imprisonment, this created a situation where 'penal institutions may be regarded as "overcrowding within the high-crime society"' (WP 2004: 319). When this White Paper ended with a sigh, stating 'we hope, in midst of urgency to regenerate social order' (p. 446), this was indeed a radically new tone from Government offices. Regarding crime, the country was obviously declared to be in a state of emergency.

As mentioned above, during the period between 2002 and 2006, the number of reported cases of theft was on a steady decline, while other cases continued to increase until 2004. Altogether, there was a consecutive decrease in crime for four years (since 2003), and the decrease in non-traffic penal code offenses from 2005 to 2006 was almost 10 per cent. If we look at the number of *persons* (instead of cases) the turn-around trend started in 2005, and the decrease was less than for cases (down some 3 per cent from 2005 to 2006).

While Japan obviously deserved its label as a 'Low-Crime Nation' until the early 1990s, from the mid-1990s there is ample reason for asking: *Crime in Japan: Paradise lost?* Even though official statistics indicate that a *downward* trend started after 2002, the numbers are still lingering at (for Japan) a high level (absolute numbers of crime in 2006 are similar to the figures from 1998). The challenge in the remaining pages of this chapter is to reach an understanding of this relatively abrupt increase in registered crime between 1995 and 2002. Are the official statistics telling a valid story, and, if so, what could explain such a development?

Before starting this interpretative process, we have to go into some more details regarding the statistics. My first question will be: Have people living in Japan become more *violent*?

A more violent society? Homicide[8]

The escalating fear of crime in Japan has been nurtured by a series of murders, widely reported and debated in the media. Episodes (taking place between 1997 and 2001) include:[9]

- A man (43 years) entering a branch office demanding money but failing in his robbery attempt, scattered gasoline at the spot, lit it and fled. Five workers were burned to death and four were injured. The arrested man was a taxi driver owing a heavy debt, but with no previous criminal record.
- A man (24 years) broke into a house to steal money, failed in his attempt and stabbed three small children (two of them died, the third was seriously wounded). The man was unemployed, had no previous record and lived two doors away from the victim's house.
- The severed head of a boy (11 years) was found at the gate of a junior high school in Kobe, with a message placed in his mouth, threatening further killings and challenging the police. The culprit was a 14-year-old boy who also confessed to the killing of a 10-year-old girl and attacks on other schoolgirls.
- A boy (13 years) stabbed a teacher to death after having been reprimanded. The same year, a 13-year old boy lashed out with a knife in response to harassment by some of his classmates and killed one of them.
- A group of juveniles called a victim late at night just because he had spoken ill of the hot rodders' group. Although the victim strongly denied this, they started lynching him and continued beating and kicking the victim for hours, causing his death.
- A juvenile, who had failed in finding a job and was scolded by his parents, ran away from home. He committed a robbery to obtain money and thereafter decided to kill the victim who had offered him a sleeping place.

It is not difficult to understand that media reports about cases like these (but often with more gruesome details included) disturb and frighten 'ordinary citizens'. Uncertainty is closely linked to unpredictability, and the referred incidents are all of a kind that implicitly sends a message that 'anything can happen anywhere' (even in schools!). But as Best (1999) argues in his interesting book *Random Violence,* the more we tend to view crime as a melodrama in which evil villains prey on innocent victims, the more we get a distorted picture of what the crime problem is all about. Furthermore, when more or less sensational media crime reports become the point of departure for designing preventive policies, it is time for critical examination.

Accordingly, let me take one step back from the heat of the media debate in the wake of these and a number of other cases of homicide (between 1350–1450 cases per year in recent years). In the next paragraph I have condensed some of the main information on these cases in Japan. As general background information for the next paragraphs, please note that the number of people aged 10–19 years decreased by more than 4 per cent between 1993 and 2002, while those aged 60-plus increased by over 5 per cent.

During the period from 1954 to 1991 the total number of reported cases of homicide showed a continuous and (quite remarkable) *decline.* According to Johnson (2006: 76, citing La Free and Drass) this decline is of a magnitude that has not been observed in any other nation, where the trend has disclosed a boom rather than a bust. In 30 of 34 nations the homicide rate was higher in 1998 than in 1956 (op. cit.). Since the start of the 1990s there have been only small fluctuations in the hom-icide rate in Japan. From 1990 to 1996 some 1200–1–250 cases were reported each year. Between 1996 and 1998 the numbers increased to 1388, but then declined to 1265 in 1999 and have stayed around 1350–1450 since then. On average, this is more than 50 per cent *less* than the number of homicides committed in the 1950s. In other words,

> *the intense debate on Japan as an unsafe society took place during a period where the homicide rate was at its lowest level in the last 50 years*[10].

Other characteristics regarding homicides include:

- Some 20–25 per cent (declining trend) of homicides in Japan are *gang-related* (the *yakuza,* i.e. the organised crime groups, make up 0.07 per cent of the Japanese population).
- Figures on homicide in Japan include *attempted* as well as *actual* hom-icides, but they do not include robbery resulting in homicide and rape resulting in homicide. Almost half of the registered homicides are categorised as attempts (Finch, 2001: 220; Johnson, 2006: 76).

- Statistics regarding *social background* disclose that, among persons cleared for homicide, the proportion of *unemployed* persons has gradually increased. Concerning *age*, it is people in their 50s and 60s who primarily are responsible for the (slight) increase in homicides around the turn of the century, even when calculated as a rate of person per population (WP 2003: 305). Compared to Western countries Japan has a disproportionally high share of people aged 50-plus as murderers (Johnson, 2006; Kageyama, 2000).
- Concerning *victims* of homicide, the rate for *minors* shows a *decrease* both in absolute and relative numbers (minor rate = rate of minor victims to all homicide victims). With a rapidly aging population there has been an increase in the rate of victims aged 60-plus, and among these it is females who have the highest rate (women 60-plus accounted for some 30 per cent of all victims of homicide in the period 1998–2002). *Unemployed* people have increased their share as victims of homicide during the 1990s (up from 21.7 per cent of all victims in 1973 to 43.9 per cent in 2002; WP 2003: 363–84).
- The *acquaintance rate* (among victims) in Japan is particularly high, ranging from 85–90 per cent[11] (while in the US the corresponding numbers are 50–60 per cent). *More spouses* and *parents* have fallen victim to homicide (by the Ministry interpreted as an upward trend of domestic violence, WP 2003: 295). The Ministry of Justice deducts from the high acquaintance rate that most homicides are committed with a relatively clear personal motive (e.g. a strong 'grudge'), and that indiscriminate homicide and random killings are exceptional cases (WP 2002: 286).[12]

Based on the above information on homicides, it must be assumed that Japan has *not* become a less safe country. Furthermore, some sensational cases where children have been killed are *not* a part of a more general trend. On the contrary, regarding homicide, children are probably safer than in any other period of Japan's history. This general conclusion does not imply that the economic decay has had no impact on the homicide rate. Unemployed people (and elderly women) seem to have been more targeted in the 1990s, and unemployed people are also (relatively) more frequently registered as perpetrators.

A more violent society? Nine types of violent offenses

It is reasonable to argue that until the 1990s Japan deserved its reputation as a non-violent society, at least if we limit ourselves to evaluating 'traditional', non-domestic, violent crimes. As long as we stick to the 'conventional' use of the term, it is noticeable that the proportion of violent crimes to total crimes committed is essentially smaller in Japan than in (for example) the UK (3.5 per cent against 21 per cent according to Hamai and Ellis, 2006: 161).

In the 2002 White Paper the Ministry undertook a special analysis of the following nine types of violent offenses: robbery, bodily injury, assault, intimidation, extortion, rape, indecent assault, breaking and entering and the destruction of objects. The conclusion for all these offenses was that the number of reported cases had increased rapidly in recent years. Since these crimes affected both the physical and the mental states of their victims, they had created a deeper feeling of *anxiety* among ordinary citizens.

As the public debate focused more and more on the increasing fear of crime, it was particularly the *robberies* that sent the strongest shock waves into society. Even though this type of crime accounted for only 0.24 per cent of all reported cases in 2002 (as compared to 0.05 per cent for homicides) the influence upon people's feeling of insecurity was immense. Except for the chaotic period immediately after the Second World War the number of reported cases of robbery had gradually declined, and then showed a flat or slightly decreasing trend from 1975 to 1988 (i.e. a period of rapid economic growth). From 1995 to 2002 the numbers increased threefold (but dropped to approximately 6.000 in 2005), and the same trend could be registered in the number of cleared cases and the number of persons cleared.

Other characteristics of robbery offenses include (WP 2003: 292–304, 363–385):

- Number of reported cases resulting in bodily injury started to increase from 1991, but escalated further from 1996. Robberies resulting in death increased from 1995.
- Regarding the *victims* of robberies, the upward trend is evenly spread between acquaintances and non-acquaintances. The acquaintance rate has been stable (around 10–20 per cent) for a couple of decades. The *female* rate increased sharply from 1996 after having been on a continuous decline since the early 1980s. *Elderly* victims of robbery increased 5.5-fold from 1991 to 2002, but when controlling for the increase of this group in the total population the Ministry concludes that 'it is not appropriate to go so far as to say that elderly people are being particularly targeted for robbery more frequently' (op. cit.: 371). The number of victims increased 2.6-fold among *employed* persons, 3.3-fold among *students/school children* and 4.1-fold among *unemployed* persons.

- The *clearance rate* for robberies, which used to be about 80 per cent until 1998, fell below 50 per cent in 2001, and this, according to the Ministry, was due to the drastic increase in the number of reported cases.
- An increasing share of the robberies was committed by persons *without previous convictions* or criminal histories.
- As for *motives* for committing robbery, it appears that 'poverty' and 'obtaining entertainment expenses/extra spending' (the two most common motives) increased among adults from the early 1990s and rose sharply from 1998. The number who committed robbery with the exclusive motive of 'debt repayment' increased significantly (tenfold) from 1995 to 2002.
- There are significant differences between *regions* (prefectures). It appears that the increase in robberies is particularly strong in prefectures where there has been an increase in what is called 'dormitory towns'; residential areas close to large city centres, giving name to what is called the 'doughnut phenomenon'. There are significant gaps between prefectures regarding the rate of increase in the number of juveniles cleared. Such information is of great interest both regarding a discussion of an asserted 'moral decay' among youth (a specific *regional* moral decay?) and in connection with the debate on changes in police work as explanations for increase in registered crime (*regional* changes in police work?).

I shall not bother readers with detailed information about the other eight violent offenses. It is sufficient for *my* analysis to notice that for all these offenses the upward trend has already started in the years 1995–98 and continues through the next five to six years.

To the extent that the discussion on crime increase in Japan is related to a debate on a general brutalisation of society, such a tendency is not mirrored in trends regarding *use of weapons*. If anything, the 'weapon use rate' showed a general declining trend between 1995 and 2002 (especially for bodily injury and assault) and the use of firearms has been almost non-existent. In the case of bodily injury, assault and extortion, the weapon use rate is approximately 10 per cent. Many criminologists have pointed to strict regulation of weapons (especially guns) as an 'explanation' of Japan's general low crime rates. To the extent that the asserted crime wave since the mid-1990s exists, it should be reassuring (according to public figures) that this is, in effect, an unarmed crime wave[13].

However, in order to understand the increasing fear of crime better, we can note that there have been some incidents where organised crime groups (the *yakuza*) have settled conflicts in the public sphere, using hand guns and with a scared audience as spectators (*Japan Times*, October 13, 1997). Such episodes imply the breaking of a tacit but well known rule that the *yakuza* should never be any bother to ordinary citizens. Even though in this case we are talking about very rare incidents, we are also talking about spectacular incidents which most certainly trigger an already heightened feeling of insecurity among people.

As a preliminary conclusion regarding the nine types of violent offenses referred to (i.e. *reported* crimes), official data support the assertion that there has been a 'particularly significant increase' (WP 2002: 273). The point of time when the negative trend started varies between the different offenses, but *1996* seems to be one onset year, while an even further escalation took place from 1998. For the debate on *which mechanisms* might have triggered the abrupt increase in registered crimes, this information regarding the onset year is important. In general, we notice that the steep crime increase started *before* the police scandals in 1999 and 2000 (to which I shall return), and (to some extent) also *before* the second financial breakdown (in late 1997). These observations do not permit any simple conclusions, regarding either crime-triggering mechanisms or the relationship between crime and economic decay. I shall return to this topic.

A more thievish society?

The number of reported cases of theft has been on a gradual increase in Japan since 1975 (i.e. long before the start of the economic backlash). This trend was amplified from 1996/1997 to 2001, before the trend turned in 2003 (a reduction of 27.4 per cent thefts from 2002 to 2005). The main data are presented in Figure 4.2.

Between *1973 and 1995* bicycle theft and motorcycle theft constituted the main group of cases and these offenses increased the most (bicycle theft doubled from some 200,000 to approximately 400,000 during this period, while motorcycle theft increased from less than 5000 to 20,000–25,000 cases). Shoplifting fluctuated all through this period at around 8000 to 12,000 cases (with a decrease around 1990) while theft from vending machines (these machines are omnipresent in Japan)[14] had the opposite trend (a steep increase from the early 1990s, lasting until the turn of the century, when there was a correspondingly steep *decrease*). Car thefts remained at a constant level all through the period from 1973 until the end of the century.

Between *1995 and 2002* almost all types of theft increased, especially theft from vehicles (27 per cent of the total increase in theft). The exception was motorcycle theft and theft from occupied property.

Snatching represents a small share of total thefts (2.2 per cent in 2002) but these offenses increased rapidly after 1991. The Ministry comments that snatching is an easier and more violent modus operandi than pick-pocketing, which requires specific skills. Pick-pocketing accounted for more than double the number of cases of snatching in 1990, but this situation was reversed during the five years from 1995 (53,000 reported cases of snatching versus less than 25,000 cases of pick-pocketing). Non-burglary theft is the only category within this group where the increase starts as late as in 1999.

Between *2003 and 2005* a downward trend started for all types of theft except for shoplifting, which increased until 2004. It is the so-called 'street thefts' (theft from vehicles, theft from vending machines, vehicle parts theft, car theft, motorcycle theft, bicycle theft and snatching) that mainly explain the ups and downs since 1995.

The link between the economic crisis and crime among *elderly people* was identified in an interesting article by Alex Martin in *Japan Times*, October 16, 2008. According to Martin (using statistics from the National Police Agency), the number of those over 65 convicted of criminal offenses increased almost fourfold from 1998 to 2007. Theft and fraud represented the most typical crime committed by these people, and the article contains a telling illustration of this problem:

> In August, a 79-year-old woman went on a slashing spree in Tokyo's bustling shopping and entertainment district of Shibuya, wounding two female passersby before being arrested by police. The attacker reportedly said she was homeless, had no money and thought if she committed a crime the police would care for her.

Professor Koichi Hamai at the Ryukoku University commented on this case by saying that some elderly people committed crimes intentionally in order to come under the care of the police instead of facing a bleak future in a society unable to adapt to the newly evolving demographics. This perspective was confirmed in the same article by a Health Ministry official who claimed that these days, 'prisons are turning into welfare facilities for the socially disadvantaged, and we need to do something about it'. What is especially noteworthy about this is that some elderly people actually react by 'striking out' rather than by 'striking in' (see Chapter 5).

In a *comparative* perspective it should be noted that, compared to countries like the USA, UK, Germany and France, Japan still has a low rate of theft. However, among these countries Japan is the only one with an *upward* trend during the 1990s (WP 2001: 230).

In conclusion, thefts (in general) have been increasing for a long period of time in Japan, but the situation worsened in the 1990s. The important observation for our discussion is to note that there are big differences regarding from *which time* the number of reported cases escalated (varying from 1990 for theft from vending machines to 1992 for shoplifting, 1996 for theft from vehicles and 1997 for theft from houses in the absence of the occupiers, while bicycle thefts experienced a new wave in 1999). This observation is important in relation to theories that suggest police scandals are the most important explanation for increasing crime (see below). I think one important conclusion from the data presented above is that, while 'crime' in some regards could be designated as one single phenomenon (actions prohibited by society), 'criminal actions' and 'criminal offenses' are extremely complex. When Braithwaite (1989: 1) reminds us about the enormous diversity of behaviour subsumed under the crime rubric, he illustrates this by saying that, 'clearly, the kinds of variables required to explain a phenomenon like rape are very different from those necessary to an explanation of embezzlement'. But this argument should be taken further. To paraphrase Braithwaite, we could argue that, clearly, the kinds of variables required to explain a phenomenon like crimes for profit may be reciprocally very different. This is partly due to the fact that different groups of people commit different types of (economic) crimes, and that the triggering mechanisms (for example, the opportunity situation) might be very different for the wide variety of crimes called theft. The data presented here confirm that these types of crimes have increased as economic conditions have worsened in Japan, but with widely different patterns (e.g. motorcycle theft went *down* while bicycle theft *increased* during the 1990s). While the general trend is clear (increasing thefts), there are exceptions to this trend, and the time of onset for increase varies quite a bit.

Juveniles – the main crime problem?

In a society with a strong belief that human conduct (especially among juveniles) can be guided and governed, and in a society where adaptation and subjugation are valued, it is not a big surprise that juvenile delinquency receives special attention. What *is* a surprise, when we know the strong reactions to youth crime in the 1990s, is to notice the historical changes in reported juvenile delinquency in Japan (see Figure 4.2): Juvenile offenses reached higher figures, both in absolute and relative numbers, in the 1980s than in the 1990s. It is interesting to notice that in the 1981 White Paper on Crime (when juvenile delinquency was approaching its peak) the Ministry stated that Japanese society was characterised by a 'well-maintained public peace' (quoted in WP

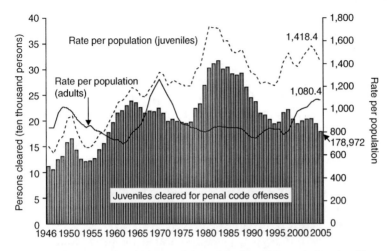

Figure 4.2 Trends in the number of juveniles cleared for penal code offenses and their rate per 100,000 population (1946–2005)

Note: 1. Including juveniles of illegal behavior who are guided by police.
2. The number and the rate since 1970 exclude those for negligence in the pursuit of social activities in traffic accidents by juveniles of illegal behavior.
3. 'Rate per population (juveniles)' refers the ratio of juveniles cleared for penal code offenses per 100,000 juveniles aged 10–19, and 'Rate per population (adults)' refers to the ration of adults cleared for penal code offenses per 100,000 adults aged 20 or older.

Source: White Paper on Crime, 2006: 164.

2005: 471). In other words, 'the story told' by public authorities and the media is very different in these two periods even though the reasons for such a dramatisation were more justified in the 1980s than in the 1990s. This represents a good illustration and an important reminder that crime is more than a social 'fact': people's historical memory is short, and it is what happens today compared to the situation *yesterday* that is the relevant comparison to be made.

The police figures referred to in the media for the period 1993 to 2003 showed that the rate of arrests within the 14–19 age group increased by some 50 per cent and according to Maeda (a well-known professor of criminal law at Tokyo Metropolitan University) there had been 'an undeniable increase in the number and severity of crimes committed by juveniles' (cited in Ryan, 2005: 178). It is this fairly recent historic view that is the basis for the outcry among 'ordinary citizens'. Accordingly, when the Ministry of Justice declared that 'issues of juvenile delinquency and juvenile delinquents have generated enormous public concern', (WP 2005: preface) this was hardly an exaggeration. What is cause and what is effect regarding signals sent by the Ministry, the National Police

Agency and the public audience is not easy to tell, but the way juvenile delinquency was dramatised at the turn of the century is quite noticeable from a criminological perspective[15]. As Hamai and Ellis (2006) have shown in their analysis of 'police scandals' referred to in the *Asahi Shinbun* (1993–2003), 'these articles tend to depict young offenders as cold-blooded monsters' (Hamai and Ellis, 2008b: 32). Correspondingly, Fenwick (2005: 134), in an article about youth crime in contemporary Japan, comments how 'the task of understanding why large numbers of young people are seemingly out of control has become something of a national obsession'. Against this background it was not very surprising that 80 per cent of the respondents in a poll (2004) were in favour of an even tougher Juvenile Act than the one that was implemented in 2001 (Ryan, 2005: 179). Let us take a look at some more details behind this dramatised picture of juvenile delinquency.

The *absolute* numbers of juveniles cleared for penal code offenses peaked in 1951 (166,000), in 1964 (239,000) and in 1983 (317,000). Since 1992 the number has remained at approximately 200,000, except for a two-year high in 1997 and 1998 (passing 220,000). In 2004, around 179,000 juveniles were cleared for penal code offenses. In other words, the chances of falling victim to juvenile offenders were higher in earlier periods than in the 1990s. However, the population of juveniles has been on a declining trend since 1986. This implies that the *relative* numbers (rate of juveniles cleared per 100,000 juveniles) decreased from 1981 to 1995 before increasing again until 2003 (then declining until today). But even in this year the juvenile delinquency rate was less than in 1981 (1553 against 1721) (WP 2005: 218–19). Accordingly, the statistics support a conclusion about a *relative* increase of juvenile delinquency from the mid-1990s, but for people's *experience* of crime one should expect that it is the absolute numbers that count. In this regard, the rate of juvenile crime is similar to or less than that in the 1960s.

The public debate on *homicide* that became increasingly intense towards the end of the century was often directed towards juveniles. Spectacular cases made people ask what was happening to the coming generation. The official figures are noteworthy. The main reason for the falling homicide rate in Japan since the 1950s is the younger generation, who these days not only commit fewer murders than the young in other countries, but who are also far less murderous than those at the same age in earlier decades. Nevertheless, in the public debate one gets the impression that juveniles are more murderous than ever. Fenwick (2005: 134) explains this paradox by pointing out that murders committed during the last decade are more 'nihilistic' and therefore

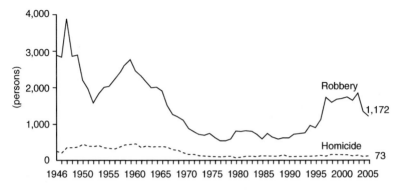

Figure 4.3 Trends in the number of juveniles cleared for homicide or robbery (1946–2004)

Note: Including juveniles of illegal behavior who are guided by police.

Source: The White Paper on Crime, 2006: 170.

harder to understand than for example the politicised murders committed in the 1960s by teenage right-wing extremists.

As can be seen in Figure 4.3, it is hard to find statistical support for dramatic reports about murderous juveniles since the burst of the bubble economy. Actually, for a very long period of time young Japanese people have rarely been sentenced for homicide. If we look at the rate (i.e. controlling for the number of persons per 100,000 in this age group) of juveniles cleared for homicide, it increased only 0.2 points from 1995 to 2002. From 2003 the total numbers of murders committed by juveniles went down from 93 to 69 in 2006 (NPA, 2007, unpaginated). Of course, one can discuss, as many do, if these homicides have been committed in a more cruel and aggressive way than before[16]. However, if we limit our analysis to the absolute and relative numbers of homicides committed by juveniles in the 1990s, one can really talk about 'deviancy amplification' and a 'signification spiral' leading to a media-led moral panic (Hamai et al. 2003: 5).

The trend during the last decade regarding *robberies* is very different from homicides. As shown in Figure 4.3, the increase in cleared persons aged 14–19 is noticeable, especially when controlling for the decreasing population of juveniles. The increase starts around 1990, and then escalates further from 1995, showing a 10.6-point increase (rate per population) until 2002, and then a significant drop from 2003 to 2005. According to the White Paper on Police (2006: 33), some 60 per cent of persons arrested for street robbery were juveniles. Also, there was an increase in the number of robbery offenses committed by two or more juveniles in groups. The *accomplice rate* increased from 52 per cent in 1987 to 71.2 per cent in 2002. According to the Ministry this has had an influence on the amount of damage caused by the perpetrators to victims due to the group mentality that triggers what are designated as 'show off' crimes.

About half the juvenile robbery cases were committed with the motive of 'obtaining entertainment expenses/extra spending money'. One gets the impression that a combination of increased 'mental immaturity' and 'normlessness' among young people is the main reason behind this 'deterioration' (WP 2003: 316). According to the official figures it is groups of both unemployed and employed juveniles together with high school students who are the main people responsible for the increasing robbery figures, while university students and vocational school students have mostly avoided the asserted decay (WP 2003: 321). Between 1995 and 2002 the number of unemployed juveniles cleared for robbery increased 2.5-fold. When analysing these data the Ministry concludes (op. cit.: 324) that 'the existence of such a large number of unemployed juveniles who cannot find their places in society may be one of the reasons for the increase in the number of unemployed juveniles who have committed robbery' (i.e. a *structural* explanation).

Data from 2004 show that more than 50 per cent of *thefts* committed by juveniles were shoplifting, some 20 per cent were bicycle theft and 11 per cent were motorcycle theft (WP 2005: 231). *Embezzlement* among juveniles has been on a continuous rise since the 1970s, both in absolute and relative numbers. Almost all of these cases (98 per cent) concern embezzling unattended articles like bicycles (Goto, 2004: 25).

In Japan, juvenile delinquency includes three types of conduct (WP 2006: 163):

- Criminal acts by juveniles aged 14–19 (the minimum age for criminal liability is 14);
- Illegal acts committed by juveniles under 14 (punishable offenses without criminal liability due to age);
- 'Status offenders' or 'pre-delinquency acts' (juveniles under 20 years who commit acts that are deemed likely to result in future offenses due to disobedience towards the lawful supervision of guardians, staying away from home without justifiable reason, contact with persons with criminal or immoral tendencies or frequentation towards acts that are detrimental to the morality of themselves or others).

Following these distinctions the Japanese criminal justice system splits juvenile delinquents (subjected to family court hearings) into three groups: Those aged 14–19, those under 14, and the pre-delinquents (cf. the third bullet point above). Since many have been worried about the moral development of Japanese youth it should be noted that the number of pre-delinquents dealt with by family courts for status offenses ('moral crimes') declined significantly between the mid-1980s and the mid-1990s. Since then, the numbers have been remarkably constant.

While this type of data gives little support to the 'moral decay' thesis, the number of juvenile delinquents who have received what is called 'police guidance' has shown an upward trend for some years (some 40 per cent increase between 1998 and 2007[17]). However, as much as 90 per cent of this 'misconduct' (as it is called) in 2007 is accounted for by 'smoking' (some 600,000) and 'late night loitering' (some 800,000), and what is most surprising about these figures (at least from a Western perspective) is probably the fact that this type of conduct is reported at all. But again, statistics should be interpreted in their rightful cultural context.

In comparison, let me finally add that international data indicate that Japanese young people still distinguish themselves as being well behaved. Miller and Kanazawa (2000: 24) refer to the United Nations Survey of Crime Trends (1995), in which the rate of juvenile suspects per 100,000 in 1995 was 848 in the US, 189 in France and 105 in Japan, and conclude from these numbers that 'Japan enjoys a relatively low number of juvenile offenders per capita'. Foljanty-Jost and Metzler (2003: 13) maintain that 'besides South Korea, Japan has the lowest numbers of criminal offenses in juvenile delinquency, including violence and homicide'. When we know how closely Japanese police are monitoring young people, these data do indicate that the young in this country are comparatively quite peaceful. This conclusion is further confirmed if one adds that drug offenses among the young (*and* adults) are at (comparatively) low levels, and statistics indicate they are on a *de*creasing trend (although media reports often give the opposite impression)[18]. The number of juveniles referred by the police to family courts for drug offenses declined from almost 30,000 cases in 1982 to some 1600 cases in 2005 (WP 2006: 173). Even though there are a lot of methodological precautions to be taken, available data indicate that drug abuse can hardly be the primary cause for concern regarding the younger generation of today. The same could be said regarding the use of alcohol (Leonardsen, 2006).

Reading the facts: Some methodological deliberations

When the media (in Japan and abroad), politicians, public servants and public opinion (surveys) all have spoken with one voice about the new crime situation in Japan, it is not very surprising. Except for personal experiences people might have had regarding 'everyday crime', the general opinion in this field is based on the same source: figures published by the police and by the Ministry of Justice. How valid is the information from these actors? Criminological research tells us that the majority of crimes go unreported[19]. Could it be that changes in the methods of reporting and recording of crime have changed so that more of the 'crime iceberg' has become visible? Could this type of argument 'explain away' almost all of the asserted crime wave? Some scholars (like Brunelli, 2003; Fenwick, 2005; Hamai et al. 2003, 2006, 2008b; Miyazawa, 2008) have put forward arguments that to some extent support such a hypothesis (varying from rejecting any significant crime increase to pointing out the disproportions between 'crime talk' and the actual crime situation). Let us take a closer look at this perspective.

Police scandals

In addition to a general critique of crime statistics, which, of course, has also been directed towards crime statistics in Japan (see Finch, 2000; Fujimoto and Park, 2006; Tanaka, 2006), the essential argument concerns changes in the methods of reporting and recording of crime (Hamai et al. 2003, 2006, 2008b) and a struggle within the police to preserve their organisational autonomy (Brunelli, 2003).

Hamai and Ellis argue that the Japanese media are not providing an accurate picture of current crime trends in Japan and that official figures disclosing an increase in crime are 'more apparent than real' (2006: 159). Based on data from the White Papers on Crime they confirm that violent crime increased by nearly 80 per cent between 1991 and 2001. However, since the homicide trend (as one of the most reliable crime statistics) is quite contrary to these figures there are 'strong grounds to question media's over-simplistic representations of increasing violent crime' (2008b: 70). In other words, since the numbers of recorded homicides have remained almost constant since the early 1990s, why do other violent crimes not show the same pattern? More importantly, the authors stress the increasing influence of the victim support movement on Japanese crime policy during the late 1990s. As documented in detail by Miyazawa (2008) this movement had a strong influence on a series of changes in legislation in the direction of increased punishment around the turn of the century. A general climate of fear and retribution developed in this period, resulting in a sudden rise in the prison population and a stronger pressure to 'establish the police for the people' (National Public Safety Commission and

National Police Agency, quoted in Hamai and Ellis, 2006: 163). Finally, and most important, a series of police scandals in 1999 and 2000 'fundamentally changed the way the press reported policing issues. These changes provoked policy reactions that ensured that more "trivial" offenses were reported, boosting overall crime figures' (op. cit.: 157). The intense critique that was launched against the police after their inaction in two murder cases in particular resulted in a readjustment of police routines. According to Yamada (quoted in Johnson, 2003: 33) 'Japan's scandal wave has generated movements for increased openness and accountability which police have stubbornly resisted'. The National Police Agency was forced to issue a new instruction safeguarding that more effort would be made to prevent crimes or accidents before they were committed. Hamai and Ellis (op. cit.: 163–64) report:

> One key outcome was to ensure that all reported incidents were now recorded without police discretion, either at the 'crime desk' or at the 'consultation desk'. Indeed, the consultation desks were opened up more widely and this is where more 'trivial' incidents would most likely to be reported. This change marked severe restrictions on *kaiketsu* [informal resolution] for a whole raft of previously under-recorded offences, and, in effect, an end to 'cuffing' at the police station. The impact of such changes on recorded crime was profound. Firstly, the number of 'incidents' recorded at the consultation desks increased dramatically'.

Another argument put forward by these two scholars concerns data from the International Crime Victim Study (ICVS) from 2000 and 2004. These data show that incidents of most types of crime in Japan have dropped during this period (except for theft from cars and attempted burglary). Even though this type of survey data also contains significant biases, they confirm the critical way of reading the official numbers from the Ministry of Justice.

In sum, these critical remarks point out that Japan has been witnessing a 'train of events' starting with the victim support movement in the late 1990s, then a series of police scandals in 1999/2000 accompanied by unprecedented media criticism, which in turn led to changes in police policy and practice with more trivial crime reported as a consequence. The main reason for the increase in crime rates is, according to Hamai and Ellis, to be found in mechanisms like this. The well documented escalation of fear and insecurity among citizens is to be found in *socially constructed* realities rather than in real deteriorations in society. In accordance with theories of 'deviancy amplification' Japan has ended up in a classical moral panic. 'The folk devils' are the criminals (especially juveniles and foreigners) and 'the moral entrepreneurs' (Cohen, 1973) are the police, the victim support movement and the media[20].

To be sure, Hamai and Ellis admit that direct causality is difficult to prove, and they also admit that 'there might be that there is an underlying trend of gradually increasing crime in Japan' (p. 168). Nevertheless, their conclusions in a number of articles on this topic stand firm, and, together with authors like Miyazawa, Brunelli and Fenwick, they are representatives of a well-known criminological tradition of scholars who warn against different types of 'moral entrepreneurs', entrepreneurs who, on the basis of quite mixed motivations, have an easy and open admission to broadcasting their warnings and worries.

I have sympathy with this criminological tradition. During some 25 years of neo-conservative and neo-liberal hegemony in Western *and* (for a shorter period) in Japanese politics there are plenty of illustrations giving support to this theoretical approach. Since modern societies from the mid-1970s experienced *The Great Disruption* (Fukuyama, 2000) characterised by a *Liquid Life* and a *Liquid Fear* (Bauman, 2005, 2006) there has been fertile soil for crusaders canvassing a message of moral decay. Also, there has been fertile soil (in Japan as well as in the West) for moral entrepreneurs who have found it easier to 'blame the victim' (often juveniles and foreigners[21]) than to address economic and structural conflicts of interest. Accordingly, I listen carefully to a message warning against intuitive and simplistic interpretations where data are taken at face value. Nevertheless, there are too many irregularities and inconsistencies in the linking of data and logical deductions that make me question only an 'apparent' crime increase. No doubt, the years after the police scandals do show an abrupt increase in registered crime, but much of this increase (as I have documented above) originated some years earlier. Also, from a general sociological point of view, I would find it surprising if the economic, social and cultural changes I have described in Chapter 3 were to leave crime statistics untouched. Of course, this might actually be the (very interesting!) case. In my first book on crime in Japan I made a point out of the fact that Japan really challenged sociological theories about the link between crime and modernisation/urbanisation. It appeared from my analysis that 'Japanese culture' really was the entrance to a deeper understanding of low crime in this country. Might it be then that Japanese culture inoculates against crime not only in days of prosperity but also in days of decline? However, the data I have presented earlier in this chapter indicate that the economic crisis and the general depression have left some direct 'fingerprints' in the crime statistics.

It is correct, as pointed out by Hamai and Ellis, that most of the increase in reported violent crime (using the period 1993–2003) was due to the enormous increase in *less serious* violent crimes. Reporting of these types of crimes was specifically encouraged by the NPA in its campaign to regain lost legitimacy and to show its willingness to get tougher on crime. Accordingly, it might sound reasonable, when the increase of *less* violent crimes constituted almost 93 per cent of the total increase (severely plus slightly injured) in violent crimes from 1999 to 2000 to conclude as Hamai and Ellis do. However, this is not a very meaningful basis for calculating percentages. Since the category 'slightly injured' constantly constitutes some 85–90 per cent of all violent crimes one has to calculate percentages of each category separately. If we do this, the figures show that the number of victims slightly injured increased 33 per cent from 1999 to 2000 while the number of severely injured increased 22 per cent. If we look at the full period for which Hamai and Ellis give data (1993–2003) it appears that 'slightly injured' increased 45 per cent, while 'severely injured' increased 43 per cent, and in the period before the police scandals (1993–99) 'severely injured' increased 15 per cent while 'slightly injured' increased 12 per cent. This way of calculating tells us that, yes, the increase in slightly injured victims was bigger than the increase in severely injured victims, but *both* categories showed a strong upward trend. This makes it reasonable to conclude that changes in reporting and registration of more 'trivial' violent offenses had an effect on the total numbers of offenses recorded within this category. However, such an observation does not nullify an argument about a real deterioration in the crime situation in general. What we can say is that the *relative share* of slightly injured (compared to all injured) increased after the police scandals, but for sure, 22 per cent increase of severely injured should not be disregarded compared to 33 per cent increase of slightly injured. Furthermore, the development of reported cases of robbery shows a gradual increase all through the 1990s (except for 1994–95), but with an especially steep increase from 1997 (i.e. before the police scandals). So when it comes to violent crimes my conclusion is that, except for homicide, Japan *really* seems to have become a more violent society in the 1990s.

If the request to be more alert regarding reporting of offenses to the police was a universal call (provoked in 1999/2000), it is worth taking a closer look at the following information (from the White Papers on Crime throughout this period):

- The rate (per 100,000 persons) of *rapes* increased from 2.3 in 1995, via 2.6 in 1997 and 2.9 in 1999 to 3.5 in 2000 and then 3.4 in 2001.
- The rate of *indecent assault* increased from 5.5 in 1995 to 6.3 in 1997, 6.9 in 1999, 8.3 in 2000 and 11.5 in 2001. While the rate of rapes (in the main) stabilised after 2001 indecent assault continued to increase for two more years, ending at a rate of 15.4 in 2003.
- *Property damage* (robbery, extortion, theft, fraud, embezzlement and conversion of lost property) experienced an even upward trend from 1995 to 2002, with no exceptional break in 1999–2000. If one looks at the total amount of property damage related to these crimes the picture is quite inconsistent, with some increases and some decreases depending on the year and type of offense. As we have already seen, the number of reported cases of non-invasive robbery increased significantly after 1996 and invasive robberies experienced the same development from 1998, respectively three years and one year *before* the police scandals.
- Cases reported for *snatching* increased from some 10,000 in around 1990 to 20,000 in 1996, but from *that* year cases increased to more than 35,000 in 1998, and then continued an upward trend (on a slightly less steep curve) until 2002. Accordingly, the most abrupt increase in these types of offenses appeared between 1996 and 1998.
- *Street theft* (theft from vehicles, from vending machines, vehicle parts theft, car theft, motorcycle theft, bicycle theft *and* snatching) increased steadily from the mid-1970s until 1996 (from almost 40,000 cases in 1976 to 110,000 in 1996, and then evenly mounted to 160,000 cases in 2001; i.e. there was no clear change in 1999/2000).

The referred types of offenses do not fit in with the 'reporting hypothesis', i.e. where the increase in crime primarily refers to the police scandals in 1999/2000. Actually, the official data disclose a much more inconsistent pattern than that conveyed by this assumption.

Finally, it should be observed that there is a time lag between the police scandals in 1999/2000 and when some of the formal changes in police investigation methods took place. Even though the police reacted promptly to the critique, quite a few of the implications of the revisions would be registered in the statistics only after 2001. The 2006 White Paper on Police accounts in detail for this process. As a result of scandals appearing after September 1999 the National Police Safety Commission called for a police reform council in March 2000. This council held 11 meetings over a short period which culminated in a compilation called 'Urgent recommendations for police reform' in July 2000. In December 2000, the Police Law was revised, and in the following years a number of measures were implemented[22]. Even though the National Police Agency had already issued new instructions in March 2000 (including strengthening the reception process for complaints, instructions about also registering charges for 'relatively minor offenses' and procedures for handling of rape cases, Hamai and Ellis, 2006: 162; Goto, 2004: 25), and even though media articles on police scandals boomed during 1999–2000, a lot of the practical police reforms took place in the following years. In the White Paper on Police from 2006 one can read that, at that time, 'police reform is only half-completed' (p. 133). It should also be pointed out that new police scandals were constantly being disclosed in the following years. As Curtin (2004e) comments, 'the Japanese police have been plagued by various scandals for more than a decade, but during 2004 their troubles reached a crisis point, with new and devastating scandals being uncovered almost every month' – while reported crime went down!

In sum, to the extent that the reporting of offenses has changed due to changes in police policy, this mechanism can represent only some part of the explanation. My analysis of the data rather proposes a 'compromise' than an either/or explanation. It is always important to have an open eye to changes on the control side of the crime enigma but data supporting this type of hypothesis should be more consistent than I have found to be the case. However, as Tanaka (2006) points out, there are two other mechanisms that *might* have had an impact on the number of cases reported during the 1990s:

- Fewer women are tolerating their husband's abuse. 'The increase in indecent assault against women is considered to be influenced more by the fact that more women now call for public intervention whenever they are subjected to sexual harassments' (Tanaka, op. cit.: 26). The Law for the Prevention of Spousal Violence and the Protection of Victims was implemented in 2001, and (as I shall come back to) this law had a huge impact on reporting.
- Increasing numbers of 'Dial 110' alarm telephones (especially in 2000 and 2001) in combination with a rapid expansion of numbers of cellular phones has facilitated reporting of crimes (especially street crimes). The same effect is most certainly related to the increasing

number of neighbourhood watch groups. The effects of new communications technology are probably undercommunicated within
criminology in the endeavours to understand new crime patterns.

Tanaka (who now is a professor at Keio University, but has long experience as a police officer) concludes his well argued analysis of changes
in the crime situation in Japan by *rejecting* the assumption that the new
police reporting/recording system can explain the crime increase: 'It
can be proved that this theory is wrong if we look at the difference in
the trend of each category of street crimes known to the police which
are relatively minor'. In short, data are not as unequivocal as they should
be to support the hypothesis[23].

Data speak. Data tell stories. But these data and these stories are not
unambiguous. They have to be interpreted. This interpretation is always
contextual. It will be based on a combination of our values, ideologies,
pre-understandings, professional knowledge and analytical conceptualisation. As already mentioned, I regard crime as a mirror of society.
Knowing the crime pattern in a given society gives us an important
intake for understanding this society in itself. In Chapter 3 I gave an
outline of Japanese society in the 1990s. It was a story about turbulence, about economic and socio-structural change and about Japan
becoming a more exclusionary society. It was also a story about changing mentality structures and about an initiating change in values and
beliefs. From a sociological point of view I find it reasonable to expect
(but not to take for granted) increasing crime in times of economic and
mental depression. As I shall elaborate further in the next chapter, data
presented in the White Papers on Crime since the turn of the century
support this assumption. The economic crisis seems to have made some
types of crime a more likely option for those hardest hit.

Victim reporting

The literature suggesting that the victim support movement strongly
increased its influence on crime policy towards the end of the 1990s
is, to the best of my knowledge, indisputable. But as Miyazawa (2008)
documents, this trend, with a stronger focus on the victims' situation,
started with the Crime Victims Payment Law in 1980, continued with
the Crime Victim Relief Fund (CVRF) in 1981 and was further strengthened in 1990 with the establishment of the Japanese Association of
Victimology. In 1992 the first crime victim survey was conducted
(funded by the CVRF) and in the same year a crime victim counselling office opened in Tokyo. The Aum attack in 1995, and not least the

Kobe earthquake the same year, amplified the importance of a stronger focus on the situation of victims in Japan. Then, in 1999 the National Network for Victim Support was established. As Miyazawa points out, up to this point the most salient issues were financial and psychological needs among victims and the danger of secondary victimisation due to insensitive and incompetent work by the police and the media. Then, from the year 2000 the victimisation debate intensified further with the implementation of the so-called *Two Laws for Crime Victims Protection* accompanied by symposiums receiving a lot of media attention. According to Miyazawa, this year is considered 'year one of the crime victims' movement in Japan' (op. cit.: 65), and the story culminates with the implementation of the Crime Victim Basic Law in 2005 and the amendment to the Code of Criminal Procedure and other laws in 2007 (strengthening the victims' influence in criminal proceedings). My intention with presenting this brief history is, also in this regard, to argue for *continuation* rather than a sharp break in development. Attention towards victims' rights intensified in 2000 (as did attention towards the police scandals) but hardly in a way that rates as a qualitative rather than a quantitative change. In this regard it should also be noted that the victims' movement has strengthened its position in countries where crime has decreased, which really indicates nothing more than a warning not to jump to conclusions based on simple unilateral co-variations.

Despite the focus on the victims' movement in Japan, there is one crime that has received little attention within the official statistics to date, but which nevertheless relies heavily on victims for its detection and clearance rates. That crime is domestic violence, and I would like to explore briefly whether Japan can be conceived of as a relatively low-violence society only if we leave the domestic sphere out of the discussion.

Domestic violence

It is a well rehearsed methodological thesis that 'where you sit (i.e. your position) decides where you stand' (i.e. which standpoint you take). This perspective holds true especially in a debate on the level of violence in a society. The number of reported cases of violent offenses can give us important information about some characteristics of a society. These data (to varying extents) are valuable for our interpretation of social integration and trust in a society. However, 'the iceberg' is bigger in these cases than in many others. It is only a tiny part of violent actions in a society that are 'observed' from the position of the police. Data from Australia disclose that while 94 per cent of the victims of motor vehicle theft, and 79 per cent of breaking and entry victims reported the incident to the police, only 25 per cent of the victims of sexual assault did the same (Anleu, 1999: 133). According to a study by Dussich and Shinohara (1997, cited in Burns, 2005: 48) only 14 per cent of Japanese women who had experienced a sexual assault reported the crime and the percentage for rape was even lower. Violence committed within the private sphere is particularly difficult to define, report and prosecute. We know from victimisation studies that small nuances in questions asked can give widely different responses. As an illustration, Balvig (1995) compared three different victimisation studies undertaken in 1984 in Denmark. In two of these surveys people were asked (with some diverging formulations) if they had experienced any violence within a period of half a year before the interview. The figures varied from 0.9 per cent in one survey to 8.0 per cent in the other. In the third case, people were asked about experience of violence during the last year. Six per cent answered this question in the affirmative. Balvig (1995: 44) concludes that 'one can hardly imagine any better illustration of how impossible it is to give a clear and distinct answer to questions about how much violence there is in a society'. As Lea (2003: 61) comments, domestic violence comes to take on some of the same characteristics as business crime: 'It takes place behind closed doors, the offender is "legitimately present" at the scene of the crime and the victim will have motives for not reporting the crime as it may reflect badly on her character'.

Partly due to an increasing public attention on sexualised violence, especially in the private sphere, and partly due to a gradual recognition that these cases had to be taken more seriously, in 2003 the Research and Training Institute of the Ministry of Justice published a special 'Study Concerning Perpetrators of Domestic Violence (DV)' (defined as 'spousal violence'). The report admitted that it was only recently that this type of violence had begun to be treated as a serious problem in Japan and declared 'we must never leave DV in the deepest recesses of society' (p. i). It was only in 2001 that the 'Law for Prevention of Spousal Violence and the Protection of Victims' was passed and this was (according to the Ministry of Justice) the first law to address comprehensively the problem of spousal violence. It goes without saying that relatively small changes in the inclination to report domestic violence will automatically result in dramatic increases in registered numbers. Therefore, it is almost impossible to give an authoritative and valid answer to the question: has domestic violence increased? Unfortunately, this observation contributes to additional uncertainty about my presentation above. If the biggest part of the iceberg regarding violent crime is hidden in the domestic arena, then the referred increase of sexual violence might mirror nothing but an uncovering of what has always been hidden behind the scenes. Regrettably, in this question we are all deemed to give our answer more or less based on qualified guessing.

Nevertheless, since I raise the general question to what extent Japan should be described as a violent society I find it appropriate to give a few comments based on what information we actually have on this topic.

In the book *Sexual Violence and the Law in Japan* Catherine Burns (2005) presents a clear analyses of judicial decision-making in Japanese cases involving sexual violence. A distinct message in this book concerns what she defines as a culture of eroticised violence which locates culpability in the feminine body. There are at least two interesting perspectives to be found in Burns' examination. First, she points out the paradoxical and thought-provoking idea that those small communities that traditionally have been attributed the honour of creating a cohesive society, are exactly the same arenas that produce a lack of safety for women. 'The reliance on informal social mechanisms to control crime or maintain conformity to social norms means that abusive forms of patriarchal control, in all but the most extreme cases, may be exercised with relative impunity within these localised networks of gendered social relations' (op. cit.: 45). Second, Burns elaborates this point by anchoring her analyses in some of the same general perspectives I presented in Chapter 2. Japanese culture is characterised by values like endurance and perseverance, will-power and self-control, 'and social proscriptions against drawing attention to oneself or problems within one's family and the shame (*haji*) that this incurs, and these values have particular social currency for Japanese women' (op. cit.: 51). It is honourable not to 'give in' or even to show a masochistic sense of martyrdom in hardship, to remain silent about private difficulties and to show strength in adversity. Furthermore, Japanese culture is based on what Sugimoto (1997: 25) describes as 'double codes', which implies a clear distinction between front stage and back stage, between inside and outside, between truth and 'correctness'. In our perspective of domestic violence these cultural traits make openness about internal relations a non-topic. As Burns points out, even within their own home, women should suppress their true feelings to safeguard the superior value of *wa* (harmony). Besides, it would be regarded as selfish and to put an improper burden and inconvenience on the other person if one disclosed private secrets. Finally (which goes for any country, but not least for Japan), the family is a basic social unit and disclosure of (sexual) violence would disrupt the very fabric of Japanese society.

The cultural characteristics referred to bring a central perspective in this book to the foreground. 'Realities' about a country or a culture have to be put in brackets until we *contextualise* our presentation. Reported numbers, be they about unemployment or suicide, alcohol consumption or crime, traffic accidents or sexual abuse, should be analysed against a culturally specific background. So many filters are to be passed through before 'the true story' can be presented that we continuously run the risk of bringing a distorted version of the facts. The above presentation is meant as a background for being able to put the subsequent information in perspective.

The data that actually are available are not easy to interpret. Burns (2005), comparing figures from the US Department of Justice with Japan National Police Agency figures, discloses that in 1995 the rate per population of rape per 100,000 population in the US was 37.1 compared to only 1.2 in Japan. The difference is overwhelming but it is hard to decide to what extent this is due to variations in legal definitions, police priorities or inclination to notify. As we have seen, the increase in some types of violent offenses has been noticeable at the turn of the century. The special study that was undertaken by the Ministry of Justice in 2003 shows that the number of reported cases for bodily injury (spousal) increased from some 22,000 in 1999 to almost 34,000 in 2001. Probably this significant upward trend is mirroring a gradually lowering threshold for reporting and this effect was (according to op. cit.: 49) further amplified with the new law on spousal violence (from 2001), which had 'quite a dramatic impact on reported cases' (even though Burns does not document that there exists a causal relationship here). Iwao (2004), who for ten years served on the National Public Safety Commission (supervising the National Police Agency) reports that over recent years the police have become more and more involved in cases of domestic violence and child abuse, 'which were formerly not regarded as matters for official intervention'. Furthermore, available information (cited in Burns, 2005) indicates that the private sphere is as safe/unsafe in Japan as in Western countries (where variations probably also exist). For those who petitioned for divorce through the family court in the 1980s, 'violence' was referred to as the most, or second most, common reason. The first national survey on violence against women (from 2000) found that almost 1 in 20 wives were 'subjected to life-threatening violence'. Data from a government survey in 2006 (*Japan Times* March 25, 2009) reveal that 33 per cent of married women had experienced physical and mental abuse (14 per cent in the past five years) and 13 per cent had feared for their life. Fifty-three per cent of these women did not ask for any help, while only around 3 per cent consulted police or a hospital, and 1 per cent turned to prefectural help centres, lawyers or private shelters.

Are there any indications that the economic crisis since the early 1990s has had any effect on the spread of domestic violence? Has increasing unemployment made the family institution a more risky place to stay? Again, this is a question that is hard to answer in a convincing 'positivistic' way. From a commonsense basis one can of course construct causal relations between unemployment, increased consumption of alcohol, a greater male presence at home, more stress, etc. *and* increasing domestic violence. As a likely trend, such scenarios seem plausible (but far from deterministically so). The special study undertaken by the Ministry of Justice found that of the 322 perpetrators who were interviewed, roughly 70 per cent were employed in some occupation and approximately 30 per cent were unemployed. Among the unemployed, 63 per cent had been unemployed for one year or longer. When the reason for the perpetrator's violence was analysed from the victim's point of view it appeared that next to 'daily trifles' and 'need to dominate the victim', 'the perpetrator's economic problems' was the most often cited reason for the infringement.

Even though these comments on domestic violence do not bring us much further in the discussion about increasing crime in Japan, I have chosen to include this section both because of the salience of this topic (Braithwaite, 1991, defines domestic violence – together with white-collar crime and traffic violence – as the most threatening crime of today), and in order to bring some nuances to the debate on increasing crime in Japan. It seems reasonable to argue that part of the increase in (registered) violent crime is reflecting an increase in the *victims' inclination to report* such crimes. Furthermore, it is important to have domestic violence in mind when discussing preventive measures against crime. The conservative cry for bringing the family back as a corner stone for building a safer society has to include more than a nostalgic belief in the restoration of a primary group that always has contained dark sides. To call for a 'protection of the family' without linking such a policy to a broader frame of welfare policy and gender equality[24] is hardly a contribution to a safer life for children and women. To many people the family institution could certainly be described as being a 'Haven in a heartless world' (Lasch, 1979b), but we know today that such a characterisation is far from the complete story about this institution. There is no reason to believe that Japan represents any exception in this regard.

Conclusion: Is Japan still unique?

If Japan in recent years has lost some of its innocence there are still notable differences between Japan and some of the main Western countries. Table 4.1 compares crime rates for Japan and four Western countries for the period 1995–2004.

Table 4.1   Crime rate (number of reported cases per 100,000) for major offenses[25] in five countries

	France	Germany	UK	USA	Japan
1995	6.317	8.179	9.529	5.275	1.420
1996	6.110	8.125	9.470	5.088	1.440
1997	5.972	8.031	8.651	4.927	1.506
1998	6.072	7.869	9.878	4.620	1.608
1999	6.097	7.682	10.208	4.267	1.710
2000	6.421	7.625	9.917	4.125	1.925
2001	6.880	7.736	10.552	4.163	2.149
2002	6.932	7.893	11.220	4.125	2.240
2003	6.666	7.963	11.241	4.067	2.187
2004	6.386	8.037	10.633	3.983	2.007

Source: White Paper on Crime 2006: 43

There are two characteristics to be read from these data. One is that Japan still seems to deserve its label as a low-crime nation, even though this is somewhat more contested than before. The other is that the *trend* has been in disfavour of Japan during most of these years. While France, Germany and partly the UK appear to have a great deal of stability in their crime situations, and the US has been in a continuous decline in numbers in this period, Japan's crime rate (until 2002) has, as far as the official data disclose, increased.[26] Thus, Brunelli (2003: 2) concluded (i.e. *before* the crime peak was reached in 2002) that 'although overall levels remain relatively low compared to the other OECD, Japan is quickly closing the gap'. Is this a sustainable assumption?

I think Brunelli's prospect for Japan is premature and out of proportion. I have four counter-arguments to the 'closing-the-gap' theory:

1. In spite of the negative crime development I have presented above, available data disclose that Japan is still 'unique' compared to main Western countries like those presented in Table 4.1.
2. Drawing conclusions based on (relatively) short-term trend analyses is a risky business. Crime development in Japan since 2003 indicates

that trends can be turned. Latest data disclose a *downward* trend for four consecutive years (down 7.9 per cent from 2005 to 2006).
3. If the low crime rate in Japan has been due to *cultural* characteristics, it is not evident that Japanese culture has changed in ways and to an extent that should produce significantly more crime. I will return to that topic.
4. *Part* of the crime increase until 2003 is probably due to changes in reporting and registration rather than real changes in crime.

Japan's relatively favourable position is confirmed by the International Crime Victims Study (ICVS) from 2000. For violent crimes like robbery, sexual assault and assault with force, Japan has the lowest reported victimisation rate of all the participating countries, and for burglary (including attempts) only Finland has a lower victimisation rate (van Kesteren et al. 2000). In addition, one could add that 'in per capita terms Japan is one of the most under-policed among OECD-countries with only one police officer for every 550 people in 2000' (Brunelli, 2003: 16), which is more than one quarter less than the United States and two and half times less than Italy.

It is far too early to dethrone Japan from its position among 'Nations not obsessed with crime' (Adler, 1983). Neither empirical data, nor a 'cultural interpretation' of how informal social control operates in this country, indicates that Japan within a few years has closed the crime gap vis-à-vis Western countries. However, such a conclusion should not be read as an 'end-of-danger' message. As I shall discuss in Chapter 6, Japanese society is already confronting serious social challenges, but these challenges are probably more linked to phenomena other than crime.

It is noteworthy that Tamura (a counsellor in the Cabinet Information Research Office) in 2004 declared that 'indeed, Japan appears quite crime-free compared to almost all other nations' (p. 17). This statement stands in clear contradiction to the relatively alarming messages sent in the White Papers on Crime through many years. In the broad context, and in an international climate characterised by retributive and punitive attitudes[27], it is perhaps more important these days to worry about *reactions* to crime than to crime itself, as the following chapter illustrates.

5
The Authoritative Interpretation of the Crime Situation

Three analytical perspectives

From the premise that the real crime situation in Japan *has* actually deteriorated, let me now proceed to the following questions. How do Japanese authorities *interpret* and then *react* to this situation? How do they explain that an increasing number of Japanese citizens (per definition) have left the company of their fellow citizens in exchange for a life outside the traditional group society? Living in a culture that celebrates the indisputable importance of being in harmony with 'society', and with very strong informal sanctions against those who turn their back on this, how is the threatening new crime situation made intelligible for the political-administrative system? Answering these questions is important because some observers have designated Japan as being unique not only regarding total crime figures, but also regarding *reactions* to crime. Braithwaite (1989: 62) has proclaimed Japan a prototypical country of reintegrative shaming with an 'extremely lenient' criminal justice system. According to this scholar, the assumption in Japan is that criminals can be restored to the community by prudent intervention and that 'nurturant acceptance' is regarded as the appropriate response to deviance. This perspective takes as its point of departure some of the same cultural characteristics that I presented in Chapter 2 regarding people's 'willingness' to subjugate themselves to authority, to adapt to collective obligations and to accept monitoring and guidance. Tough, punitive reactions should, according to this point of view, be unnecessary since proper guidance should be sufficient to bring wayward deviants back on track. Leaving aside the discussion of the 'correctness' of Braithwaite's description of Japan *until 1990*, how well does this notion describe the criminal justice system *today*?

Based on the White Papers on Crime, published by the Ministry of Justice, I discuss this topic and also try to map what kind of counter-measures are proposed to prevent crime. At the rhetorical level it appears that the Ministry of Justice operates with a quite 'holistic' approach to understanding crime, since *economic* variables (unemployment and poverty), *socio-structural* variables (disintegration of community and family, etc.) and also *cultural* variables (values and morality) are all included in the analyses. However, when it comes to the sphere of *Realpolitik,* Japan (like many Western countries) seems to be moving in a more *punitive* direction. The 'traditional' Confucian value structure of Japan could still be described as a 'crime prevention mechanism' (Japan is still a low-crime nation). However, with the implementation of more economic liberalism in combination with a welfare state that is not too generous, and with a more fragmented family institution than previously, it seems that since the early 1990s Japan has turned into a less caring society. As market reforms and a tougher climate in the economy have taken hold, Confucianism is no longer a sufficient insurance against social disruption, and it seems that it is the more authoritarian aspects of this system that have gained the upper hand.

As an analytical tool for discussing these questions, let me use Offe's (1984) instructive scheme, dividing society into three different subsystems (the economic, the socio-cultural, and the political-administrative system). Applied to our criminological analysis one could argue that (increasing) crime can be explained by taking one or more of the following perspectives:

1. Crime as a result of societal transformations generated in the *economic* system. How people are situated with regard to the sphere of labour and income and how they can compete with demands from the anonymous 'market forces' are of primary relevance to understanding what has been called the 'root causes of crime'. This is often defined as a 'critical' or 'radical' perspective on crime, in the tradition of Young, Taylor, Lea, Garland, Currie and Muncie. Also included in this perspective would be technological changes and how these affect social relations.
2. Crime as a result of more or less autonomous processes going on in the *socio-cultural* system. A typical explanation from this perspective would be to make crime the final result of unsuccessful socialisation, broken families and a loss of moral standards, whether in the family, school or society in general. Crime in this perspective is about social structures and social relations, about values and culture and about

attitudes and norms that are transmitted through primary and secondary groups.
3. Crime as a result of decisions made within the *political-administrative* system. This is a constructivist perspective, arguing that crime, after all, is nothing but what people in authoritative positions have decided to define as crime. This perspective brings forward the important reminder that crime in society can increase (or decrease) even though nothing has changed within the economic or socio-cultural systems. If legislative authorities have become more (or less) punitive, imposing/deleting laws or activating/deactivating formal control, this will be reflected in the crime statistics.

Crime from an economic system perspective

As documented in Chapter 3, Japanese society has unquestionably turned into a more exclusionary society in economic terms. Increasing unemployment, economic inequalities and poverty; the end of life-long employment contracts together with new labour laws (1999/2004) allowing the use of temporary workers; changes in the system of school-to-work transitions and bankruptcies are some of the disturbing characteristics we commented on. As Japan moved into the twenty-first century, the economic order that every citizen had until then taken for granted was gone and the future seemed more unpredictable. As already pointed out, this triggered an atmosphere of *declining hope* and *feelings of injustice* that to an increasing extent came to mark Japanese society.

The criminological relevance of economic turbulence and uncertainty has been repeatedly discussed. It would take another book to document these questions in depth[1]. We all know that most unemployed people live law-abiding lives, and we know that rich as well as poor societies might be high-crime societies. Simple bivariate analyses at the macro level can only give us some indications of possible interconnections, and statistical covariation is not the same as causal relations. Furthermore, as pointed out above, 'crime' is a composite social phenomenon and aggregate numbers might well hide contradictory trends (e.g. increases in some types of violence for some groups, decreases in other types of violence for other groups). However, the essence of the argument for those who make 'economy' the starting point for understanding crime goes like this:

> Without a move towards justice in the distribution of reward there will never be a tranquil social order... For the incessant competition

of one against another, the grading of other human beings in their monetary value in 'the race of life' scarcely promises social tranquillity or human altruism. And the effect on the individuals concerned can be deleterious: to turn themselves into commodities to be priced and marketed. (Young, 1999: 153)

According to this perspective a criminology that does not include some kind of 'materialistic' perspectives will never catch the 'deeper causes of crime'. While this approach (as already underlined) cannot be reduced to some simple argument about unemployment, poverty, inequalities, etc.[2], the argument still holds that people living in relative poverty, people with insufficient incomes, no stake in society and bereft of hope for any change will be more vulnerable to crime than others. Japanese scholars have supported such a view. Based on Japanese data, Yonekawa (2003) presents information that indicates how poverty/single-parent family status affects crime. In an interesting article entitled 'Inequality based on family background as a reason for juvenile delinquency', Yonekawa concludes that 'juvenile delinquents are more likely to come from poor families than from other families' (p. 117), and 'the incidence of juvenile delinquency in non-two-parent families is much higher than in two-parent families' (p. 118)[3]. Also with reference to Japan, Miller and Kanazawa (2000: 59) maintain that 'employed young males are far less likely to participate in criminal activities than are unemployed young males'. Without elaborating on this topic any further (and, of course, these quotes are no proof), the main message for those developing theories about crime and economic parameters is, as expressed by Currie (1998: 135), that 'market society promotes crime by increasing inequality and concentrated economic deprivation'[4].

To what extent do Japanese authorities regard economic miseries a relevant approach to understanding increasing crime? Does the Ministry of Justice make any causal links between the economic decay and the asserted crime increase? Here is a small sample of the many statements on this topic from the White Papers on Crime from recent years:

WP 2002: Since the end of the bubble economy ... Japan fell into economic recession, and this recession has lasted for more than 10 years. In the meantime, Japan witnessed the fall of big enterprises, the collapse of financial institutions, intensified business restructuring and rises in the unemployment rate, none of which we had ever imagined could happen during the period of rapid economic growth. The recent crime situation of Japan seems to be closely related to these social and economic factors. (preface)

WP 2002: In recent years, the cases where adults committed impulsive, momentary, and simplistic offenses have also increased, and it can be presumed that a category of 'adults who lose their temper easily' has emerged. As the reason behind this, it can be considered that the environment surrounding adults has deteriorated markedly, as seen in weakened family bonds, accumulated daily stress, the unstable economic situation, and anxieties related to unemployment etc. (p. 345)

WP 2003: Thus, the existence of such a large number of unemployed juveniles who cannot find their place in society may be one of the reasons for the increase in the number of unemployed juveniles who have committed robbery. (p. 324)

WP 2003: As for robbery, the majority of the defendants are unemployed persons and those who have changed or lost jobs 3 times or more account for 79.0%, suggesting unstable employment situations among robbery offenders...job loss had an influence on the commitment of the offense in a considerable number of robbery cases. (p. 424)

WP 2003: Among visiting nationals who commit offenses, some have been legally employed but lost their jobs due to recession and finally dared to commit offenses to overcome financial difficulties. (p. 479)

WP 2004: As for economic situations, the effect of the prolonged recession is still evident in statistical data, such as the unemployment rate among newly admitted prisoners, parolees, and probationers. (p. 444)

The White Papers on Crime in recent years have referenced the link between an increase in registered crime and high unemployment/the unstable economy. In a special analysis of heinous offences for which a sentence of death or imprisonment with labour for life had been demanded (during the five-year period 1998–2002), the Ministry of Justice documents that in the cases of homicide (106 persons) and robbery (290 persons) some 50 per cent of the defendants were categorised as 'unemployed' (WP 2003). Furthermore, in the case of robbery almost

80 per cent of the defendants (some 60 per cent in cases of homicide) had changed or lost jobs three times or more. In discussing what is defined as 'background factors' behind the increase in robberies the 2003 White Paper points out that:

> as robbery is an offense committed with intention of obtaining gains through robbing people of money or articles, mostly money, it inevitably has something to do with social background factors such as the increase in the number of unemployed persons as well as the increase in persons suffering financial failure or in need of money. (p. 351)

The Ministry presents statistics showing an exponential increase in the numbers of *petitions for bankruptcy* (up from 10,000 in 1990 to more than 220,000 in 2002) and a steep increase in the number of *inquiries for consultation on multiple debts* (up from a handful in 1990 to more than 50,000 in 2002, p. 352). Official numbers confirm an increase in the relative share of unemployed people committing robbery, and this share is bigger than the increase in the number of unemployed should imply. When one looks at persons cleared for robbery it appears that until 1982 both the number and percentage of employed persons committing robbery were larger than those of unemployed persons. However, from 1992 unemployed persons exceeded those of employed persons cleared for robbery and the gap between the two gradually widened in the following years. According to the Ministry, available data support a conclusion that 'job loss had an influence on the commitment of the offense in a considerable number of robbery cases' (p. 424).

The above presentation should not lead us to conclude that the Ministry of Justice operates with simplistic conclusions regarding joblessness and the commission of crimes for gain. Of course, a situation of unemployment *might* generate a need for money (not least in Japan, with lean welfare benefits), but this need could manifest itself even for people *holding* a job. The 'need for money' is primarily a question of the relationship between expenditure and income. Therefore, one should not focus merely on the unemployment situation in itself. Also, the reader should be reminded that this study does not include white-collar crimes, where it is not necessarily unemployment but the relative disproportion between income and expenditure that represents the main problem. As Aristotle wisely pointed out more than 2000 years ago, 'poverty creates revolutions and crimes, but the biggest crimes are not committed out of want but to obtain luxury' (quoted in Balvig,

1996: 72). As the above quotes from recent White Papers indicate, it is obvious that when looking at the changing crime situation in Japan the link between poverty and offences is an explicit part of the analysis.

Among adults, from 1990 there was an upward trend in the number of those committing robbery due to poverty (with the motive of obtaining living expenses), and this was strongly amplified from 1998 (a 2.1-fold increase from 1997 to 2002). The same trend is apparent regarding 'debt repayment' as the exclusive motive for robbery. This motive increased 10.2-fold from 1995 to 2002 (all figures: WP 2003: 315). Among juveniles, however, the main motive (in approximately 50 per cent of cases) for committing robbery has traditionally been 'obtaining entertainment expenses/extra spending money', while 'poverty' and 'debt repayment' (naturally) are rarely mentioned motives.[5] However, in the White Paper published two years later, the same Ministry admits that when comparing the labour market for juveniles in 1995 with the situation in 2004, 'employment has become even more difficult for discharged inmates in recent years' (p. 337). It is most of all juveniles who have been hardest hit by the recession. The White Paper on the Labour Economy from 2005 (cited in Tanaka, 2006) points out how unemployment among junior high school graduates rapidly increased in 1998 and 1999, and, according to Tanaka (op. cit.: 25), 'this is considered to have contributed to the rapid change of crimes, especially street crimes, which occurred in 2000 and 2001'.

At both the empirical and theoretical levels there is an expressed awareness of how macroeconomic changes filter into Japanese society and make crime a more likely alternative for many people. As we have seen, figures indicating 'crime for gain' (robbery, extortion and theft) in the White Papers are explicitly linked to variables related to expelling and excluding factors. With the decline in the number of new job openings and with the end of the periodical blanket recruitment system (cf. Chapter 3), the Ministry of Justice admits that an important crime prevention mechanism has been 'devalued'. In this regard, the Ministry is in accordance with scholars like Ôta (2004), Tamura (2004: 4) and Yuji (2005), arguing that 'the increase in crime since the early 1990s stems primarily from the nation's economic stagnation'.

Crime from a socio-cultural perspective

Man cannot live by bread alone. There is more to social well being than the safeguarding of people's material basis. Belonging and being normatively integrated are other prerequisites to having a well founded stake in society. Such a *socio-cultural* perspective on crime is widely covered in criminological literature (usually under the label 'control theory'). This approach covers a socio-*structural* dimension (the importance of social bonding that results from face-to-face interaction in primary groups) as well as cultural *codes* for behaviour (norms internalised via primary socialisation and via macro cultural values). *Causal* as well as *volitional* perspectives are included here. In Leonardsen (2004) I gave a broad presentation of this perspective, both as a general criminological perspective and as a main way to understanding low crime in Japan. I shall not repeat the full argument here, but limit myself to a summary of that earlier analysis (see, for example, Durkheim, 1952; Gottfredson and Hirschi, 1990; Murray, 1984; Wilson, 1993).

It is from the primary groups (*structure*) and the socialising agents (*cultural values*) like the family and the school that an (inner) self-control is joined together with an (outer) social control. What keeps individuals from committing crimes is (according to this approach) a combination of attachments, commitments and involvements in relation to significant others and a cultural learned code which implies an acceptance of obeying the rules of society. Even though criminologists representing different 'ideological' schools have underlined the importance of stability and trust in primary relations to prevent crime, the focus on socio-cultural dimensions is traditionally attached to a socially conservative position. Protection of the family and implanting of morality have often been the message broadcasted. If people could stay true to original close relations and to 'traditional morality' the world would be better galvanised against crime. However, as well as this socially conservative and 'micro oriented moralistic' explanation of crime, there is also a 'value approach' to explaining crime that focuses on the *macro* level and goes beyond one single ideological orientation. Garland (2001: 88) gives a condensed expression of this perspective:

In the post-war period, moral absolutes and unquestionable prohibitions lost their force and credibility, as the rigid and long-standing social hierarchies on which they relied began to be dismantled. This, in turn, weakened the moral powers of the church and the state, and encouraged the spread of a more relativistic, more 'situational' moral sensibility. In the course of a few years, quite radical changes occurred in the norms governing such matters as divorce, sexual conduct, illegitimacy, and drug taking. With the development of new social movements, and more and more groups asserting the legitimacy of their particular values and lifestyles, a much more pluralistic politics began to take shape. The result was an identity politics that disrupted the old political party system and a more diversified public opinion that questioned the possibility of moral consensus and the power of a singular dominant culture that it implied.

Even though Garland with the above description most likely refers to Western countries, it is not without relevance for Japanese society, albeit several decades later. Instead of supporting a thesis about 'moral decay' in society, meaning that *individuals* have become less moral, one can argue that 'collective parameters' have changed in a way that challenges modern man in a new way. This is what is implied in Garland's account, and, as I shall return to, also has validity for Japan.

In the debate on Japan's status as a low-crime nation these different socio-cultural perspectives have all been represented. A combination of structural conditions (Japan as a society permeated by small groups) and Confucian/Buddhist values (obedience, adaptation, consensus, endurance and shame – both as a collective structure and as guiding principles at the individual level) is what has brought general conformity. Do Japanese authorities refer to changes in this field when finding explanations for the new crime situation? Are there any references to weakened social and cultural structures and to a moral decay in society in the discussions that are presented in the White Papers? Here are some illustrative quotations:

> **WP 2002:** Education both at home and at schools does not fulfil its function well. Social ethics have deteriorated. There is [a] lack of traditional sense of solidarity in the local community, which used to function as a deterrent to crime in Japan. (preface)
>
> **WP 2003:** Behind the occurrence of an offense, there is a complex combination of various factors including the offender's personal predisposition, level of consciousness of norms, …. (p. 322)
>
> **WP 2003:** [within] families of many juvenile robbery offenders, parents leave their children to their own devices and fail to exercise proper guiding ability or become aware of the actual status of their own children, who have committed robbery. Also in such families, the family relationship is often poor. Thus, the family system does not function sufficiently in many families. Most recent juvenile robbery offenders lack a sense of belonging in society and a bright vision for the future. (p. 403)

WP 2003: ... the majority of inmates in juvenile training schools have suffered bodily harm at home. This indicates that such child abuse is likely to prompt juveniles to leave home and commit delinquent acts. Thus, it is evident that delinquency can be either allowed to blossom or nipped in the bud at home. (p. 403)

WP 2004: In addition, people, especially in urban areas, became less inclined to be involved with other people. Together with changes in values and lifestyles, social solidarity also seems to be weakening. (p. 444)

WP 2005: Under the rapid changes of the population structure with a low birth rate and longevity in Japan, the environment surrounding juveniles has also changed significantly. Those changes, such as a decrease in family members, an increase in [the] divorce rate, diffusion of the Internet, and diversification and liquidation of employment, have affected juveniles in various ways... Furthermore, the most urgent issue for overall society is to make up for insufficient supervision by families and provide juveniles with support and guidance so that they can root themselves in local communities. (p. 215)

WP 2005: Many juvenile delinquents drop out of school at early stages due to academic failure or being bullied, can not blend in well with local communities and strengthen ties with friends in similar circumstances, only to be led into delinquency.

As can be seen from these quotations, the Ministry of Justice is in accordance with the criminology that has its roots in structural functionalism and social control theory. Perspectives pointing out that primary groups are the crest of humankind (Cooley, 1964), that social bonding is the fundamental prerequisite for social integration and, by implication, that informal and formal control systems are essential for a well functioning society are inbuilt in the way the Ministry understands the crime problem. That human actions have to be guided by inner and outer sources of control is a central postulate of such criminological thinking *and*, as expected, the Ministry agrees. In Leonardsen (2004) I described Japan as a typical socially conservative society, stressing the importance of social institutions, social ethics and communal values, and this is clearly mirrored in the White Papers. As shown in Chapter 2, from the government down to each single neighbourhood, kindergarten, school and family, the confidence in moulding people into one harmonious whole is largely uncontested. Ackermann (2004) maintains that in Japan a collective unit is almost by definition something good. Consequently, if something goes wrong, it is easy to conclude that it has to be the fault of the individual. Corrective measures towards this individual are therefore the appropriate reaction, and in Japan there is a huge amount of 'direction' as to what makes 'a good human being'. While parts of Western crime prevention ideology have gradually turned into a 'realistic' perspective on crime (the managerial or actuarial approach to crime), another part of it (the conservative, educative and control theory) still finds a strong resonance in Japan. As we can see from the quotations above, 'communal' perspectives on crime are coupled with a strong belief in educative approaches when crime increases are to be analysed. Volitional and structural perspectives go in tandem. Value changes, at both the individual and at collective levels (cf. 'social ethics have deteriorated') are included in the analysis.

This optimistic view about the effectiveness of guidance, monitoring and rehabilitation of juveniles was strongly underlined in an action plan issued in 2003 called the 'Guidelines for measures on the cultivation of youth' (Goto, 2004: 24). In the 2004 White Paper on Crime, the same perspective was carried further in a section called 'Treatment of offenders' (150 pages). Even though imposing appropriate punishment was to be a central task for the criminal justice agencies, 'they should also strive for reduction of recidivists and maintenance of public order through effective treatment for rehabilitation and social re-integration of offenders' (op. cit.: preface). Crime and criminals should still be condemned with deserved punishments, but it was added that 'criminals too are members of society, thus society needs them to repent from re-offending. Therefore it also is an important role of criminal justice to maintain public security by providing proper treatment for regeneration and social re-integration of offenders' (op. cit.: 289). However, as I already have commented, it is not only this silk glove that is present in the criminal justice system today. The iron fist has become more and more importunate. (It should be added that many scholars have never accepted the presentation of the Japanese criminal justice system as particularly lenient. Miyazawa (2008: 74) illustrates this position when arguing that 'shaming in Japan was not reintegrative and criminal justice was not benevolent from the beginning').

While the Ministry of Justice recognised that confrontation and 'responsibilisation' represented an important approach in curbing crime, 'excusing circumstances' for misbehaviour were indicated at the same time. The 2005 White Paper on Crime covered a broad documentation on these matters pointing out 'an increasing number of parents are apt to abuse their children' (p. 384), that 'the percentage of juveniles' parents with problems such as "neglect/negligence", "abuse/maltreatment", and "abandonment of child/refusal of child-rearing" has been on a rise' (p. 382) and that 'most of those male juveniles [where the father had been the victim] had a history of family violence' (p. 392). In the special study on juvenile delinquency the Ministry made a separate analysis of what were called 'serious juvenile offenders'. Offenders were divided into four different groups (offences committed by two or more persons, by single persons, towards family members and traffic type offences) and then analysed further. The first group accounted for nearly three-quarters of overall serious juvenile crimes and the data disclosed:

> Many of them did not do well in school or could not continue their jobs and spent most of their time in pursuit of pleasure. Their attitude of trying to assert their power by violence and alleviating their boredom caused them to commit serious crimes. They did not have a sense of belonging to schools, working places, or local communities, and seemed to have tried to resolve their maladaptation and maintain their power by strengthening connections with similar companies and senior delinquents and by associating with them. (WP 2005: 434)

Offenders in the third group mentioned above ('family type' of offences) included cases of infanticide where girls, who wanted to maintain their position at home as good daughters, remained silent about their pregnancy to their parents, and decided to kill their babies. In cases like this, we get an illustration of how a shame-based culture not only operates in a crime preventing way but also might *trigger* some types of crime ('females who killed their new-born babies were all unmarried and did not tell their family about their pregnancy', WP 2005: 391). Of course, this 'shame mechanism' will have relevance for a number of other offences as well (see WP 2003: 476).

From a very broad, but sometimes quite confusing database, it appears that the Ministry of Justice often draws a link between crime and family/school conditions. The same sort of story is repeated time and again in the White Papers, namely about delinquent children who are emotionally disturbed or harmed due to different types of familial neglect or problems at school. Even though the Ministerial surveys do not permit an 'everything-has-got-worse' conclusion, there is a lot of documentation on juvenile delinquents with broken families and troubled relationships throughout the educational years.

However, these delinquents are not simply presented as innocent *victims* of a breakdown in close relations. Even if a collapse in family and school life is framing the everyday life of many juvenile offenders, such social circumstances do not exclude perspectives of 'rational choice' among these youngsters. The strategic criminal, the conscious criminal, the sensation-seeking criminal, the gambling criminal, the calculating criminal are all included in the complex web of criminogenic variables, and therefore a language of sharper sentences is also present. As I will come back to, an increasing *punitiveness* in criminal justice policy is easy to identify in Japan in recent years. Sentences for rape and other sexual offences have been extended, and 'this is because the public is likely to seek for imposing heavy sentence upon the offenders who committed sexual offenses, which might remarkably impair human rights of victims and cause serious damages to them bodily and mentally' (WP 2002: 323). In connection with the amendment of the juvenile law in 2000 the Ministry underscored that in the light of the major heinous crimes committed by juveniles, and in order to state clearly that even young people would be liable for punishment, it would be necessary to lower the possible age for criminal responsibility to 14 years (WP 2001: 175). When discussing the increase in heinous crimes in the 2003 White Paper, the Ministry underlined that 'it is necessary to impose severe punishments for them [malicious crimes] while giving due consideration to feelings of victims', and continues to stress the importance of 'nipping crimes in the bud' (p. 479). Expressions about juveniles 'lacking in consideration for other people' also indicate a rather volitional perspective on crime. By implication, the judicial system was recommended as an appropriate institution to handle these challenges, even for juveniles down to 14 years. However, the official way of arguing was all the time 'double tracked': the necessity for severe punishment and discipline went in tandem with a strong belief in educational measures, with programmes focusing on sentiments and morals and a fostering of juveniles 'full of humanity' (WP 2003: 480).

In conclusion, the Ministry of Justice does not only adopt a 'radical' (economic) perspective, explaining crime as the result of exclusionary forces; it also gives support to a paradigm where committing crime is defined as a conscious decision[6], but one which is triggered by unfortunate circumstances (which, obviously, young people could hardly be blamed for). Together with expressions about short-sighted, spontaneous and hedonistic actions among juveniles (expressing weakened moral standards) one finds references to material structures of affluence and easy availability, and wanting social bondings among people, as explanations of increasing crime. Changes on the 'demand side' (the quest for material goods and weaker moral barriers), together with changes on the 'supply side' (more goods and easier availability), represent a new challenge. In short, most of the relevant 'variables' that have been introduced in criminologists' endeavours to explain crime are included in the official documents referred to here. Everything is mentioned, nothing forgotten; then it is all up to the sphere of *Realpolitik* and the implementing authorities to decide where to start and what to do on crime. And at *this* point, when it comes to proactive initiatives to prevent crime, I am afraid that the documents referred to offered little else but more or less wishful proclamations like 'restoring the family', 'restoring the community', 'bringing back values based on solidarity principles', etc. The symptoms are registered and then, without any further reflection as to how these symptoms are linked to more fundamental societal structures, economy and power relations, a variety of 'good hopes' is proclaimed. As Gottfredson and Hirschi point out, 'nothing is more dangerous than a policy justified only by the ambitions of politicians and bureaucrats' (quoted in Young, 1999: 132). What implications the causal explanations presented in the White Papers might have for welfare politics in general, housing and labour market policies and the social benefit system, etc. are left without any further discussion. In comparison, this approach has some similarities with the Western, Etzionian, communitarian movement, where social and moral dimensions have a stronger say than material conditions. Consequently, the Ministry of Justice seems to fall victim to the same type of critique as the communitarian movement has received (see Hughes, 1996; Young, 1999). This relates to critical remarks about too little focus on injustices in society, too much focus on control and a simplified understanding of what the family institution represents in present-day society (there is probably more violence and sexual abuse inside the family than outside it). Alternatively, I have found a precise expression of what an important aspect of the crime problem is all about in the following statement by Walker (quoted in Shaftoe, 2004: 42):

> The truth is, we are not facing a foreign enemy. We are up against ourselves. We need to deal with our own social institutions, our own

values, our own habits and our own crime control policies... We will reduce crime when we make basic changes in all of our social policies that affect families, employment and neighbourhoods. There is no quick, easy 'miracle' cure for crime.

From a critical perspective one could argue that the Ministerial analyses of social disruption referred to above might seem to replace symptoms with causes, and, consequently, the counteracting measures proposed seem to represent a reflex action to, more than a reflection over, the social problems that are disclosed. To re-establish social integration in a postmodern, turbulent, open economy, where basic social structures and societal ligatures ('deeper bonds' and 'moral beliefs', Dahrendorf, 1985: 25) are seen in a broader context, will demand a more thorough development of interventionist, welfare oriented measures. A reinforcement of the family institution[7] will obviously have to invite welfare as well as labour market strategies that so far have been little discussed. To give juveniles hope for the future, give them a stake in society and make up for insufficient supervision by families is easy to proclaim but will not be realised without a more extensive, sociological analysis of how economic and social variables are interlinked. An appeal that juveniles will have to learn not to let themselves be pressured by other youngsters is definitely an interesting recommendation. Sociological analyses related to social preventive work has shown how young people, due to pluralistic ignorance, act in a performative way with deviance and delinquency as a likely outcome (Balvig et al. 2005). But once again, to take this perspective seriously implies coordinated programme strategies that presuppose extensive and skilful intervention.

It remains to comment on the last (ideal typical) perspective on crime. To what extent and in which way could crime, and changing crime patterns, be a reflection of decisions made by *political-administrative* actors. This is a constructivist perspective where public decisions rather than citizens' actions are made the subject of analysis.

Crime from a political-administrative perspective

Crime increases in Japan during the 1990s could be a reflex, not only to changes in police work, but in legislation activity in general. Even though the connection could go in both directions, it could be argued that the more we strengthen the police and the more we criminalise certain actions, the more crime we will experience. Anyway, changes regarding what we label crime and how resources are prioritised in detecting crime will affect the final outcome.

Criminologists arguing like this (Becker, Kitsuse, Lemert, Pfohl and Schur, to mention a few) move their primary attention away from the delinquent and focus instead on people in positions of power (i.e. the political-administrative system). Becker (1963: 8–9) has given a precise statement of the essence of this perspective:

> The sociological view I have just discussed defines deviance as the infraction of some agreed-upon rule. It then goes on to ask who breaks rules, and to search for the factors in their personalities and life situations that might account for the infractions. This assumes that those who have broken a rule constitute a homogenous category, because they have committed the same deviant act. Such an assumption seems to me to ignore the central fact about deviance: it is created by society. I do not mean this in the way it is ordinarily understood, in which the causes of deviance are located in the social situation of the deviant or in 'social factors' which prompt his action. I mean, rather, that *social groups create deviance by making the rules whose infraction constitutes deviance,* and by applying those rules to particular people and labelling them as outsiders. From this point of view, deviance is *not* a quality of the act the person commits, but rather a consequence of the application by others of rules and sanctions to an 'offender'. The deviant is one to whom that label has successfully been applied; deviant behavior is behavior that people so label. (emphasis in original)

If this classical statement ever had relevance it should be in Japan. Japan has for centuries been a society where the central authorities have had omnipotent power in defining, implementing, supervising and enforcing formalised control (Henshall, 1999). The institutionalised system of justice has always reached with its tentacles into the smallest bits of society, down to the level of neighbourhood control and even into the family institution (*ie*). There are few modernised societies where the belief in a centralised, governmental control has been stronger than in Japan, and there are few societies that have been known to make the most of this power to a larger extent. When the alarm bells started ringing towards the end of the century (due to the crime situation), there were obvious reasons to mobilise the state apparatus as a rescue centre. According to Fenwick (2004), Hamai and Ellis (2008a), Johnson (2008) and Miyazawa (2008), this was actually also what happened, and it was the *repressive* and *punitive* (more than the welfarist) state that appeared on the scene. The interesting research question in this regard concerns how changes on the *control* side might affect the total amount of crime. So far, we have seen that Japanese authorities make a causal link between economic and socio-cultural changes and increasing crime rates. Do they draw any corresponding links between formal control mechanisms and crime? Let me first of all give a few illustrations of how the Ministry of Justice and the police regard the role of the formal control system in fighting crime:

> **WP 2003:**.... it is more important than anything to enhance criminal justice. To this end, it is necessary at first to improve human and material resources of the criminal justice authorities that are engaged in the process of law enforcement, starting from crime prevention activities including the reinforcement of immigration control system, through the clearance, prosecution, and trial of offenders, to correction and rehabilitation of offenders. (p. 481)

> **WP 2006:**... the upper limits of penalties were raised by the recently revised Penal Code, which enables the courts to provide wider-ranging sentencing, considering the possibility of a defendant's repeating offenses along with other circumstances. Furthermore, as fines were newly established for theft and obstructing performance of public duty, etc. as optional punishment, the impact of punishment is likely to affect the minds of offenders with relatively less advanced criminal tendencies. (p. 368)

> **WP 2006:** While clarifying the reality of crime damage, crime victims should be given sufficient opportunities to state their opinions concerning penalties to be imposed on perpetrators and criminal dispositions should be determined taking such victim's opinions into consideration in an appropriate manner. (p. 369)

> **MM 2003[8]:** Reinforce the police activities during times and in areas that crimes frequently occur. Do not overlook crime and disorder committed in public even when they are trivial. Create a society intolerant to these conducts with appropriate measures by the police as well as cooperation with local residents. (p. 8)

> **MM 2003:** Investigate juvenile crimes strictly and promptly. Sending juvenile delinquents to family courts as soon as possible may contribute to the restoration of juvenile's rehabilitation. In order for prompt investigation, streamline the procedure for making investigation documents. (p. 15)

MM 2003: To solve the cases committed by juveniles under 14 and treat them properly, the amendment of the law that clarifies the police authority and procedure to investigate such cases as a precondition for trial will be considered. (p. 16)

MM 2003: To respond aptly to the people's demands, such as prevention of street crimes and improvement in the ability to investigate various crimes, the police will increase the number of prefectural police officers and increase the number of officers at the National Police Agency... To carry out investigations promptly, the government will increase the number of prosecutors and their secretaries. (p. 36)

No wonder, representatives of the criminal justice system will propagate their own role in combating crime. The idea behind the 'broken window' theory (Wilson and Kelling, 1982) was explicitly referred to when the 'Action Plan to Create A Crime-Resistant Society' from 2003 was presented. This perspective argues that if a small violation is ignored, a sense of disorder will rapidly grow in society, and problems will escalate. The 'Action Plan' (p. 2) referred to the success this strategy had attained in the US (which, of course, implied that more resources had to be allocated to the police and also to voluntary crime prevention groups). The importance of 'acting strictly and promptly', especially in cases of juvenile delinquency, was frequently underlined as a premise for reviving Japan as the safest country in the world.[9]

The impression that Japanese society has reacted to the increase in registered crimes in a more punitive way is confirmed by criminologists. Miyazawa (2008: 74) is perhaps the most distinct voice in the chorus of critics regarding the trend Japanese crime policy has taken. At an early stage of the debate he rejected characterisations of Japanese criminal justice policy as 'benevolent paternalism' (Foote, 1992) or 'reintegrative shaming' (Braithwaite, 1989). Today, Miyazawa describes Japanese criminal justice policy as a type of 'penal populism' that we already know from Western countries. According to Miyazawa, since the early 1990s there has been a clear turn-around trend in the direction of more punitive reactions to crime, nourished by a strong victims' movement. As referred to in chapter 4, the public has become more and more fearful and stereotypical depictions of juveniles have become omnipresent. Concern has moved from the predator to the public and the victim; these are the ones who need protection. In his article 'The politics of increasing punitiveness and the rising populism in Japanese criminal justice policy', Miyazawa (2008) focuses on changes in the Criminal

Code in 2004 and in the Juvenile Law in 2000, with the main points being (cf. the White Paper on Crime, 2006: 268–72):

- a general increase in punishment provided by the criminal code (upper limits raised from 15/20 years to 20/30 years, depending on types of crime).
- easing conditions for the death penalty.
- life imprisonment and death penalties for juvenile crime.
- lowering age limits (the upper age limit for sending a case back to the prosecutor was reduced from 16 to 14 years), seeking harsher treatment of offenders younger than 14 years (the Juvenile Law was amended in 2000 and its aftermath).
- the creation of a new crime category for dangerous driving (in 2001), with penalties of 1 to 15 years imprisonment for death and up to 10 years imprisonment for injury.
- amendment of the Child Prostitution Prohibition Law (in 2004), increasing punishment for buying services of child prostitutes from up to three years/1 million yen to five years/3 million yen.

Of course, one cannot make direct deductions from implementation of new laws, amendment of older laws or harsher punishment to conclusions in the direction of a new punitivism. These are *normative* questions that must be evaluated in a broader context. For example, Miyazawa does not mention stricter laws against organised crimes (Organised Crime Punishment Law, enacted in 2000, see the White Paper on Police, 2006: 72). 'Technically', this could be described as a 'punitive' reaction. But without bringing in another important perspective that Becker (1967) introduced by asking 'Whose side are we on?', the discussion becomes formalistic. The same argument could be applied to legislative activities related to dangerous driving and child prostitution. Harsher punishment in cases like these is per definition a punitive reaction from the government, but, at the same time, this legislation represents an important signal concerning an intention to safeguard 'soft values'. But of course, this invites a discussion as to whether *any* type of legislation should automatically be subsumed under the term 'punitivism'.

Fenwick (2005) concludes in much the same way as Miyazawa. Focusing on the reform of the Juvenile Law in 2000, he argues that this amendment represents a profound change in the language as well as in the substance of youth justice policy. 'A traditional concern with protection and rehabilitation has clearly been displaced by a new emphasis on punitiveness, the rights of the victim, and notions of parental responsibility. As such, the new law marks an important break in the rhetoric and practice of Japanese crime control' (p. 139). It is interesting to note the revision regarding the role of parents. Under the revised law, judges are now given the power to issue warnings and instructions to parents of juveniles falling under their jurisdiction. This reform reflects, as Fenwick points out, a broader concern about irresponsible parenting as a possible cause of the current crime situation. Among other things, the government has shown its engagement in inviting parents into a more responsible role through a TV ad campaign, concluding: 'Just because you have a child, it doesn't mean you are a parent'. While Fenwick pursues an argument which unambiguously favours increasing punitiveness in Japanese crime justice policy, it is a bit unclear (to me) why more responsibility among parents should represent an expression of more punitiveness. Furthermore, safeguarding of victims' rights *might* be, but does not have to be, synonymous with punitiveness.

Hamai and Ellis (2008a) conclude that Japan during the last ten years has entered the same road (but at a faster speed!) towards penal populism as many Western countries. To these authors indices of *genbatsuka* (increased punitiveness) include a sudden rise in the prison population[10], harsher sentences for those defendants sent for trial, legislative changes permitting harsher sentences (and an increase in the number of lifers and death row inmates, in spite of unchanged murder rates), fewer lifers released on parole and, not least, an astonishing rise in the number of executions in Japan. Hamai and Ellis also note that the public prosecutors have increased their power and have gradually been pushed into more and more punitive recommendations. A complicated interaction between the media, crime victims, the National Police Agency and politicians, and lawyers ('The Iron Quadrangle'), has resulted in a growing penal populism in Japan. According to Hamai and Ellis, academics, defence lawyers, judges and other experts who these days would argue against *genbatsuka* are treated with less respect than before (p. 86).

Ryan (2005), studying the revisions that were made to the Juvenile Act in 2001, comes to the same conclusion as Miyazawa and Hamai/ Ellis. While the previous Juvenile Act aimed at focusing on 'the sound upbringing of the juvenile' (Article 1 of the Juvenile Act), emphasising respect and dignity for the individual juvenile and prioritising re-integration over punishment, the outcome of the revision process was clearly in the direction of much tougher dispositions and increased punishment. Ryan concludes his analysis by saying that the changes 'represent a significant departure from the original understanding of the purpose of the *Juvenile Act*', and that 'disposition is becoming harsher, more standardised, and incident-focused' (p. 185). Accordingly, the present juvenile justice system is, to Ryan, characterised as a 'paternalistic-benevolent' model without benevolence.

From the above argument one could say that a 'labelling perspective' on the crime increase in Japan is highly relevant. A general intensification of the formal control system took place through a series of interventions, from new legal regulations, via a strengthening of the police to a general increase in punishment. This might easily have contributed to an amplification process where a general ideology of getting 'tough on crime' alerted all levels in the control system. The 2002 White Paper on Crime (pp. 274–75) gives an account of a series of recent legislative changes related to types of violent offences (concerning organised crime, anti-stalking laws, child abuse and spousal violence). However, the relevance of these changes for understanding the new crime situation is not reflected upon in the White Papers[11], and no comment is made on the police scandals. The general intensification of police control and the increased use of neighbourhood watch groups, etc. might also have had an impact on tendencies to report crime, but even this is overlooked in silence in the White Papers. The understanding of the causal relation seems to go in the other direction; it is the increase in crime that leads to an increase in the formalised control, not the other way around (or rather seeing it as a dialectical process). When the Ministry declares that 'legislative measures are being taken one after another with the aim of preventing offenses committed in dangerous or new ways', this information is not an integral part of how to understand rising crime. Furthermore, tendencies towards moral panic among ordinary citizens are certainly not calmed down by public authorities. If anything, the public fear seems to be used as an input for an argument that would most likely lead to a further escalation of fear. Time and again, reference to a scared audience is used as an argument for not being lenient on crime.

In sum, it seems that a conclusion that Japanese criminal justice policy has turned in a more punitive direction during the 1990s is defensible[12]. Increasing liberalism in economic politics is matched by increasingly *anti-liberal* ideology in the criminal justice policy. This is not a very unfamiliar mix of policies. Social conservatism often goes in tandem with economic liberalism (Levitas, 1986).

The new punitivism in Japan is particularly apparent in the use of the death penalty and the reform of the Juvenile Law. However, there *is* more to this story than has been presented above. For one thing, the term 'punitivism' is problematic. Furthermore, I will argue that a limited conclusion in the direction of 'new punitivism' or 'populistic punitivism' represents too much of a simplification. At least my reading of the White Papers on Crime discloses a somewhat more nuanced approach to the crime enigma than the term 'punitivism' indicates. An ideology of being 'tough on crime' is in these documents paralleled with what actually could be described as a more sociologically oriented perspective. Let me elaborate this a bit further.

Japanese criminal justice policy: More sword – less chrysanthemum?

In *The chrysanthemum and the sword: patterns of Japanese culture,* Ruth Benedict (1967: 1) reminds us that the Japanese for many years have been described 'in the most fantastic series of "but also's" ': The Japanese are polite, *but also* insolent, they are aggressive, *but also* unaggressive, they are rigid, *but also* adaptable, they are loyal, *but also* treacherous and they are brave, *but also* timid. Ambiguities or paradoxes like these are numerous in Japanese society. As I have shown above, quite a few scholars have concluded their analyses of recent Japanese criminal justice policy with the label 'punitivism' or *genbatsuka*. The question is to what extent this characteristic gives an adequate and satisfactory description of present-day crime policy in Japan. My conclusion is that in this regard also we have to return to Benedict's 'schizophrenic' analytical approach, and that we have to listen carefully to Donald Levine's (1985) critique of what he labels 'the modern assault on ambiguity'. A bottom line in Levine's argument is to warn against a disposition to flee from the ambiguities of human life. Even though the *trend* in Japanese criminal justice policy is unmistakeable, this does not exclude a description that still has room for 'but also's'. Criminal justice policy in Japan is changing (like 'everywhere' else), but we should endeavour not to sweep Japan into a terminology which leaves out peculiar and specific cultural characteristics.

Criminologists have often characterised *Western* criminal justice policy during the last 20 years with labels like 'new punitivism', 'populistic punitiveness', or 'penal populism' (for an overview, see Garland, 2001; Pratt, 2007)[13]. A condensed expression of what is meant by these (closely interlinked) concepts would include:

a. Crime justice policy is run by politicians who look for policies which are electorally attractive;

b.   harsher sentencing and more use of prison should be applied; and
c.   politicians turn their back on bureaucratic advisors and expert knowledge and instead give priority to popular commonsense practice.

How does Japan score against these characteristics?

a) I think the documentation I have referred to above clearly indicates that Japan has moved in a more punitive direction. The argument in the White Papers on Crime is continuously referring back to a scared audience and what people demand or need. Frequent surveys are undertaken to tap public opinion which systematically disclose a strong support for more punitiveness. Political legitimacy is challenged and the consequence is a rhetoric that brings the electorate the message they want to hear. The broad documentation regarding the role played by the growing victims' movement in Japan gives credentials to this conclusion.

b) The literature referred to above is also convincingly clear as for a general sharpening of sentences. This can be registered regarding not only laws and policies that promote *genbatsuka* but also regarding judicial decisions (changing age limits, increases in punishment by the criminal code, stricter sentencing, life imprisonment and death penalties for juvenile crime, to mention just some). I find it well documented that Japan, concerning both formalities (the criminal code) and realities (sentences passed) has moved in a significantly more punitive direction during the last ten years.

c) While this perspective has been generally advocated by Pratt (2007), Miyazawa (2008) is the most articulate critic in Japan concerning the missing role for empirical criminologists in criminal justice policy-making. As an illustration he refers to a symposium in 2004 aimed at undertaking a re-examination of policy-making processes in recent legislation and policies on criminal justice. At this gathering criminal law professor Yuji Shiroshita examined the legislative process behind the increase in penalties provided in the Criminal Code in 2004 and concluded that the Ministry of Justice had justified the amendment on three grounds: changes in the public conception of justice, an increase in the number of reported crimes and *genbatsuka* of sentencing, resulting in many sentences reaching upper limits. However, from a professional point of view there was no basis for supporting these three grounds and no evidence for the claim that increasing penalties would have a deterrent effect (Miyazawa, 2008: 71). According to Miyazawa, in

present-day Japan one has ended up in a situation where political correctness has taken priority over intellectual integrity.

I find it well documented that Japanese society turned in a more punitive direction during the 1990s. As a result of climbing crime figures in
combination with a general feeling of unease and uncertainty among
'ordinary people' there has been a fertile soil for implementing a 'tough
(or at least 'tougher') on crime' strategy in Japan. 'Nurturant acceptance' is hardly a fitting label for criminal justice policy in this country
in recent years. However, I have three supplementary comments to add
to the presentation above:

The role for empirical criminologists.   As indicated by Pratt (2007) Japan is
hardly a very special case when it comes to the role for criminologists in
criminal justice policy-making. Politicians all over the world, and especially when it comes to criminal justice policy, have never shown much
interest in seeking professional support, where such support does not
resonate with public opinion. Criminal justice policy is probably the seg-
ment where politicians have the most to lose by listening to professional
advice. Politicians who want to be re-elected should probably keep professionals within this field at arm's length. However, my main point in
this regard concerns the implicit argument in Miyazawa's presentation,
namely that social science, *qua science,* can give more or less unequivocal
answers to how criminal justice policy should be run. Criminal justice
policy is certainly a contested area, but the same goes for research within
this field. There is certainly no problem in criticising separate political
decisions, bills or strategies within this field on the basis of 'evidence-
based' research. However, politics is not about separate and singular
rationalities, but about 'packages of truth', where questions about 'what
works' by necessity will have to include much more than what a strictly
scientific argument should indicate. It is the legitimate right of politicians to act according to the dictates of common sense, and the alternative to this would probably point in a direction where 'technocracy'
would replace 'democracy'. Professional criminologists, as much as professional economists, or professional militarists, should not be in a position to reassess political 'trade offs' between different considerations and
different interests. That is why it is called 'policy'. When the final history
about the financial crises starting in 2008 or the Iraq War in 2003 is written, the critique might easily well be that the politicians based too much
of their final decisions on expert knowledge from the professionals.

The definition of punitiveness.   If *any* extension of legislative measures is
automatically defined as increased punitivism, we easily leave out one

important perspective in the debate. As mentioned above, evaluations in this field are replete with normative questions. As long as the legitimate use of legal regulations is the accepted premise for any state, the interesting criminological discussion is not primarily about *quantitative* changes in the use of this instrument, but about *qualitative* changes. When a state turns to legal solutions in order to solve a problem, the most important question to clarify is *whose interests are taken care of* through such a regulation, and *then* comes the question of if this is an efficient or sustainable strategy. As long as our discussion concerns criminal *justice policy*, it is the two words in italics that deserve attention ('justice' and 'policy'). I cannot enter this complex discussion here, but I do miss this perspective, in both the present debate about *genbatsuka* in Japan and also in the broader international debate on this topic. Criminal justice policy is about asking (with Becker, 1967) 'whose side are we on?'. Criminal justice policy is about conflicts of interests and values and governments should be challenged on such a debate rather than on to what extent they turn to legislative solutions (even though, of course, it is right also to debate limits to legislation in a modern state). In my opinion, intensifying legal measures against people accused of organised crime, trafficking, white-collar crime, abuse of vulnerable and defenceless people, etc., should not be discussed in the same context as when we discuss increasing punitiveness against perpetrators who already might be defined as 'victims', be they among 'the excluded', 'the outcasts', 'the outsiders' or the oppressed who have experienced domestic violence. This observation, of course, also has implications regarding a topic that is hugely undercommunicated in Japan, namely *social class*. As Yoder (2004: 10) underlines, 'like in other modern industrialized societies, class is a major factor in youth crime in Japan'. One of the most important issues to confront in the present debate on increasing punitiveness in Japan is the question of *what types of crime,* and *which social groups* are confronted with public attention (be it in the form of 'guidance' or 'punishment'). In a hierarchical society like Japan I think scholars should raise this topic very clearly, rather than limiting their arguments to a general warning against the new punitivism.

The supplementing story[14]. If we limit ourselves to what political authorities in Japan have expressed verbally, we have seen above that the increase in registered crime in Japan since the end of the 1990s is partly explained by pointing to *economic* variables and partly by pointing to *socio-cultural* variables. Within the last category one will find both *structural* (disruption of social networks like the family, etc.) and *moral* perspectives (a breakdown of values related to respect, trust and decent behaviour in general). The blame is sometimes (especially) put on young people as individual actors for being hedonistic, impulsive and short-sighted, and sometimes the blame is directed towards representatives at the institutional level, criticising parents and 'schools' for failing to teach 'the values of society' as Foljanty-Jost and Metzler (2003: 3) put it[15]. When it comes to the first of these 'causes' ('moral decay'), programmes subsumed under the headline 'life guidance' for (especially) *juveniles* have been strengthened during recent years. It seems that the traditional Japanese 'apology and repentance culture' still lingers on, and the belief in a systematic 'inner search' as the road towards living a more decent life is unabated. The core idea is to detect juvenile delinquents at a very early stage (cf. the wide definition of 'status offences') and then provide the necessary and appropriate treatment. Whatever viewpoint one might hold regarding 'treatment' or 'guiding' as a relevant strategy for curbing crime, the story about an escalating punitivism in Japan should be supplemented with a story about 'life guidance' (and of course, the principle of 'life guidance' is not necessarily in contradiction to a punitive approach to crime).

Metzler (2003) gives an informative introduction to how this principle of guidance is operationalised in Japanese training schools. In a chapter about 'Teaching Young Serious Offenders How to Live and "How to Be"', she gives a close-up presentation of daily life in these training schools. The 'corrective education' is subsumed under the headline 'life guidance', and is said to be the most important part of the educational curriculum. The life guidance is divided into six components: 'educational/occupational guidance', 'guidance related to problem behaviour', 'training regarding life style and basic daily habits', 'cultivation of aesthetic sentiment', 'guidance related to the regulation of living environment' and 'therapeutic education'. The 2003 White Paper on Crime (p. 144, pp. 147–48) gives an overview of what 'programmes' different groups of inmates are subjected to, and according to this source 65 per cent of the inmates are classified as belonging to the group needing 'life guidance'[16]. As registered crime has increased, a lot of governmental energy has been put into a further elaboration of these programmes.

Another element in what I defined above as 'the supplementing story' has been told by Feeley (2007). According to this scholar it is really not clear what media coverage of asserted crime waves or the mobilisation of victim rights' groups add up to, since 'police and courts continue to act more or less as they always have, and at best the changes in the criminal process have been minimal' (p. 14). Furthermore, he contends that Japan, being in a group of strong democratic states that are more immune to penal populism, 'is much more resistant to any deep culture of control than are the United States and the United Kingdom' (p. 20).

Accordingly, one should not expect that victims' rights groups will gain much influence in Japan. Even though both of these arguments could be contested, it is appropriate not to jump to conclusions on this complex topic. As Feeley wisely adds, only the future can tell.

Even though a more punitive 'climate' seems to have reached Japan, it should also be underlined (cf. above) that the Ministry of Justice offers a multitude of perspectives when discussing crime. Crime as a mirror of society and as a consequence of basic economic and socio-cultural changes is clearly reflected in the White Papers. This conclusion is evident both when discussing 'causes' of crime and even more so when the topic turns to prevention. The following passages represent an illustration of this broad approach to understanding crime in a modern society:

> In short, not only the authorities concerned with criminal justice but also the whole society surrounding juveniles including parents and families, schools, work places, and communities, should make efforts to ensure that juveniles recognize themselves as irreplaceable members of the society and as persons who will be responsible for the future of the society. Such efforts will be a significant driving force to stop the increase in robbery offenses and other offenses committed by juveniles. (WP 2003: 403–404)

> When aiming at realizing a safe and secure society, we face not a few problems that are difficult to solve only through criminal justice. For this reason, it is absolutely necessary that the criminal authorities, which play a central role, as well as other ministries concerned and all organizations and individuals, including families, schools, workplaces, communities, and volunteer groups, will cooperate with one another beyond boundaries and make consistent efforts to design and carry out radical measures to prevent heinous offenses while offering opinions from various perspectives. (WP 2003: 481–82)

Even though declarations like this are vague and give relatively little guidance as to what this actually means when it comes to implementation and priorities among conflicting interests, those who would try to appeal to the authorities to avoid the pressure in the direction of retribution and 'blaming the victim' can find support for their arguments in the documents mentioned above. Sure enough, there are few signs of a broader, binding welfarist perspective in the Ministerial analyses of crime[17]. However, the White Papers include references that involve corporate as well as civil society, the labour market as well as a deteriorating morality, the family and the role of the parents as well as the schools and their very competitive demands and the delay in social independence of juveniles of today as well as an increased marketisation and consumer pressure on youngsters. When all these perspectives are turned into practical measures, the 2006 White Paper presents no less than 150 separate crime prevention measures, divided into the following categories: 'Prevention of familiar offenses that may threaten peaceful life', 'prevention of juvenile offenses that should be coped with by the whole society', 'response to threats coming beyond national borders', 'protection of the economy and society from organized crimes' and 'infrastructure development for restoring public safety'. As an illustration of how the government works to heighten residents' awareness of crime prevention, more than 100,000 essays were submitted for an essay contest for elementary schoolchildren and junior high school students. One of the aims of such a contest is to 'deepen local residents' understanding and concerns on rehabilitation of people who have once committed offenses or delinquency, prompt local communities to accept them as part of their community and help their rehabilitation, and thereby prevent them from committing offenses or delinquency again' (op. cit.: 267).

In many ways one could say that the approach to crime prevention presented here comes close to strategies that Western governments through many years have tried (see Garland, 2001; Hughes and Edwards, 2002, 2007; Lea, 2002; Tilley, 2002, 2005). Be it strategies like situational crime prevention, target hardening and actuarial risk management, or be it community crime prevention programmes backing the idea of multi-agency safety strategies, they are all included in the broad repertoire presented in the White Papers. In the mid-1980s The British Home Office had already declared that 'every citizen and all those agencies whose policies and practices can influence the extent of crime should make their contribution. Preventing crime is a task for the whole community' (quoted in Shaftoe, 2004: 107–108). This way of involving 'every citizen' in the crime prevention project is what Garland (2001: 124) designates 'the responsibilisation strategy'. This implies the extension of state agencies by linking them up with actors in the private sector and the community. The challenge of securing a safe society is (according to this perspective) no longer the single responsibility of central government and its formal control agencies but becomes a joint task in close cooperation with a network of non-government organisations and actors. Consequently, when crime control becomes a 'democratised' project where each citizen is authorised or empowered to fight crime, this can easily be designated as something different from a centralist, punitivist approach. In this perspective crime control is *not* necessarily and unambiguously the authoritative, monologist, strong state showing muscles and seeking popularity by getting tough on crime, but rather a negotiating state, trying to redistribute and deregulate the unruly common people. Of course, there is no elevated, neutral point of observation for describing 'the responsibilisation strategy' in fighting crime, and in today's variegated, multi-faceted approach to this problem it is easy to find empirical 'evidence' for different characterisations. For those who stick to a 'governmentality' perspective it is urgent to warn against the revival of the old, authoritarian, omnipresent Japanese state apparatus with its tentacles entering into the smallest fibres of society. An 'involving' state should not be confused with a 'dialogical' state. 'Civil society' and non-governmental organisations have not played any important roles in Japanese history, but for those who have a hope that a stronger civil society might develop in this country (like Hirata, 2002, and Kingston, 2004) and who agitate for the strengthening of communitarian values, some of the political signals in the White Papers on Crime might be interpreted more optimistically. It is the running discussion of the criminal justice policy that will decide to what extent the sword will replace the chrysanthemum in Japan.

6

Social Disruption? Self Destruction and Social Phobia in Modern-Day Japan

Framing the problem of social withdrawal

The main question asked in this book is to what extent Japan's collectivistic, Confucian culture as a system of thoughts (and not as an institutionalised welfare system) protects people in times of economic decay. For a long period of time (1960–90) Japan was admired by many observers for being a socially inclusive and harmonious society (which, to me, is true only with essential reservations). Be that as it may, in Chapter 5 I concluded that Japan (whatever the 'starting point' may have been) has been moving in a more punitive direction. As long as the focus is on implementation rather than on the rhetoric, a development in the direction of populist punitivism away from elements of nurturant acceptance has been the bottom line of my presentation.

It has been argued that the true quality of a society is disclosed in the way it treats its 'losers' (Bauman, 2004). In the present book I am not only asking if Japan still deserves its reputation as being 'unique' regarding crime, but also, in a broader sense, to what extent Japan is a society that succeeds in taking care of the 'drop outs', the 'outsiders' or those who do not succeed in competing when the wheels are spinning faster. Is Japan really a society that could be defined as 'inclusive', 'caring' or 'solidaric'? When asking this type of question, the crime rate, as well as reactions to crime, is only one indication of anomic or punitive tendencies. As already mentioned, crime could (analytically) be described as a 'striking out' reaction to a deeper social unrest in society. Other ways of reacting to situations of 'unrest' might be described as 'striking in', i.e. different expressions of withdrawal from society.

To the extent that crime could be described as an active response to a humiliating situation, to what extent do others end up in more passive or resigning roles? To what extent do Japanese people end up 'blaming themselves' rather than 'blaming society' (or others)? Or to express the problem in this way: if crime is more of a 'damn you' reaction, then the focus in this chapter is to look at types of 'damn me' reactions, where people actually 'opt out', withdraw from communal participation or, even worse, look for the 'exit'[1], and where the silent message is 'I take the blame'. Does Japanese culture represent more of a burden to people who cannot compete or does it instead represent a support and a lever for such people? Bearing in mind that my perspective delimits the analysis to recent years, the challenge is to answer how inclusive and caring Japanese society is in times of economic turbulence.

When discussing this I shall focus on two social phenomena: *hikikomori* (social withdrawal) and *suicide*. Of course, it could be questioned whether these ways of acting have anything in common and, in which case, if this could be expressed as a 'striking in'. A lot of crimes could actually be described as 'passive' actions, while, conversely, some suicides could be labelled 'exposive', not to say 'explosive'. However, it is not so much the final act (suicide, withdrawal) that catches my attention in this discussion but the process *behind* these actions. What could be described as a kind of common denominator between these two concepts is an expression of 'giving up' and an expression of an active decision by choosing to 'disappear'. The individual renounces his/her role in a communal setting and turns his/her back on society. Nonparticipation is what links these two phenomena together.

As with crime, bringing forward 'facts' about retreatism is (almost by definition) a very complicated affair. Even though suicides are registered as 'hard facts' in official statistics, both the dark and the grey figures are significant. As one can imagine, this is even truer when it comes to defining and then registering people who withdraw from public participation (mainly education or work). As I shall come back to, *hikikomori* is a transient and blurred phenomenon that makes it hard to know what one really is studying. Consequently, the methodological warnings I made in Chapter 4 about crime should, for even stronger reasons, be repeated here. There are many uncertainties. Nevertheless, uncertainties about quantities do not remove our possibilities for discussing qualities. If the 'real' number of retreatists is closer to 200,000 than to 2 million, this does not remove our chances for general learning based on an observable phenomenon. If one novel can bring us interesting insights about society, then, for sure, thousands of 'real cases' should be able to do the same. My interest in decoding the *hikikomori* phenomenon lies in using this as a radar that might tell us an interesting story about Japanese society in the age of late modernity. But before I begin this topic let me first explicate the importance of *contextualising* our empirical presentation (cf. Chapter 2).

Social phenomena should be interpreted in their culturally specific context and the *meaning* of such phenomena should be deducted with reference to this context. What does this mean regarding *hikikomori* and *suicide*? When people 'prefer' to choose 'exit' as a way of solving their personal troubles, my assertion is that, *ceteris paribus*, this will more likely happen in Japan than in an average Western country. Due to a stress on conformity, adaptation, harmony, form, guidance, endurance, discipline and, eventually, resignation, the lesson taught from early childhood and all through life is to avoid annoying other people, creating any troubles for your companions or exposing your troubles to anyone near you, and to accept being supervised by superiors. Society should be like a calm lake that, at almost any cost, should remain in tranquillity. As long as the surface of the lake is in stability one should avoid disclosing currents or troubles deeper down. Harmony at the *tatemae* level (i.e. formal politeness) is the thing of overarching importance that wipes out most individual rights and needs. 'Don't pour out your troubles' and 'hold no grudges' are essential expressions describing this mentality. Or as expressed by Watabe (2001: 20):

> Even when the position a person has held in society has been taken away unfairly, almost no one resorts to acts of aggression against society. Instead such people think they were unlucky and resign themselves to their fate. In these situations, they do not feel like violating social norms, nor are they inclined to commit crimes. When they can bear the situation no longer, it is not to crime they turn, but suicide. They do not resent society or other people and instead feel personally responsible when their affairs fail to go well.

Watabe's interpretation is echoed by Sadatsugu Kudo, who heads the privately funded *Youth Support Center* outside Tokyo. He claims that youthful social withdrawal is 'a very Japanese phenomenon' and continues with reference to his clients: 'In Japan you are trained to be the same as other people and that a single individual's existence is not seen to be very important, so these people feel it's very difficult to live here'. Kudo argues that young people who feel they do not fit in or feel they are different from others sometimes withdraw, living off the support of a concerned and confused family[2]. Add to this the time-old characteristic of Japanese culture where *celebrating solitude* stands out as a value in itself and one can imagine the relatively strong leads that point in the direction of personal withdrawal rather than opposition and 'striking out' reactions.

Japanese culture is characterised by a general approach to understanding the human mind that has been described as 'anti-psychology' or 'anti-psychiatry' (Lock, quoted in Borovoy, 2008: 554). This attitude could be interpreted equally as *negligence* (denying facts about people's problems) or as *empowerment*. Since an understanding of these cultural characteristics is important for the way we interpret *hikikomori* let me trace this last perspective by referring to a very interesting passage in Borovoy (op. cit.: 554) where he discusses the *hikikomori* phenomenon. In Japan there is:

> a web of ideas and institutions that militate against pathologizing the individual and that, instead, make it possible to view a vast array of human differences and distress as potentially manageable and containable through reliance on self-discipline, coping and support from family and others. Both mental health care and Japanese public school pedagogy emphasize the effects of the environment in learning and human development, minimizing the consequences of innate abilities and predispositions. The assumption that, if the environment is healthful, children will thrive underlies the tendency to resist categories and labels. It also leads to the treatment of a vast array of psychological and social problems as correctible.

What it is important to highlight here is that Japanese culture (in general) regards problems related to interpersonal relationships and communication in quite a different way than a Western approach would suggest. While, for example, American institutions seem to manage these types of problems 'through aggressive diagnosis, individual educational plans and high rates of prescriptions of stimulants and psychopharmaceuticals for youths under age 20' (op. cit.: 573), there is in Japan (according to Borovoy) a heavy emphasis on 'mainstreaming' people[3] and equating health with social integration. A lot of energy and care is invested in including every citizen into a group and this is done in ways that appeal to each individual's capacity for self-correction. Correspondingly, Desapriya and Nobutada (2002: 1866) underlines the importance of willpower in Japan and that people 'are socially programmed to feel a sense of shame if they lack this willpower'. It is only when massive inclusionary endeavours fail, when a person is unable to exercise willpower that custodial forms of care take over.

As noticed, it will depend on one's viewpoint how this approach to interpersonal problems is evaluated. Is non-intervention primarily an expression of irresponsibility or is it rather an expression of the opposite? Based on an ethnographic study, LeTendre (2000) has brought this topic into focus through his discussion of *Learning to be adolescent* in Japan. When comparing how schools as institutions affect adolescent development in the United States and Japan he concludes that in Japan there is a preoccupation with endurance, tenacity and perseverance. Interestingly, these qualities were seen as preconditions for *self-realisation* and a sense of *in*dependence. Empowerment of students and a strengthening of their volitional capacity are thought to be realised through discipline and hard work. 'If young adolescents could not persevere a difficult tasks, they would not become successful adults' (p. 181), LeTendre concludes.

The point I want to make is the relevance of general cultural characteristics (like those referred to above) for our interpretation of tendencies of retreatism in Japan today. Illustrations of retreatism like *hikikomori* and *suicide* are unambiguously and clearly distinguishing *negative* features of Japanese society. However, the cultural characteristics that are often brought to the forefront when explaining social withdrawal are, I would say, *ambiguously* rather than unequivocally negative. Concepts like patience and tenacity connote other qualities and are confined to other universes of meaning in Japan than in the West. But of course, it should go without saying that in a culture that clearly tells you not to bother your companions unnecessarily, there will be a dangerously short distance between stoic perseverance and stoic withdrawal.

Hikikomori – youth in crisis or just another moral panic?

Social withdrawal is a general phenomenon that could be discussed as much in relation to old people as to juveniles. Especially in times of shrinking labour markets involuntary escapes into the private sphere are probably becoming an escalating problem (not only in Japan), and people of all age groups (often, but not necessarily, women more than men) are vulnerable. It is important to underline this, since most of the attention regarding social withdrawal is addressed towards youth. In itself, this is logical, since this is the group of people who are supposed to be *leaving* their nest, not desperately clinging to it. However, exclusion from the labour market for people in their late 50s, who might expect to live for another 30 years, is probably a challenge that too easily is overlooked.

The experience of being excluded from joint participation in public life is presumably extraordinarily painful in a typically group and shame based culture (like Japan) and where *seken* ('the others', cf. Chapter 1) watch you all the time. In fear of losing face, people who are (more or less) forced to resign from active participation in society try to hide their defeat by becoming 'invisible' to close acquaintances. Saito and Genda (2005: 16) gives a good expression of this: 'By pulling down shutters, closing the curtains, and in some cases even taping black papers across the windows, they're [i.e. the *hikikomoris*] trying to shut out the looks of the people who live in their neighbourhood'. Ogino (2004: 128, referring to Ishikawa) tells that the question *hikikomori* patients were most afraid of being asked was 'What are you doing?' The decision to withdraw was described as a strategy employed to defend their dignity or self-esteem. A recurrent topic in articles on *hikikomoris* is the focus on the shame that not only these people themselves feel, but even their families experience. One of the reasons that it is difficult to calculate the approximate number of *hikikomoris* is that these families are often unwilling to ask for counselling for anything that might suggest that problems exist (Watts, 2002: 1131).

Dziesinski (2003: 18) has developed a 'model' consisting of seven phases in the progression of the *hikikomori* syndrome, where the fourth is described as 'parental collusion'. Parents, usually the mother, help the victim to withdraw owing to shame about the condition and fear that neighbours will know. Actually, the parents may contribute to a self-escalation of the problem by encouraging the shut-in person to *stay in* and spare the family from neighbourhood gossip (p. 27).[4] In Leonardsen (2002: 212) I described Japan as an other-directed, relational and contextual society where it is important not to lose face. It is reasonable to argue that in such a culture the problem that retreatism represents will be further amplified by the strong shame attached to this syndrome. As I have already pointed out, in Japan 'society' is by definition something good. If problems occur, then (principally) it has to be the individual that is to blame!

There seems to be broad agreement among scholars that negative and sensational *attention* towards youth problems has been on an upward trend in Japan during the last ten years. Kotani (2004: 32) talks about a general 'youthphobia' where 'adults have created dreadful monsters out of youth', and Watabe (2001: 1) observes that 'public interest in youth problems is noticeably higher than it was twenty or thirty years ago. There is a strong perception that Japanese young people today are somehow facing a crisis'. Even though a general worry about 'what will become of the youth' has been present in Japanese society for a long period (Mathews and White, 2004: 6)[5], this topic has entered the public debate in a far more intensified and fierce way. As a general report from this debate, McVeigh (2004: 115) concludes that 'Japanese media are filled with reports on how the latest crop of Japanese youth is challenging the status quo'. Included in this overview (in addition to youth crime) one finds stories about

- students who suddenly explode into violent rage for no apparent reason
- promiscuous lifestyles among juveniles with accompanying sexually transmitted infections
- 'compensated dating' where high school female students engage in prostitution
- intergenerational fury (termed 'old-man hunting') with an openly outrageous behaviour which is new
- youths who have lost their manners in most regards, from eating habits to the (mis)use of cell phones
- loitering juveniles spending their time at convenience stores, smoking cigarettes, playing boom boxes (ghetto blasters) and uttering threatening epithets.

McVeigh could have added additional complaints about a lack of social competence, loss of values, drug abuse, truancy, bullying, classroom collapse, parasite singles, lazy part-time workers and youths who stay overnight at internet cafés (Foljanty-Jost and Metzler, 2003: 1). As extensively reported in Mathews and White (2004), towards the end of the twentieth century there were clear signs of a *fin de siècle* mood in Japan, with a particularly deep pessimism expressed for the coming generation[6].

Are these alarming reports nothing but media hype where history, from Socrates until modern-day society, repeats itself? Do present-day juveniles in this country really represent a 'new breed'[7] where basic values in Japanese culture are challenged?

Mathews and White (2004) address this question in their informative book *Japan's changing generations*. Based on ten different contributions, the bottom line in this book is ambiguous. After having asked if young people are creating a new society they admit that 'it is remarkable how profoundly the different chapters of this book disagree on this question' (p. 189). However, at least in the words of the editors, Japan today might actually be facing something more than a moral panic and their conclusion is rather sensational: 'The young may indeed be acting so as to help destroy the postwar Japanese social order' (p. 6). This challenge to the Japanese social order does not come from rebellious youths who engage in street demonstrations or political protests. Present-day youths are not a group of anti-establishment people who plead for an alternative society based on alternative values. The fear about youth is as much addressed to tendencies of *withdrawal* from society as it is addressed to aggression and crime. According to Mathews and White (op. cit.: 6) the coming generation represents a group of people that 'tend to accept without protest their apparently diminished prospects in life'. In the face of increasing unemployment and a loss of hope for the future it is resignation and lowered ambitions that have entered youth culture. As documented in Chapter 3, many scholars (Eades, 2005; Kingston, 2004; Mathews and White, 2004; Möhwald, 2000; Morishima, 2000) have pointed out that Japan during the last couple of decades has become a far more pluralised society than before. However, in tandem with this increased pluralisation some scholars will argue that today one can register less commitment for collective values and a stronger self-orientation among young people. When Mathews and White (2004) refer to youths who challenge the established social order in Japan today they are talking about people who have a higher degree of relaxation in how to live their lives. *Parasite singles, NEETS, freeters* (cf. Chapter 3) and *hikikomoris* are examples of people who refuse to become traditional 'corporate warriors' and who (often willingly) 'opt out' in different ways.

Kotani (2004) has challenged this perspective on 'disengaged youth' in an article entitled 'Why are Japanese youth today so passive'? According to this author, these youngsters are in a miserable situation, and, consequently, they should have a lot of reasons to rebel. Kotani continues: 'This is the kind of situation where it would not be strange if young people started large-scale riots. But in Japan today, nothing happens; young people don't even stage demonstrations to protest their miserable prospects' (p. 31). Instead, 10 million prefer to vegetate as single parasites, unmarried young people who enjoy living with their parents after graduation from university and using their own salaries (those who have a job) as pocket-money. They 'prefer' to live a depoliticised life with little or no involvement in society, 'rather then arguing whether or not society can be changed, the existence of society itself is left out of the thinking of young people today'

(Kotani, 2004: 42). They even 'prefer' to withdraw into their own bedroom and stay there for years, taking advantage of parents who are totally centred on their children and who have enough money to support adolescents living at home. They also prefer to live a more or less virtual life or a life as 'media addicts' ('wrapped in the cocoon that the media spin, young people will probably remain passive', op. cit.: 36).

Kotani is but one of a series of scholars who bring up this unambiguous negative picture of a narcissistic, parasitic and passive generation, living in 'a community of me' (Internet users), and with little fostering of human relations. This type of presentation is often coupled with assertions about a general moral decay among youths, who live their lives dependent upon the wealth of their parents. There is often an implicit (or sometimes even explicit) moralising voice in these texts, especially those found in magazines and newspapers.

As one close observer of Japanese youths points out, 'it is not easy to determine whether Japanese young people are, in fact, in crisis or changing for the worse' (Watabe[8], 2001: 1). Are these juveniles more self-indulgent and passive than before? Available data do not provide us with a univocal answer. Some scholars have pointed out that the degree of youth passiveness or involvement has appeared cyclical. In the latter half of the 1960s the 'baby boomers' revolted against the indulgent *amae* mothers who wrapped their children in excessive love and made them completely dependent and passive (Sakurai, 2004: 20). In the 1980s, the discussion drew attention to 'the mental state of lethargic youth who felt enthusiastic about nothing and indolent about everything' (op. cit.: 21). The debate among social scientists at that time had quite a few parallels with the present situation. Sakurai refers to students who were shutting themselves up in a capsule and avoided becoming involved with each other. The Japanese psychiatrist Okonogi suggested in 1977 that the coming generation seemed to avoid growing up and that the period of adolescence had now been extended to the age of 30. This observation made by Okonogi and other Japanese scholars parallels what (with Western eyes) Christopher Lasch in 1979 famously labelled *The culture of narcissism* – the unrestrained cultivation of the self, of 'me', of a culture where the individual had been set free from traditions, prejudices and intimate bonding.

When it comes to the more *acute* form of self-centredness and social withdrawal represented by the *hikikomori* phenomenon, Furlong (2008) maintains that this can be traced back to the mid-1980s. The concept was used for the first time in an academic context in 1986 by Kitao ('Dropout, apathy and withdrawal', printed (in Japanese) in *Journal of Education and Medicine,* 34, no. 5), but this topic became broadly debated in the media only at the turn of the century.

In Japan, as in Western countries, this increasing introvertedness was further facilitated and amplified with the introduction of the cell phone and Internet. In the 1980s the Japanese media wrote about the *shinjinrui,* the new species of human being who fled into a visual culture of videos, internet and comics, and who became increasingly self-obsessive. Both the cell phone and Internet made it possible to avoid face-to-face interaction while still preserving an illusion of being 'linked' to society (according to Huus, 2003). Today, there are 1.5 mobile phones for every person in Japan. In the latter half of the 1980s the concept of *otaku*[9] was applied to young people so encapsulated in a virtual media culture that they turned their backs on living relationships. According to Sakurai (2004: 23, cf. Furlong, 2008: 321) the word *otaku* came to depict 'a young generation completely divorced from the social and moral world of their elders'.

What this short retrospective tells us is that the worry about social withdrawal among young people is a recurrent topic in recent Japanese social history. It is the classical story about new age cohorts finding new ways of expressing their autonomy before entering the established and responsible social order. It is also a story about a culture where inclusion and participation in a network of groups are of superior importance, and, accordingly, where signs of non-participation in these groups become very alarming signals. In this perspective the cry about 'a new breed' among juveniles is the traditional moral worry (or panic?) among the establishment, and this is a well traded topic. According to Goodman (2002: 7) social panics in recent years (starting in the mid-1980s) 'seem to have followed an unusually predictable two-year sequence in Japan and have mostly been connected with the perceived "problem of youth"' (shifting focus from violence by children against their parents, to violence by children against teachers, then bullying, then school refusals and, finally, abuse of children by adults). This warning about overdramatising youth problems is further supported in Foljanty-Jost's (2003) book *Juvenile delinquency in Japan. Reconsidering the 'crisis'* (note the quotes!). In the introductory chapter Foljanty-Jost and Metzler take a clear stance about the narrative of troubled youths. While mass media commentators, academics, educators and public institutions (schools and the police) all 'share deep concern about their "children in crisis"'[10] (p. 3), these authors do not find support for such a pessimistic view. Even though they can confirm that there really was an increase in violence and bullying at junior high schools in the mid-1990s, they point out that the moral campaign that public authorities are running is 'surprisingly unrelated to the actual degree of occurrence of problem behavior' (Foljanty-Jost and Metzler, 2003: 43).

However, the suggestions that Japanese social order (meaning: an industrious, conscientious and hard-working people) is challenged through passivity find support in Kadowaki's (2003) analysis based on three different types of surveys (covering a period of more than 20 years). He divides Japanese youth into four personality types: the 'steadily aching', the 'malcontent', the 'non-confrontational' and the 'autonomous'. The data disclose that it is the group labelled 'malcontent' that is currently dominant. Young Japanese are considerably dissatisfied with the Japan of today and the way the political system is managed. Amidst affluence they feel a deep-seated emptiness ('no real feeling that they are living fulfilling lives', p. 87), and in order to fill this emptiness they turn to delinquency, virtual lives or 'shut themselves in their own world' (p. 87). In this dreary picture Kadowaki finds an increasing distrust of others and also an increasing apathy (the voting rate amongst people in their twenties in Tokyo is less than 20 per cent). Social phenomena like *freeters* and *parasite singles* are taken as a manifestation of this change of values among young people. Like Mathews and White (2004), Kadowaki comes to the relatively dramatic conclusion that these data disclose a new situation which, as a consequence, will erode the values underpinning present-day Japan. While the *freeters* could be seen as an expression of an increasing detachment from *work*, the *parasite singles* could be expressing detachment from *family* and the erosion of 'social competence' could be taken as a manifestation of detachment from *politics*. The hope, of course, is that this new agenda can be turned into a 'decent-society orientation'.

Based on this general description of what an eventual 'youth crisis' might be about, it is time to enter the discussion of the group that has taken the 'diminished prospects of life' (cf. above) to its utmost consequence, namely the *hikikomoris* (traditionally limited to people aged 15–34). To the extent that there is more 'resignation' than 'ignition' among Japanese youth today, how does this social withdrawal syndrome fit into this picture?

Numbers, definition and public awareness of the problem

The polar estimates I have found in the literature suggest anything from 200,000 to 2 million *hikikomoris* in Japan today. Saito, who is known as one of the most widely cited experts on this topic, makes an estimate (based on the number of schizophrenics found in Japan, see Zielenziger, 2006: 60) that there are between 500,000 and 1 million *hikikomoris* in Japan. This figure has been disputed by Furlong (2008) who calculates, based on labour force statistics, that 'it is probable that numbers are closer to 200,000'. At the present moment there are no valid data that will guide us any further to a firm conclusion about numbers[11]. The nature of this problem, the difficulties in registration and too little systematic research on this topic leave us with 'guesstimates'. However, politicians as well as scholars seem to recognise that seclusion of the younger generation from the public space is on an alarming upward trend. Hattori (2005), who suggests that up to 1.4 million people are affected by the withdrawal syndrome, describes the development in recent years as 'near-epidemic'. The founder of 'The Nationwide Association of Parents of Hikikomori Sufferers', Masahisa Okuyama, comments on the situation by warning: 'It's a disease that can bring the nation to collapse' (quoted in Furlong, 2008: 182).

Estimates, however, depend on the definition applied and which methods are used for registering. The official definition (from the Ministry of Health and Welfare) includes the following characteristics (cited in Hattori, 2005: 183):

- The person shuts him/herself at home for at least six months.
- The person has no intimate relationships with other than family members.
- The social withdrawal is not a symptom of other psychotic disorders.
- The social withdrawal refers to not taking part in any social activities (school/work)[12].

Even though this might seem a precise description of the phenomenon, each one of these specifications is open to difficult delimitations. There is no clear start and no clear end to life as a *hikikomori*. 'Intimate relationships' and 'family members' are vague categories, and it is hard to say how we can know if a *hikikomori* person has no other psychic disorder[13]. Also, it is an open question how strictly one should apply the fourth point above (social participation). Registration is more than complicated. This is partly due to the liberalisation of the labour market in Japan, which has created a much more fluid and obscure situation as for registration, and partly due to who should be counted regarding those actually seeking help (Mizutani, cited in Davidsen, 2006)[14].

In addition to the agreement about the upward trend of *hikikomori*, there is also agreement that *men* are clearly overrepresented (probably 70–80 per cent are men). Actually, one might have guessed that the opposite was the case since studies of deviant behaviour suggest that men are likely to 'strike out' when problems occur, whereas women are more likely to participate in more self-destructive or 'introvert' behaviour (Edwin M. Schur, quoted in Miller and Kanazawa, 2000: 48). The usual explanation of why men are overrepresented in the group of *hikikomori* is that Japan still has a relatively 'traditional' gender pattern where expectations about career and visible success primarily impact the male part of the population. As Shizue Kato, the first woman elected to Japan's parliament, disclosed in an interview in 1997, Japanese men have not changed their behaviour during her lifetime. They had remained samurai, only now camouflaged in their business suits. To Kato, Japanese men are a group of trapped people who cannot speak their minds (Zielenziger, 2006: 122).

Ishikawa (cited in Furlong, 2008) has charted the number of articles referring to the *hikikomori* phenomenon in two major Japanese newspapers between 1983 and 2005. Her data disclose an exponential increase in articles in 2000 (from four articles in 1985 to 794 in 2000), and this sudden interest was most certainly linked to three crimes allegedly committed by *hikikomoris* in this year (Kaneko, 2006: 234; Larimer, 2000; Ogino, 2004: 121; Ueda, 2000: 1). In particular, the murder of a primary school pupil in Kyoto (where the perpetrator was defined as a *hikikomori*) became a high-profile case in the newspapers[15]. As Watts (2002: 1131) reports, 'in the past year, newspapers have been filled with stories of reclusive teenagers suddenly turning on their parents, teachers, or classmates – at times with murderous consequences'. However, these cases, linking *hikikomori* to crime, might be the exception rather than the rule. Most experts are quick to point out that people who suffer from a withdrawal syndrome are simply antisocial, not violent (Barr, 2000; Larimer, 2000: 2), even though Hattori suggests that 60 per cent of his patients had attacked one or both of their parents (cited in Zielenziger, 2006). It is lethargy rather than aggression that is associated with *hikikomori*[16]. If there is a link between crime and social withdrawal it is more likely the opposite of what is popularly presented in the media: as Saiko (quoted in Ueda, 2000: 3) points out, people who seclude themselves from society 'contribute to the low crime rate of the youth'. When confronted with personal problems these people choose the defensive solution to their problem rather than the offensive one (i.e. crime). Nevertheless, the passivity of the *hikikomoris* seems to create no less anger and fear among ordinary citizens than the aggression of the criminals. However, the public *attitude* towards people who withdraw tends to be rather hostile. Hattori (2005: 198) refers to a number of scholars when he concludes that among the public a *hikikomori* is typically referred to as a person of moral weakness, spoiled and lazy, who wilfully disregards their parents and wilfully adopts a role of non-participation. In a society where thousands of people die from overwork, one that preaches the importance of endurance, discipline, self-inhibition and group harmony, it is obviously threatening that others opt not to contribute at all.

It has been generally assumed that the *hikikomori* phenomenon is unique to contemporary Japanese society and that it can be linked directly to some main characteristics in this (Saito, cited in Kaneko, 2006). Even though truancy, Asperger's syndrome and other expressions of disengagement from communal ties have been registered in most countries and cultures, Japan seems to be the only country where the problem has been 'consolidated' to such a degree that it has received its own label. However, this is not tantamount to making it an exclusive Japanese phenomenon. It is probably not, even though it might be a more extensive problem in Japan than other places. From countries like Taiwan, South Korea, Hong Kong and Oman, there are reports that indicate some of the same symptoms among young people (Krysinska, 2006: 12). Different mechanisms might be in operation, but big pressure in combination with failure/bullying at school, problems in the job market and a deep-seated fear of failure in the face of significant others, seem to be common traits. All of these countries contain elements of a collectivistic ideology where each individual is pressured to conform and submerge their own wishes to what is best for the group, and where efficiency and contribution to a wider collective unity are paramount. A telling illustration of this is the tradition in Japan of defining a workman as 'an economic warrior', i.e. a person from whom one can expect a willingness to channel all energy and give all priority to work. To my mind, this perspective is the main one in understanding the *hikikomori* phenomenon in its rightful context. Based on these arguments it is reasonable to assume that social withdrawal, in the *hikikomori* version of it, will be more common in cultures like Japan's than in other cultures.

It is probably not very surprising that in Japan today, there are strong differences in the interpretation of this type of social withdrawal between psychologists, sociologists and those held by the public at large (Furlong, 2008). However, in the literature about this topic, three main perspectives have been crystallised as a frame for interpretation. One is related to the family (a micro perspective), one is related to characteristics within the school system (a meso perspective) and one is related to a broad socio-cultural context (a macro perspective).

Explanations at the micro level: The family

From a 'pure' psychological point of view, a *hikikomori* person suffers from a cognitive malfunction that calls for a combination of drugs and psychotherapy. According to Furlong (2008: 310) 'triggers can include dysfunctional family relations as well as clinically diagnosable mental disorders, such as depression'. Some have described *hikikomori* as a psychopathic sickness (contrary to the official definition), some have termed it 'Apathy Syndrome' (see Dziesinki, 2002: 34) while others have suggested a link between this type of social withdrawal and the pathology of narcissism (Ogino, 2004: 122). To make a parallel, from a Western context we have become acquainted with the concept of 'the curling generation' (Hougaard, 2005)[17], referring to a society where children grow up surrounded by overprotecting parents who have swept away all obstacles for their offspring (children as 'pets')[18]. The worry about these children is that they will turn into a generation that can tolerate very little hardship. This perspective links directly to what I referred to in Chapter 2 about *amae* relationships in Japan. This relationship is about indulgent dependency where the child develops a strong desire to be loved, but, as importantly, where the mother experiences satisfaction through overindulgence of her child. Krysinsky (2006: 74) stresses this point in a passage that should be referred to in full:

> Since mothers feel lonely, they forge a symbiotic, co-dependent relationship. For the same reason they don't want to see their children grow into independent adults, because the children living with them are their reason for existing. Japanese parents, especially mothers, are 'addicted' to their offspring and, as Satoshi Kotani describes it, 'they have lived by such maxims as *ko-wa kasugai* (the child is the clamp that binds together husband and wife)'. Without parental roles, parents may not have anything to communicate about. As a result, children grow [up] overprotected and tend to get hurt easily. They become adults, who cannot defend themselves, and who are not ready to face the world with all its flaws. Scholars argue, then, that parental overprotectiveness incapacitates children in a sense that they become powerless and unable to live an adult life. Combating obstacles becomes an issue they cannot deal with by themselves. According to scholars, what causes the children to feel

lost, without anyone to turn to with their concerns, are two characteristics of Japanese families: poor communication originating from
the traditional, authoritarian model of family, and loosening of family ties in contemporary times.

Of course, it should be noticed that (a) *amae* relations penetrate all of
Japanese society, and (b) such relations have characterised Japan for a
very long period of time. So what is the relevance of the time-old conception of *amae* for explaining the incidents of *hikikomori*? The answer
to this is, as always when ideas about simple uni- or bivariate relations
are suggested, that *amae* relations are but one relevant indicator for the
occurrence of *hikikomori*. When *complex* social phenomena like *hikikomori* appear, then *complex* social processes have to interact – over time.
But so far in my analysis, the cultural characteristic of *amae* relations,
which penetrates into the early 'micro socialisation' of every child in
Japan, represents only *one* influence behind this syndrome[19].

Explanations at the meso level: The school

The educational system in Japan has for many years been the subject
of intense interest from social scientists. The evaluations have varied
from panegyric admiration to fierce critique. I can see reasons for both
positions. When it comes to characteristics of the school system that
are of relevance to social withdrawal, it is academic pressure that has
caught interest. While the Japanese school system in many ways has
been *negatively* described as an inclusive system, always striving to keep
each pupil within the group context, this changes when one reaches
the age of entering high school. Japan is a meritocracy, where school
achievements decide the trajectory of the rest of one's life. Education
is the primary means by which to accomplish the best in life and the
decisive years are when one enters high school. The test results from
entrance exams at this point in life and the degree of success during
high school decide which university one can enter. It is this part of the
Japanese educational system that has been labelled the 'exam hell' and
that has received the strongest critique. And it is this part of the system
that has also been linked to the *hikikomori* phenomenon.

Furthermore, a lot of scholars have pointed out that the Japanese education system is highly regimented and single tracked. In this country it
is important to make the correct choices right away. Becoming an adult
is often a demanding process in all cultures. In Japan, it is important
not to 'fail' or to make wrong choices. In this sense, Japanese society
represents a tough challenge for young people. Saito (quoted in Furlong,

2008: 315) links the emergence of acute social withdrawal to Erikson's term 'psychological moratorium'. Young people struggling to find their path in life might experience a lot of frustration during transitional periods. Many will need time to orient and re-orient themselves before finding out where to go. For those who do not successfully find their 'new' identity as a member of adult society, confusion will be the result, often with retreatism as the final outcome. In Japan there is less leeway for 'wrong' decisions for youngsters than in many Western societies. As Professor Ikeda explained to *Times Online* (June 19, 2008) 'the young feel a sense of deadlock' since 'society does not accept minor mistakes'. Or as Furlong (op. cit.: 316) expressed it: 'As young people and their families are aware, it is important to 'get it right' first time; those who fail to do so may be sentenced to a life in the secondary labour market'.

School refusal and bullying have been recurring problems in Japanese schools since the early 1980s (Erbe, 2003; Foljanty-Jost (ed.), 2003; Fujita, 2003; Taki, 2003). According to Dziesinsky (2003: 20) the number of school refusals at the turn of the century was twice the number only ten years earlier (134.400 absent for 30 consecutive days ore more in 2000–2001). Of all countries participating in the PISA surveys in 2003 Japan had the highest number of students classified as unmotivated (Furlong, 2008: 315).[20] The principle of 'groupism' has huge advantages as long as one is inside the group, but for those failing to match the standard, life can become complicated. The Japanese group ideology easily leads to ostracism of those who differ from others. As Watabe (2001: 2) argues, 'attacks on individuals tend to be directed toward a group's weaker members. In a sense, the Japanese people as a whole can be said to have a national character that makes them prone to bullying'.

However, these characteristics of the Japanese educational system are not new. On the contrary, and as discussed in Chapter 3, school reforms through the 1990s should not indicate an increase in the pressure to which students are exposed. A reduction of the school week from 6 to 5 days is just one of the reforms that points in the other direction. But again, the general pressure to perform and contribute, the highly regimented environments, the demands for conformism and adaptation *and* the general deterioration in employment prospects (next section) all represent a general background that might erupt in retreatism for vulnerable individuals. As underlined in Chapter 1, it is only in relation to specific *contexts* that 'factor a' and 'factor b' will interact and produce a certain result. This specific context, I think, is to be found in changes in Japanese economy and the changes in 'mentality structures' that we have discussed in Chapter 3. Let me elaborate this perspective.

Explanations at the macro level: Wider society

Amae relations and strong pressure in schools do not explain social withdrawal in itself. On the contrary, under given circumstances such forms of social relations may as well contribute to social inclusion, at least at the surface level. A combination of ('internal') emotional ties and ('external') incentives can create social conditions that 'bind' each individual to a tight network of implicit and explicit social expectations. Japanese society succeeded in its inclusive endeavours for a long period of time, as long as economic optimism reigned. When the Japanese economy went into turmoil, when demands for efficiency increased[21] and when an increasing number of the population became redundant, things changed. To me, the main approach to understanding the increase in *hikikomoris* is based on a general sociological principle: people with no stake in society will easily opt out in one way or another. One of Zielenziger's (2006: 18) informants, the mother of a *hikikomori,* declared that for a person who in one or another way challenges the established order there are only two options, either you leave the country or you become a *hikikomori*. The Japanese way of adapting to a situation of being superfluous or feeling 'different' has for many adolescents been to escape into the private sphere (while some few have moved abroad). The *material* precondition for withdrawing into the private sphere is the simple fact that parents these days can afford to have their child living 'parasitically' at home. The *mental* precondition is the fact that parents (especially the mother) are willing to encapsulate an 'adult child' in their cocoon. These two factors represent what we could designate 'pull factors'. In addition, an active 'push factor' is to be found in the competitive educational system, in combination with bullying of those who deviate in one way or another, and in society in general (conformism and a monitoring public eye).

Against this backdrop it is important to direct one's attention to the road ahead, i.e. the future chances for finding one's stake in society. As long as optimism endured and the labour market could absorb every juvenile who completed school, this transition (school-to-work) was relatively painless. With waning hopes and fewer options the situation was completely new. When a shrinking labour market operated in combination with a 'high pressure' school system, the chances increased that more people would become resigned and opt out.

People who look for an exit in this way are a well covered topic in sociology. They are sometimes labelled 'outsiders' and sometimes 'retreatists'. The last concept connotes Merton's (1968) development of Durkheim's *anomie* theory. While Durkheim applied the concept of anomie (normlessness) to the division of labour and suicide, Merton laid the foundation for a more general theory of deviance in his seminal work on 'Social structure and anomie'. Merton made a distinction between society's *cultural goals*, the *norms* prescribing the means that may be applied in the pursuit of these goals and, finally, the *institutionalised means* that are more or less unevenly distributed among people. It is the *relationship* between all of these three dimensions that decides the outcome of an anomic situation. What has happened in Japan since the early 1990s is that the cultural goals of progress and affluence have become devalued. Today, there is much less appeal in monetary and quantitative goals than before. Nevertheless, people are still searching for a meaningful role within a broader collective, although the distribution of opportunities for achieving cultural goals has changed. However, the official norms regulating legitimate means have remained the same and have been further underlined. As we have seen, school reforms have aimed at strengthening moral education and community obligations. The economic and social crisis has been met with different strategies and appeals for re-moralisation. In sum, the Japan of today is a society with less commitment to traditional goals and fewer options for finding one's place within a broader social network, but with even more instructions and supervision linked to what is regarded as 'decent behaviour'. Accordingly, the situation is not without anomic characteristics.

In Figure 6.1, I sum up the main aspects of my approach to understanding the *hikikomori* phenomenon.

	Push factors		Pull factors
School:	Bullying Pressure to succeed Lack of second chances	**Family:**	*Amae* relations Overprotection Good economy
Labour market:	Changed opportunity structures Shrinking job offers		
Society/culture:	Conformism *Seken* ('others') Shame Pressures of time and efficiency Loss of hope for the future		

Figure 6.1   A model for understanding *hikikomori*

Of all the characteristics mentioned in the above figure it is the changes in the labour market and loss of hope for the future (*and* good family income) that could be defined as something 'new' and, thereby, of special interest to understanding the relatively recent phenomenon *hikikomori*. I think Furlong (2008: 320–21) has summed up the situation in a concise way when saying:

> Here it is argued that the link between changing transitions and the *hikikomori* phenomenon are significant and reflect conditions of normlessness. In a situation where traditional opportunities have all but collapsed for large sections of the younger population in the space of around a decade, where previous predictabilities have been undermined, signposts become obscure and traditional sources of advice rendered useless, the preconditions for a classic situation of anomie (Durkheim, 1947) are all present. A labour market charac-terised by extreme stability and rigidity, with transitions largely structured by forms of educational participation and controlled by teachers as gatekeepers working closely with employers, has been replaced by a situation where many young people are forced to navi-gate a sea of uncertainty. Under such circumstances, it should not surprise anyone when large numbers of anxious travellers withdraw from social and economic life.

In other words, it is the changes in the 'material sphere' in combination with the accompanying disillusionment in the wake of economic decay that seem to be the significant variable to understanding the new form of retreatism in Japan. The drama of this story should not be exagger-ated since social withdrawal is hardly a new phenomenon, in either Japan or other countries. However, current evidence supports the view that these tendencies have become more common. Without being able to elaborate this topic any further, the story about a growing number of women being isolated in an empty nuclear family is but another expres-sion of loneliness among Japanese citizens (cf. Muriel Jolivet's (1993) book *Japan: the childless society? The crisis of motherhood*). It is no exag-geration to describe Japan at the beginning of the twenty-first century as a country of disillusion and resignation. Actually, such a message was implicitly transmitted from the government itself in the White Paper published in 2005, which outlined a 'twenty-first century vision' of a new Japan. Zielenziger (2006: 269) reports: 'It accurately diagnosed a Japan that, if it failed to reform and rejuvenate itself, would be saddled with "an increasing number of people [who] lose hope" and a "Japan that will be left behind in globalization"'. This recognition brings us to the second topic about modern 'exits', namely changing patterns of suicide.

Japan – a suicide culture?

> Japanese people have been traditionally socialized to stifle aggression in the interest of group harmony. Not only self-restraint but also self-negation is often required for adaptive adjustment in Japan. When aggression is not directed at an external object, it may be directed at oneself. (Iga, 1986: 140)

A search on Google entering the words 'suicide' and 'Japan' gave 1.2 million hits (68,000 hits for *hikikomori*). Ozawa-de Silva (2008: 526) found 3,140,000 Web sites when searching the word 'suicide' at the Japanese-language site (Google) and he received 22,600 results when searching the phrase 'suicide methods'. A Japanese Web site called 'Suicide Site: A Relaxing Place for Suicidal People' reports having had more than 3 million hits since it opened and registered more than 1000 hits on one single day in December 2006. Fujita et al. (2008: 184) searched for all medical reports in English on suicide in Japan indexed by PubMed during the period 1990–2005 and found 223 papers. Eighty of these papers were published between 1990 and 1997 and 143 during the period from 1998 to 2005 (almost doubling).

Suicide is a 'hot topic' in scientific as well as popular literature referring to Japan, and it is a topic that is widely covered in the newspapers. Fact and fiction are not always easy to discern. Since my discussion is related to the question 'what happens to the social web in Japan *when confronted with the economic decay*', I shall concentrate on *recent* developments. However, since my *interpretation* of current data is dependent on some kind of cultural perspective I have to give a short introductory statement.

I regard *hikikomori* and *suicide* as two expressions of a joint syndrome, namely as 'retreatism' or social withdrawal. In both cases problems are 'solved' by attacking oneself instead of taking external avenues for discontent. As already mentioned, this analytical distinction ('striking in' or 'striking out') represents a simplification that, as we now turn to suicide, has to be further nuanced. How could the *kamikaze* bombers during the Second Wold War (suicide attackers by military aviators) be described as retreatists? These were 'human bullets' (Ueno, 2005) who fiercely attacked others and who did it in what has to be described as a performative way. They were people who 'voluntarily' gave their lives in the most aggressive and 'spectacular' way.

In his classical work on suicide, Durkheim (1952) made a distinction between four types of suicide (egoistic, altruistic, anomic and fatalistic), but he did not relate these ideal types to what Ozawa-de Silva (2008: 543) describes as 'the social and historical construction of ideas about the meaning of death'. Approaching suicide in a more phenomenological way, focusing on the *meaning* aspect, discloses common elements in altruistic and egoistic suicides that Durkheim neglected. Consequently, before addressing some empirical data about suicide in Japan, let me make a comment on the ontology of suicide in Japanese culture.

Especially in popular articles, Japanese society is often presented as a suicide accepting culture[22]. Traditional argumentation points to ritual and honourable suicides (*seppuku*) among the samurais[23], they point to double suicides by lovers, to parents taking their children's lives or other cases of joint suicide and they point to the *kamikaze* bombers mentioned above. It is quite common (probably in more than 50 per cent of the cases)[24] for people who commit suicide in Japan to leave a note explaining why they did it. By writing such a message, intended to reach a broader audience, one has restored the balance between the individual and the group, and one has regained an honourable position. As Kawanishi (2006) observes, the Japanese have an idiomatic expression, 'apologise by dying', and this refers to a culture where harmony within the group is the all-embracing value. Committing suicide represents a last resort for balancing accounts vis-à-vis the wider society. The suicide will thereby communicate a message of taking responsibility and of expressing a form of cultural atonement, and thereby, as Durkheim noted, there is social prestige attached to these suicides. Ono et al. (2002: 14) confirm this perspective when saying that 'within the Japanese cultural context, suicide remains an understandable, even virtuous act, and is not looked upon in a pejorative way, like in the West', while others maintain that 'death puts an end to everything, and the victim becomes a god, and becoming free of criticism' (Yukiko Nishihara, founder of the Tokyo branch of international organisation 'Befrienders Worldwide', quoted in *Associated Press*, 2007). The types of suicide referred to could all be described as expressions of 'striking in', as suicides that are acceptable or even honourable because the individual settles conflicts with 'the others' by ending his/her life (even though there might also be clear elements of *punishing* others in these suicides). Thus, these suicides have sometimes been regarded as 'unique' to Japan, and 'analyzing suicide was regarded as tantamount to decoding Japanese culture, society, and its people' (Ueno, 2005: 1). It is the association with meanings of valiance and vindication linked to Japanese suicides that has especially caught attention.

However, other types of suicide are contemptuous because they are expressing a different meaning. The recent increase in Internet-assisted group suicide (34 people killed themselves in 12 group internet suicide incidents in 2003, Curtin, 2004d) represents an illustrative case. These are suicides where victims meet online, using anonymous screen names, and then join each other to complete their lethal project. However, Japanese culture does not put these suicides on an equal footing with those mentioned above. It is only in certain prescribed circumstances that suicide is accepted in Japan. This point is important to notice for my discussion since many scholars have explained increasing numbers of suicides in Japan in recent years by referring to Japan as a 'suicide nation' where the culture permits or even promotes suicide[25]. Such an argument is only partly true, depending on the context within which the suicide takes place. The Internet suicide pacts referred to do certainly illustrate actions of resignation or 'acting in' but they do not represent actions that are regarded as honourable and thereby initiated or supported by the wider society. On the contrary, these actions are widely condemned and they are *not* culturally accepted. As Ozawa-de Silva (2008) has interestingly shown, Internet suicides are regarded as people who are weak-willed and who can only justify their lethal actions by joining a spontaneous and temporary group. If the suicide is 'something that the group chooses, then it is not a question of them as individuals violating a communal standard. The decision of the group, then, becomes something that they can follow – are indeed obligated, according to cultural prescriptions, to follow; social obligation is thereby reconciled to individual choice' (op. cit.: 546). In many ways these people are types of *hikikomoris* who (in the eyes of the public) have distanced themselves from a communal life. They are people who (as expressed by themselves) can find no meaning in this world, they have no intention to punish others by their actions, and it is their disconnectedness with the world that makes them give up. To the extent that these suicides represent any blame, it has to be a silent message about modern society as a totally meaningless project. From this perspective Internet suicide seems to be a kind of *anomic* suicide which might tell an alarming story about Japanese society at the turn of the century. I shall return to this discussion.

Traphagan (2004) gives another illustration of the complexity of the concept of suicide. In an interesting article about interpretations of elder suicide among rural Japanese, he shows how various forms of suicide are interpreted in various ways and how different terms are used to identify these various forms. It is of great importance how self-killing is motivated, and the significant distinction concerns the degree of altruism and egoism behind the action. A suicide that minimises any consequential burdens for others is different from a suicide that can be regarded as selfish and that places a burden on others. Even though there are elements in Japanese culture that have made suicide an acceptable solution to a given set of problems, this is not tantamount to saying that this goes for *all* types of suicides. Suicide is culturally accepted only in certain prescribed circumstances. With such a point of departure, one could contest the popular impression of Japan as a typical 'suicide nation'.

So far we have only addressed to what extent some *cultural characteristics* (religion, basic values related to shame, apology and not bothering others) represent a framework that does not actively obstruct suicide. The next question concerns the empirical data: to what extent does Japan distinguish itself as a suicide-prone nation?

Empirical data: *Is* Japan really a suicide nation?

According to one of the (so-called) foremost experts on this topic, suicide is the single biggest healthcare issue in Japan today (Saito, cited in Zielenziger, 2002). Saito maintains that Japan at the turn of the century is at a turning point, moving in the direction of a more individualistic society where the citizens will be unable to survive unless they have their own individual strength. From being a 'convoy-type' of society, where each individual was embedded in *amae* relations with close social ties, Japan of today seems to have turned into more of a Western-like 'survival-of-the-fittest' society, according to Saito. This is most of all mirrored in suicide statistics.

Questions have also been raised as to possible media hype also in *this* regard (cf. the debate on 'youth crisis'). As was the case with crime, changes in suicide patterns have rapidly been mirrored in the media, and it might seem that it is the Japanese themselves who most of all portray the picture of their country as being a 'suicide nation' (the term was actually coined as early as in the 1950s, when suicides went up). Broad media coverage might be a special problem related to cases of suicide since there is strong evidence that media portrayal can lead to so-called 'copycat suicides'. This is particularly the case if the reporting is sensationalised or glorified (Ueno, 2005: 4). Mathews (2008: 6), who has studied media reports on Internet suicides in Japan, contends that the sensationalistic media reporting in these cases actually acted 'to trigger a spate of further Internet suicides through repetitive and elaborate reporting practices'. Contrary to what we found in the case of crime reports, it is difficult to argue that media attention in this field has been 'out of proportion' due to an imbalance between 'realities' and coverage. Even though some scholars have talked about undue sensationalism regarding Internet suicide pacts, and even though it has been argued that youth suicides have been unduly focused upon (Holloway, 2000)[26], one could easily reply that these cases really *are* sensational and the fact that young people killing themselves really *deserves* serious attention. As Curtin (2004b: 3) observes, one could contend that 'youth suicide appears to have become such a common phenomenon that it no longer grabs press attention and *ABC News,* July 2007 reports are usually consigned to the back pages of newspapers'. Correspondingly, Hiroshi Sakamoto, a retired local government official and volunteer suicide counsellor, points out in an interview with Curtin that reports on suicide never occur on TV, 'they say it is too gloomy, too dark, not a happy subject. I feel the whole country is in a state of denial' (op. cit.). In other words, instead of hysteria one might as well talk about active denial both from public authorities and from the media.

Do public figures disclose that suicide is an increasing problem in Japan these days? The answer is unquestionably 'yes'. The suicide death rate in Japan peaked in the 1950s (23,641 suicides in 1968); it then declined until the early 1970s, but reached another peak in 1986 (25,667 suicides) (Ueno, 2005). Since 1998 there has been a significant increase, and in 2008 no fewer than 32,000 people killed themselves, keeping suicides above the 30,000 mark for the eleventh straight year (*Japan Times*, March 7, 2009). This amounts to some 90 suicides per day or almost one every 15 minutes. Males account for some 70 per cent of the 'voluntary' deaths (this figure comes closer to 50 per cent in the age 15–34 group, and a case study from one prefecture indicates that females exceed males in the group of *attempted* suicides, Fushimi et al. 2006: 289). Almost 60 per cent of all suicides are committed by people over 50 years of age. Suicide rates by age (2006) are presented in Table 6.1. Even though the figures are relatively low among younger people, one has to add that the data do not correct for the size of each age group (Japan is an aging nation)[27]. Suicide is the number one cause of death for women aged 20–9 and for men aged 25–39. Among the youngest, suicide is the number two cause of death for women aged 15–19 and for men aged 15–24 (Inoue et al. 2008: 384).

Table 6.1   Suicide rates in Japan (per 100,000) by age (2006)

	5–14	15–24	25–34	35–44	45–54	55–64	65–74	75 +
Total	0.7	14.1	22.1	26.0	32.9	35.3	28.8	29.6
Male	0.9	18.2	30.5	38.5	51.9	55.5	41.2	43.1
Female	0.3	9,7	13.4	13.1	13.7	15.8	17.8	21.5

Source: World Health Organization.

Table 6.2   Suicide rates per 100,000 in 2005 by country and sex

Country	Male	Female
Japan	35.6	12.8
US	17.7	4.5
UK	10.4	3.2
Lithuania	68.1	12.9
Russian Federation	58.1	9.8
Norway	15.7	7.4

Source: World Health Organization.

The current ratio of suicide to population is about double that found in the United States or most European countries. Table 6.2 presents some comparative data. According to figures published by the World Health Organization, in 2005/2006 Japan had the eighth highest suicide rate among the nations of the world, surpassed primarily (except for Sri Lanka) by the Russian Federation and some of the former members of the 'Soviet bloc' (ranked: Lithuania, Belarus, Russian Federation, Hungary, Kazakhstan and Latvia)[28]. It goes without saying that comparing international rates is a risky business due to varying degrees of evidentiary standards when defining suicide, so these figures are presented with great caution. Also, one should keep in mind that the number of suicide attempts is considerably higher than registered figures indicate. According to Takahasi (cited in Ozawa-de Silva, 2008) there are 100–200 times more unsuccessful suicide attempts in Japan as there are actual suicides.

Chen et al. (2009) have compared suicide rates in Japan with 25 high-income OECD countries. They conclude that, among these countries, Japan's male suicide rate ranks second highest (highest for females) from 1998 to 2001, and highest (second highest for females) from 2002 to 2004. When analysing the period from 1950 to 2004 Chen et al. (op. cit.: 141) found that 'Japan's suicide rates are stubbornly higher than the average of other OECD countries, with a sharp increase in 1998' (op. cit.: 141). (According to *Japan Times*, January 25, 2009, Japan registers 50 per cent more suicides than the average of the OECD countries). However, even though Japan on the whole has ranked above the *average* during the postwar period this does not permit a characterisation of Japan as *unique* when it comes to suicide figures. Iga (1986: 17) presents suicide rates from 1973 that rank Japan behind countries like Hungary, Denmark, Finland, Czechoslovakia, Austria, Sweden, West Germany and Switzerland, and Pinguet (1993: 14) finds that the suicide rates in France and Japan (except for the 1950s) have been quite comparable for a long period of time. It is only the rates in the 1950s and the boom in 1998 that make Japan a special case, and both these periods represent periods of economic and social upheaval in Japan. The important 'message' in this information is that 'despite that Japanese society often having been presented as a 'culture of suicide', available data make such a characterisation ambiguous. In a comparative perspective, Japan is more 'unique' when it comes to crime than when it comes to suicide. It is the abrupt increase in 1998 (and the 1950s) that needs to be interpreted, since it is from this time that Japan stands out with a particularly high suicide rate. While such an interpretation naturally has to pay due attention to specific cultural dimensions in Japanese society, these dimensions represent nothing but a general background against which time-specific events should be included. *For most observers, it is in the economic and social turbulence during the 1990s that we should search for the decisive explanations to present-day high suicide rates in Japan. It seems sustainable to hypothesise that the economic crisis really has struck 'inwards' and the recent changes in the suicide numbers make it relevant to ask how inclusionary and caring Japanese culture really is.*

While some observers have made suicide among *adult men* the main problem (due to the highest numbers being in this group), others have noted that 'victims are mostly young adults' (Desapriya), that 'most disturbing has been the rise in suicide rates among young Japanese' (Ozawa-de Silva, 2008: 520) and that 'the recent sharp increase in the number of child deaths recorded in the latest suicide figures is perhaps one of its most troubling developments' (Curtin, 2004b). Both perspectives are, on their own premises, correct. As shown in Table 6.1, suicide rates among people under 25 are lower than for those above this age. However, if one calculates the percentage increase per group from 1997 to 1998 'women under the age of 19 show the most significant rise, with an almost 70% increase in suicides, followed by a 50% increase among men under 19' (Police Office Reports, quoted in Ozawa-de Silva,

2008: 520). Due to a huge increase in the number of elderly people in Japanese society, and a comparatively shrinking group of youths, counting numbers and counting percentages can give apparently contradictory conclusions. Without going into methodological details about which group is hardest hit, and without undercommunicating the negative effects of the economic bust on working people, this should not take our attention away from living conditions among youth. The turbulence that struck Japanese society in the 1990s has affected most groups in this country and the total number of suicides during the last ten years has sent a gloomy message about a society 'out of balance' which seems to be unable to defend its reputation as an inclusive society. I shall return to this discussion.

While the increase in registered crime in the 1990s has been disputed by some, and given varying explanations by others, there exists a striking agreement regarding suicide. Regarding both the validity of the figures and the main explanations behind the changes, there is little dispute: it is the economic crisis that carries the blame[29], as the following section illustrates.

Explaining high suicide rates at the turn of the century

Any human action is the result of a complex interplay between an individual life world and the outer environment. The life world consists of genetic, psychological and socio-psychological factors (which always will carry a *culture specific* fingerprint), while the environmental world contains structural and cultural factors. Understanding suicide, then, implies grasping the way 'inner motivation' interacts with 'outer incentives/disincentives', i.e. how individual prerequisites, abilities and values interact with a set of economic and sociological circumstances.

Sociologists with an inclination to search for broad social patterns and general explanations to social problems have often fallen victim to kinds of 'fallacies of the wrong level'. Forgetting that criminals, drug addicts or suicide candidates have a sex and an age, analyses have often become shady because explanations have been applied to groups (age cohorts, females/males) that should not have been included. So when I now turn to explaining the rapid increase in suicide in Japan in 1998 let me first return to one of the facts presented above: the rapid rise (in absolute numbers) in suicides at this time is mainly attributable to *males aged 25 to 65 years* (see, e.g. Chen et al. 2009: 143). By pointing to this statistical fact it is reasonable to think that changes in the labour market might give a key to understand rising suicide rates.[30]

The popular explanation found in the media (and which is often based on information from the Ministries) leaves little doubt about the close connection between increasing suicide rates and economic instability. Ozawa-de Silva (2008: 522) maintains that 'the vast majority of news and journal articles discussing the issue [suicide] attribute the rise in suicide to the economic recession, which they claim caused financial and psychological insecurity among middle-aged Japanese men in a society that had previously enjoyed extremely low levels of unemployment'. The broad sample of media reports presented below should give a good illustration of this focus on the link between suicide and economic crisis:

- A commuter train on the JR Kansai Line hit and killed two men and a woman in what appears to have been a multiple suicide. ... Police have concluded the three committed suicide after they found a suicide note .... 'We have decided to opt for death after thinking over and over about what to do', the note read. According to people close to the three, she [note writer] was having trouble repaying loans from an unlicensed money lender (*Japan Times*, June 15, 2003).
- Business suicides: Japan's death trap. Kitagawa mans the phone lines at a Tokyo counselling hotline called *Inochi Denwa*, or Life Phone. It's a busy place: Mirroring Japan's slide into economic stagnation, suicide-related calls have doubled since 1997 (*Business Week Online*, June 3, 2002).
- The rise in suicides has closely tracked the decline of Japan's economy, Saito said. In a decade, they have increased 67% among men. In a nation of corporate warriors who have made their companies their true families – complete with ritual obligations and enveloping social ties – the nation's rising suicide level 'is like a barometer reflecting the epidemic problems of the economy', he said (*Knight Ridder Newspapers*, December 18, 2002).
- On the morning of August 13, a 70-year-old Yokohama man hanged himself in his home – driven over the edge by debt .... He was as good as murdered by loan sharks. (*Japan Times*, September 14, 2003).
- Loan sharks fuel Japan's suicide rise. Last year, a record 7,940 Japanese killed themselves because of financial worries, 1,000 more than in 2001 (*The Observer*, August 17, 2003).
- As the suicide rate hits highs amid the prolonged economic slump, every day some 30 children lose a parent to suicide – in most cases fathers who feel they can no longer support their families. Additionally, many children are told to keep silent or lie about their

parent's death by adults in their family who fear being ostracized (*Japan Times*, March 7, 2002).

- Debts, loan sharks and culture of shame a recipe for suicide. Saito's story – told in a new book with a dozen other offspring who lost parent to suicide, mostly over money problems – had struck a chord in this nation, where tough times are now a major force driving 31,000 people a year to take their own lives (*Japan Times*, March 13, 2003).
- The per capita individual bankruptcy rate in the United States is more than three times the Japanese rate, with more than 1.5 million Americans declaring individual bankruptcy last year. But the bad debt syndrome leads far more easily to individual tragedy in Japan, experts say, because of the culture of shame that makes bankruptcy a last resort for many. People plagued by bad debts in Japan are estimated to be as high as 2 million (*Japan Times,* March 13, 2003).
- The officials said the children of suicide victims live in severe economic conditions, with average annual family income of only 1.72 million yen, less than half the lowest taxable annual income of about 3.8 million yen. About 25% of families with a mother as the surviving parent have no source of income, the officials added (*Japan Times*, December, 22, 2001).
- According to the ruling, Okayama, fearful of losing his job and being unable to support his family due to a possible recurrence of back pain, killed his then 49-year-old wife, 20-year-old son and 16-year-old daughter before stabbing himself in the neck in a suicide attempt (*Japan Times*, July 31, 2001).
- 'Suicide forest' yields 78 corpses. Most of the dead last year were men, police said, attributing the high suicide rate to depression over loss of jobs or heavy debts (*Japan Times*, February, 7, 2003).
- In particular, the number of those who are believed to have killed themselves for financial reasons surpassed the 7,000 mark for the first time, illustrating the seriousness of the prolonged recession (*Mainichi Daily News*, July 25, 2003).

The strong presence of 'shame' in Japanese culture becomes particularly apparent in these cases.

Each individual is supposed to possess a strong willpower, and those who do not have this power, 'are socially programmed to feel a sense of shame' (Desapriya, 2002: 1866). It is quite suggestive that even though the American per capita individual bankruptcy rate is more than three times the Japanese rate, this does not have the same tragic consequences in America. The so-called 'bad debt syndrome' leads far more easily to suicide in Japan because of the culture of shame. Bankruptcy in this country is an absolute last resort and suicide can in such cases represent an alternative 'solution' (see Kageyama, 2003b). 'Japanese feel it's an obligation to pay back money they've borrowed. They're determined to pay it back even if it kills them' (Kanamori, legal adviser to people struggling with bad debts, quoted in Kageyama, 2003a). In these cases it can often be a battle of semantics as to whether one defines the final outcome as suicide or murder. A huge number of Japanese (estimated to be 1 million in 2003, McCurry, 2003) have during recent years fallen prey to unscrupulous moneylenders, and 'the loan sharks have moved in to kill' (op. cit.). However, in a culture of shame, honour can be regained by conducting the execution oneself.

However, it is wrong if the above presentation gives the impression that it is the economic bust, and nothing but bust, that speaks through the suicide rates. Such a conclusion has to be nuanced. The official (i.e. those given by the police) explanations for reported suicides are usually split into eight categories: family problems, health, economic hardship, job stress, male-female relationships, school, alcoholism and mental illness and 'other' (Japan is one of the few countries to maintain such specific data). Of these, it is *health* problems that most commonly have been referred to as the main cause for suicide (primarily among the elderly, but also among young people).[31] However, as one can easily imagine, these classifications are not mutually exclusive and what is cause and what is effect can easily be mixed. The available data show that it is the relative share of the economically based suicides that has increased the most (in absolute numbers) in recent years (Curtin, 2003a). Official statistics disclose that it is suicide due to 'economic reasons' which, since the early 1990s, explains the lion's share of the increase, while suicide due to all other reasons increased only slightly. West (2005: 224) presents a case study of debt-suicides and these data (based on police data) support the same conclusion. Whilst West finds a *negative* correlation between divorce and suicide, he suggests that there has been a 'dramatic' increase in debt-suicides, since 1990. After a gradual rise from some 1,200 in 1990 to some 3,800 in 1997, the rush came in 1998 with more than 6,000 cases, with a further climb to some 9,000 in 2003. (In 2003, financial problems were attributed as the prime cause for some 26 per cent of all suicides; Curtin, 2004c). Based on information from those who left a suicide note West relates that 39 per cent of male economic suicides are committed by men in their fifties, 24 per cent by men in their forties and 20 per cent by men in their sixties. West's analysis is supported by Chen et al. (2009) who likewise observe that the effects of socio-economic factors vary, depending on gender and age. When comparing their data to other OECD countries these authors conclude that the suicide problem in Japan is very different from that of other OECD countries. The summary of their extensive analysis of data from all OECD countries gives this important overview:

> Amidst the myth and folklore about suicide in Japan, the empirical results show that socioeconomic variables explain well the anomaly of Japanese suicide. Indeed, it has been hypothesized that the recent suicide epidemic mentioned at the beginning of this paper is related to the economic recessions, in the wake of the burst of the bubble (Koo and Cox, 2006). Further, the collapse of the mega-banks in 1997 caused a crisis in the domestic financial sector, which is often referred to as a typical example of 'credit crunch' (Woo, 2003). Existing studies show that the negative impact of the credit crunch in Japan damaged small firms disproportionately, leading to debt insolvencies and personal bankruptcies among many small business owners. Indeed, the number of applications for personal bankruptcies jumped from 43.545 in 1993 to 122.741 in 1999 (Sawada et al. 2007). The social stigma and mental depression associated with personal debt and bankruptcy has led to a dramatic increase in suicides. (op. cit.: 149–50)

As can be imagined from some of the press releases presented above the life stories behind the naked statistics are tragic. The background for some of these stories is presented in a series of articles published by Japanese Institute of Global Communications (Curtin, diverse years). This is some of what has been disclosed:

- People who kill themselves in order to generate a life insurance payment that will cover the debts of the individual. In a culture where it is imperative not to create any problem for other people, suicide will 'solve' the problem. Wiseman (2007) explains in more detail how the 'rationale for suicide' might turn out: 'For an unemployed, former "salaryman", suicide can be a "rational" decision. When a man commits suicide in Japan, his beneficiaries can still collect his life insurance. And insurers pay off Japanese home mortgages when a family's breadwinner dies – even if the death is suicide'. Wiesman then refers to sociologist Yamada, who claims that 'if he dies, the rest of the family gets money. If he continues to live without a job, they will lose the house'.

- Insurance companies that have taken measures to discourage indebted people from taking out policies before killing themselves. These insurance companies have now extended the exemption period from one year to two or even three years in order to discourage these types of suicides.
- Because policies pay more for death by accident or violence at the hands of a third party, some people have taken to advertising on the internet for someone who will turn what would otherwise be a suicide into a murder or 'accident'. For the same reason, there are people who deliberately try to conceal their actions by faking an accident. Thus, it is easier to receive undisputed insurance payout for their beneficiaries.
- Cases of murder-suicide (i.e. a mother or father who murders their child(ren) or other family members and then commits suicide). The major motive behind many of these incidents is financial worries, often related to single mothers who have experienced extreme economic hardship (cf. the scant and drastically reduced welfare budget for this group of people).

Stories like these are cited only as small illustrations of some of the tragedies behind the macro data. Of course, they do not allow any easy conclusions that 'economic failure' gives us the key to understanding the rush of suicides at the turn of the century. Even though available data are in support of the decisive effect of the financial crisis on self-killing in Japan, health problems (cf. aging population), interpersonal conflicts and job stress have their say in the total picture. Furthermore, as noted earlier, the phenomenon of suicides among the younger generation is deeply worrying. Reports about schoolchildren being bullied to death, about group suicides on the Internet and, more generally, about extensive mental health problems, send a signal of a society in crisis (Foljanty-Jost (ed.), 2003; Mathews and White, 2004; Tipton, 2002). In Japan it is about 4.5 times more likely that a person will die by her/his own hand than in a traffic accident (while in the UK the figure is 1.7, Curtin, 2004a). In Japan, a book entitled *The Complete Suicide Manual* (published in 1993) has sold more than 2 million copies (a bestseller in the 1990s according to Bremner, 2002). In it one finds technically explicit instructions on how to take your own life by ten different methods (Samuels, 2007). In Japan, a national suicide hotline (called Telephone Lifeline) is struggling to meet demand, with 7,000 volunteers handling some 700,000 calls a year (*ABC News*, 2007). When Tipton (2002: 222) ends his book on *Modern Japan* with a section called 'Social *malaise* at the turn of the century', this is quite typical for much of the literature on social life in Japan from this time period.

Conclusions: 'The land of the lonely'

So what is really going on in Japanese society? The crime situation, as one indicator of social disintegration, suggests that 'something is wrong'. The *hikikomori* phenomenon points in the same direction. And, finally, changes in patterns and the spread of suicides give reason for pause. Is Japan, in addition to the financial disturbances it shares with most modern countries, also facing a *social* crisis that forces us to raise questions about how inclusionary this society really is? A short report from the world of literature and the world of film confirms the impression of present-day Japan as a nation where loneliness and resignation prevail.

In an interesting article entitled *(R)evolution in the land of the lonely: Murakami Ryu and the project to overcome modernity,* Strecher (2008) analyses three of Murakami's novels. Murakami has become famous both for his 'document novels' and for his films, and one of the recurring themes in his work (besides domestic violence, school drop outs and compensated dating) is what can explain a phenomenon like social withdrawal. The essence of Murakami's message is expressed in one of his essays in this way:

> 'Get into a good school, get into a good company. Girls should marry a man with a stable position in the company'. Children think that's what they have to do…. But many in our society no longer believe that just getting into a good school and good company guarantees happiness. Children unconsciously realize that one is not necessarily made whole simply by joining groups that are perceived to have value. (quoted in Strecher, op. cit.: 332)

For Murakami, the time has come to an end for a system of rigidly defined paths for every citizen. An indoctrinating school and a commercialised society are now losing legitimacy. Offering people who already are materially satisfied more of the same no longer has the same credibility. The bottom line in Murakami's message then, is (as formulated by Strecher, op. cit.: 329) that 'Japan has reached a point where its current social and political structures, grounded in modernization (*kindaika*), must give way to a new evolutionary stage of social development'. Today, Japanese society is characterised by an increasingly disillusioned population, described by Murakami as a *social ethos of loneliness*. According to Murakami, the main challenge today is to give people a sense of purpose and direction (see op. cit.: 340)[32]. However, Murakami maintains that the leaders of Japan, instead of addressing these problems, demonstrate an escalating urge to exercise control over its citizens by way of a variety of disciplining strategies. The result is a resigned population, members of which more and more choose to opt out.

Much of the same message is sent by the well known film director Kinji Fukasaku. In an interview with *Time* (January 26, 2001) about his controversial film 'Battle Royale', Fukasaku, who was 70 years at the time of the interview, compares conditions for juveniles during his childhood (cf. the war) and today. Even though young people in modern society have not experienced cities burnt down and destroyed, the problem, as Fukasaku sees it, concerns the whole society: 'When the bubble burst in Japan, adults, especially salarymen, lost their confidence and hope. That affected the kids.... Adults have lost hope for tomorrow. Children have no hope for the future'. Fukusaka's son, who was also involved in the film, adds to this description the following diagnosis of the situation among the young generation:

My idea about the difference between adults and children today is the word *'gambare'* [perseverance]. After World War II, Japan had economic growth. The most symbolic event was the Tokyo Olympics (in 1964). The people said *'gambare'* and believed they had a goal. Then they reached their goal. Now society itself, and the economy, is declining. The word *'gambare'* doesn't mean much to us anymore. We thought about giving the film a happy ending. But we couldn't do that. Young Japanese people don't feel *'gambare'* anymore.

Perseverance can be claimed when people are *needed*. This need for people has for some years been on the decline, and, accordingly, for many (especially: *young*) people a call for perseverance is without meaning. The story told by the artists above is about a social crisis where the motivational foundation for 'building the nation' seems to vanish for an increasing number of people. *Resignation* and *loneliness* are typical characteristics used to describe the final adaptation to this 'mental climate' of disillusion and loss of hope.[33]

In a society where confrontation should be avoided, and where bothering others is a disgrace, one has to ask how individuals, facing existential problems, can get their worries off their chest. Of course, one could imagine that a culture valuing endurance and persistence would actually be a *low*-suicide society. When 'giving in' is an unacceptable way out, then one takes the pain and continues like before. Ueno (2005: 5) talks about the 'stingy' public assistance policy of Japan, where a would-be applicant will be asked to make all possible efforts before applying for help. Strangely enough, while Japan is a culture well known for its celebration of *dependency* relations, it is at the same time a culture where becoming a 'failure', and being in need of other people's help, is shameful. This paradox can primarily be explained by pointing to the *asymmetrical* aspects in these dependency relations. Japan is a hierarchical society, and benevolence can only be anticipated if one is part of an already established group. People living *On the margins of Japanese society* (to quote the title of Carolyn Steven's 1997 book on the urban underclass in Japan) will not be in a position to count on support since they have broken with their primary network. This means that for people who have played an enduring and persisting role for a long time, there might be few other options than exit when hope is about to vanish.

The message sent by Murakami and Fukasaku illustrates in a direct way that even if the economy should recover, the deeper problems of social inclusion and commitment will not be solved. Symptoms like crime, suicide and social withdrawal would probably be moderated with a smoothly running economy, but the existential problem of *ikigai* (the worth of living) would not necessarily be solved. To the extent that the *aim* of material progress has lost some of its seductive attractiveness, equally feelings of humiliation and resignation will continue. What I find particularly important to point out in the case of Japan is the danger that tendencies of *silent suffering* which are clearly visible today will amplify in the coming years. Characteristics of Japanese society that I have presented in this book indicate that this problem, which until recently has been quite muted, should perhaps be given a higher priority than the relatively small crime problem.

7
Depression of Mind through Suppression of Crime?

The people and society of Japan are being ravaged, quietly but steadily, by insidious ailment – a potentially lethal disorder that advances from within, attacking our vital functions at the very core before it displays its outward symptoms. This is a deep-rooted internal disorder, not some seasonal malady or external injury. The responsible agent has not been identified, nor has a specific remedy been found. It may be that we are predisposed to this illness by our lifestyle or genetic makeup. All that is certain is that the Japanese disease is gradually sapping us of our energy and the will to build our own future. (Sugahara, 1994: 68)

The economic depression that began in the mid-1990s combined with the political confusion that seemed to encircle it has produced a thick cloud of uncertainty over the future of Japan. (Kadowaki, 2003: 88)

In the 70s we were not rich but we had dreams. If we studied and worked hard, we could buy TV sets, cars and so on. We've never imagined that our companies go bankrupt or we get fired for a recession. We are pessimistic and vulnerable. Once we lost a life model, we have a difficulty finding one [sic.]. Now adults in Japan are struggling to find new dreams or purposes to live. We have to change or we can't show a brighter future where young people will want to live. (Japanese man, commenting on the death of nine young Japanese who arranged a group suicide over the Internet, quoted in Ozawa-de Silva, 2008: 531)

171

The challenge today: Reflexive modernity meeting a shame based traditionalism

Let me end this book where it started in the Preface: around the fire-place in my Japanese colleague's cottage and his pessimistic expression that Japanese citizens struggled with finding a hope for the future. This observation goes to the core of my own interpretation of Japan's main challenge these days, namely *how to give people a meaningful stake in a revised project 'Japan Inc.'.* Japan has come to a turning point, not only because quite a few of its citizens have become superfluous in the endeav-ours to build an economic superpower, but also because this project has lost some of its attraction and thereby some of its legitimacy.

As a minimum, a socially integrated society has to be *structurally arranged* in a way that safeguards for everybody a *meaningful role* within a community of significant others (i.e. an institutional and mental belonging within a family, within education/work and friendship). Both of the above sets of italics should be noticed. One concerns situatedness (being an integral part of a broader social web) and the other concerns the subjective experience of playing a meaningful role beyond oneself.

If social problems like crime and social withdrawal are to be addressed in more than a superficial way, this challenge (no matter how compli-cated) has to be faced. For the broad majority of Japanese people the struggle to become an economic superpower represented a meaning-ful aim as long as everybody could participate in that project, as long as other considerations (like environmental and social topics) did not intervene and as long as they could have confidence in their leaders. From the early 1990s these preconditions were no longer present. A new uncertainty had entered Japanese society and this uncertainty referred to more than just economic matters.

The quotes introducing this chapter bring this message to the fore-front. Japan today is not only struggling (like most Western countries) with adapting its economy to new structural parameters; it is also strug-gling with a deeper motivational crisis (or 'a profound cultural crisis', as Kerr, 2001: 5, labels it)[1]. In facing this challenge, it has been interesting to find out how Japanese authorities react to recent tendencies of social disruption in society. A superior research question for me has been to analyse to what extent Japanese culture is characterised by caring and inclusionary values. Is it the cautious, benevolent, Buddhist model that dominates this country when hardship occurs, or is it rather the more repressive, Confucian inspired model that gets precedence? In this final chapter I shall develop this discussion further and approach a summary conclusion to this book. Therefore, I start this chapter from the *broad* perspective on crime and social withdrawal. If we are to understand the 'deeper causes' of these social problems in Japan today, we have to discuss what could be described as a collision between modernity and traditionalism in Japan and how this collision is tackled.

Even though principally Japan does not distinguish itself from Western countries in terms of technological optimism and belief in the blessings of economic growth, one *could* argue that these values have had an even more dominant place in Japan ('the basic policy of sac-rificing everything for industrial growth never changed', Kerr, 2001: 5). Also, one *could* argue that the Japanese population has been more united (some would say 'disciplined') behind the rush for material wealth. As I commented in Chapter 3, the restoration of Japan from the disgrace of the war was to take place through an 'economic war', this time with the US in the role, not of a *military* giant, but of an *economic* superpower that should be overtaken. Creating an economic miracle became the main preoccupation for every decent citizen ('minute pen-etration of the everyday lives of citizens', as Field, 1996: xv, describes the governmental strategy for mobilising the citizenry for prosperity). With traditional fidelity and loyalty to the political leadership, every-body took pride in reshaping the Phoenix bird of Japan.

While in the West modernisation had already become its own theme (i.e. 'reflexive modernity') in the late 1960s, in Japan the end of the 'con-sensus on progress' (Beck, 1986: 202) became apparent only some 20–25 years later[2]. During the period from the Second World War until 1990 Japan succeeded in a remarkable way in combining economic moderni-sation with cultural traditionalism[3]. In the discussion on an asserted 'Japanese uniqueness' this is what I really think deserves such a desig-nation: the ability to bring a thousand years of tradition more or less undefiled into high tech modernity. However, after 1990 this became a much more challenging task to fulfil. When the economic basis started to waver, along with confidence in the main project, it became more difficult to attain social integration by way of re-moralising strategies. To the extent that there is truth in the saying that 'meaning can't be created administratively' or that 'the state cannot make people happy' (Leonardsen, 1993: 141, 146), Japanese society is these days facing a huge challenge.

It is my contention that when reflection on the modernity project first arrived in Japan during the 1990s, triggered partly by an economic crisis and partly by a deeper motivational one, the impacts were par-ticularly tangible in this country. There are four reasons for this.

First, the *sensitiveness* characterising Japanese culture induces a more volatile reaction to social change than would otherwise have been expected. When the traditional quest for safety, order and dependency (cf. Chapter 2) can no longer be satisfied, it is the basis of people's lives that is shaken. When McCormack writes in 1996 – six years *after* the economic breakdown of 1990, and one year *before* the economic crisis deepened further– that 'the political, intellectual, cultural, and moral dilemmas facing this nation [Japan] today are of enormous concern to the whole world' (p. 6), this message had already been taken in by most citizens. When the blind belief in progress within a nation-family and care-taking system started withering, a deep ontological uncertainty invaded Japanese society.

Second, Japan is not only a culture stressing order and consensus; it is also a culture of *shame*. In such a culture one should be especially aware of the danger that problems that are *structurally* conditioned turn into *mental* problems, which, in turn, might end up as problems of withdrawal, suicide or even crime. Even though Japan is a typical *collective* culture, problems that occur are rarely handled at the collective level. Rather, each individual has to struggle with problems (unemployment, mental stress, etc.) in solitude. Accordingly, the experience of being socially excluded will certainly have a more destructive effect in Japan than in most Western countries.

Third, Japanese culture is based on principles of *hierarchy*, senior-junior relations and fidelity to the leaders. According to Confucian thought this type of vertical thinking is not necessarily repressive since it is based on *mutual* obligations. In exchange for obedience and submission, the superior will have to guarantee care and safety. Next to the Emperor, the state and after that the company have been the central carriers of citizens' interests. While this to some extent parallels the situation in at least some European countries, what differs is the hierarchical context this leadership takes in Japan. The absence of a civil society and of a critical, alternative agenda for discussion has put Japanese citizens in a direct dependency relationship with the state and with their company. A relatively blind confidence in the care-taking abilities of these two institutions was dominant in Japan until the early 1990s. When this confidence was broken, the disillusionment was noticeable.

Fourth, in this non-pluralistic, monolithic society, Japanese politicians envisaged *few other meaningful projects* but making Japan number one among the world's nations (cf. Vogel's book *Japan as no. 1*, 1979). The only relevant criterion for this was the Gross Domestic Product. Despite being a country cultivating the arts of flower arranging, the tea ceremony, calligraphy, the kimono, self-defence and flute-playing, and despite the fact that these activities had (and still have) a more than superficial influence in everyday life (Becker, 1988: 429), it was economic and technological hubris that had hegemonic power (Kerr, 2001; McCormack, 1996; Tipton, 2002). When this project lost credibility and legitimacy a main motivating force for selfless commitment disappeared.

It is against this broad historical context that the challenges of crime, suicide and social withdrawal should be interpreted. Regarded as separate and delimited problems, these challenges could be addressed as *administrative* tasks with a social engineering type of solution. However, as *public issues* (Mills, 1970: 15) we have to interpret the present situation regarding crime, suicide and *hikikomori* in Japan from a much broader scope. Let me sum up my argument concerning how, in such a broad perspective, *economic* and *socio-cultural* changes have affected the situation in terms of the aforementioned problems.

The impacts of economic and socio-cultural turbulence on crime, suicide and *hikikomori*

Economic turbulence

Crime

As underlined in earlier chapters, there is no simple and univariate link between economic problems and *crime*. Nevertheless, within the criminological canon one can certainly find theoretical and empirical 'documentation' that either supports or falsifies any causal relation between economic and social misery. In Chapter 4 I have argued (a) that there really *has* been a crime increase in Japan during the 1990s (essentially 1996–2003), and (b) that the economic turbulence *does* go a long way towards explaining this increase. In spite of different types of methodological uncertainties that always will exist when drawing conclusions from macro ('the economy') to micro ('criminal actions'), the empirical data presented over many years in the White Papers on Crime seem convincing: economic hardship is an identifiable variable behind different types of larceny in Japan. For males, especially, identity is in Japan unequivocally linked to finding one's place in the big army of 'salary men', to being a responsible breadwinner and to avoiding being a burden to anybody around you. When bankruptcy, unemployment, restructuring and downsizing occur, then *shame* enters the agenda to a larger extent in Japan than in Western countries. For an increasing number of people, these problems have ended with a 'striking out' reaction, sometimes expressed as 'crimes for gain', but sometimes also expressed as 'crimes of pain' (i.e. violent crimes).

Of course, it is too simplistic to take 'crime' in its totality as nothing but an expression of economic misery or material wants. Balvig and Kyvsgaard (1986) make an important analytical distinction between crimes of *protest,* crimes of *display* and crimes of *survival*[4]. The economic recession in Japan has obviously triggered different types of 'crimes of survival'. This has been a recurring topic in the White Papers on Crime, most notably in the one from 2000, which had 'Economic offenses' as its special topic ('as future developments in the economy remain unpredictable, many uncertain factors will affect the trend of economic offenses', preface). However, the link between economic recession and crime is probably most appropriate to *adults.* To link *juvenile* crimes to this type of explanation is more problematic, even though it is also relevant for this group. Data presented by the Ministry of Justice (2003 White Paper on Crime: 315–16) showed that 'obtaining entertainment expenses'/'extra spending money' was indisputably the most common motive given by juvenile robbery offenders for their crime, far more significant than the 'in need of living expenses' explanation. Furthermore, the percentage giving this answer was significantly up between 1993 and 2002. Of course, one *could* argue that a motive of 'obtaining entertainment expenses'/'extra spending money' could be linked to reduced parental 'pocket money', and thus one might identify an 'economic need' explanation behind even this type of motive. However, there *is* an interesting difference between juveniles and adults in the Ministry's data concerning motives for committing robberies. While it is 'simplistic motives' (like obtaining entertainment money) that dominate among juveniles (disclosing 'mentally immature youths', p. 316), 'poverty' has become a more dominant reason among adults cleared for robbery. It is important not to simplify what are most certainly very complex interrelationships in the crime triggering process, and this is why I warn against 'economic reductionism' in this discussion. When it comes to *motives* for committing crimes of gain, one should consider *age* as a significant variable for an adequate and valid interpretation. Let me elaborate this a bit further.

The data presented in the White Papers on Crime on youth offenders indicate the complexity linked to the modus operandi and how economic mechanisms interact with social and psychological mechanisms. According to the White Paper, robberies committed by juveniles were often committed more as a result of 'the atmosphere at the scene' (p. 389) than as a means of gaining money or articles from the victims.

Offenders who operate in groups account for nearly three-quarters of overall serious juvenile offenders (WP, 2005: 434), and, not least in a group oriented society like Japan, the *expectations from accomplices* are essential to the course of the crime. 'To achieve recognition', 'not to be disrespected', 'not to be alienated' and 'afraid of the revenge for not participating in the offense', are the main reasons these juveniles give when asked about motives for maintaining the relationship with accomplices (WP, 2003: 390). These motives correspond to Balvig's concept of 'crimes of display' and should be recognised as a supplementary perspective, especially as a 'triggering effect', when it comes to understanding youth crime. 'Unemployment', 'poverty' or 'economic inequality' are perhaps overly crude categories for understanding processes triggering youth crime. But once again, these types of seemingly 'show off' crimes should not be regarded as *un*related to material living conditions among the perpetrators (*and* their parents). One should not operate with *nominal* distinctions (crimes of display *versus* crimes of survival) as if they were mutually exclusive categories in *real life*. They are not. As pointed out in the special analysis on juvenile delinquency in the 2005 White Paper on Crime, the environment surrounding juveniles changed significantly from the early 1990s, and the 'diversification and liquidation of employment' (p. 215) was one of the main changes to which the Ministry referred[5].

In short: the economy has obviously had an influence on both adult and youth crime, but such a link is most *directly* apparent for the first group of perpetrators. *Performative* reasons (cf. group conformity, etc.), however, may be more influential among juveniles than among adults.

Suicide

An even more worrying reaction to the economic crisis than crimes for profit ('striking out') is the 'striking in' effect. In my opinion, the link between economic worries and *suicide* is more unambiguous than the link between economic worries and crime. Available data strongly support the negative influence the economic downturn (in Japan) has had on the tendency for people to take their own life. The detailed statistics that exist in Japan on why people have committed suicide disclose that economically based suicides have not only increased steeply in recent years (a sevenfold increase from 1990 to 2003), but that they have increased by significantly more than all other reasons for suicide. As discussed in Chapter 6, the 'bad debt syndrome' has had a strong impact on the total number of suicides in Japan, especially since 1998.

Hikikomori

When it comes to the *hikikomori* phenomenon, I have argued that changes in the labour market and in the Japanese system of transition from school to work represent the single most important explanatory variable. A general uncertainty about the future of Japanese society and a drastic reduction in the number of job openings have made *withdrawal* a more common survival strategy. As Yuji (2006: 196) points out, the difficult labour market situation for youth has not primarily given rise to anger, 'but rather to resignation and a feeling of helplessness'. What Honda (2006) in Chapter 3 described as 'a grim reality in the youth labour market' has probably affected the aspirations for participating among some youths. The 'choice' of 'not participating' (i.e. *at all*) is clearly not an active choice expressing a prioritised set of (new) values among Japanese youth; it is rather a passive adjustment to an economic structure that is outside the control of any single individual. For some, the solution has been to withdraw rather than to enter the battle for an uncertain career. Criminologists, especially those who have focused on the drug issue in modern societies, have repeatedly pointed out that apathy and retreatism are inadequately focused upon compared to the attention paid to the crime problem. The dull life that people outside the labour market resign themselves to provokes less of a political response than the more aggressive, rebellious type of action.

I have come to the conclusion that the economic turbulence that has characterised Japanese society since the early 1990s, and which was further amplified from 1997, has had a significant impact on the social environment in Japan, with a corresponding effect on crime, suicide and social withdrawal (*hikikomori*). Let me also develop this conclusion with regard to how *socio-cultural* changes have affected these problems.

Socio-cultural turbulence

As maintained in *Japan as a low-crime nation* (Leonardsen, 2004), the socio-cultural system has for years functioned as a massive crime prevention 'mechanism' in Japan. As the country underwent a very rapid process of modernisation and urbanisation, cultural characteristics functioned as a counteracting force, and they did so for as long as the economy was flourishing. While processes of restructuring in the West were synonymous with escalating crime, this was not the case in Japan. A collective shame culture, based on an elaborate system of primary groups (i.e. strong informal social control) and cultural values that invited a defensive way of behaving, was the common denominator I used to explain this phenomenon[6]. However, 'something' has also changed in the socio-cultural system and this has to be heeded if we are to understand the new panorama of social problems in Japan. This 'something' is of two kinds, related to group structure and value systems.

Group structure

Even though Japan still deserves to be called a group society, some disturbances in the *structure* of primary groups have occurred. The Japanese traditional *family* structure, once known for a value system that met people's need for affiliation and cultural identity, is now facing challenges that call for 'intergenerational programs' and activities 'for supplementing familial support systems and maintaining social cohesion' (Kaplan et al. 1998: vii). Most important are the shift in household composition in the direction of more single-mother households and the end of relatively stable employment contracts. The family is today less of a *Haven in a heartless world* (cf. Lasch, 1979). When the Ministry of Justice analyses what it describes as a deteriorating crime situation, it constantly refers to problems due to a disrupting family institution. Furthermore, there is no doubt that *the working place* could no longer be regarded as an extension of the family providing social belonging and rooting as it once did. As Vij (2007: 23) has pointed out, it is the family and the firm that have traditionally constituted the institutional basis of people's welfare support in this country. Insufficient welfare support for single mothers and the total absence of divorced fathers from their children's lives has obviously made family life more difficult for an increasing number of people. A new uncertainty regarding job security and meagre unemployment benefits point in the same direction. Even though one cannot make any simple deduction from increases in divorces or labour market turbulence and correspondingly wider social problems, instability in essential primary groups (which relates to much more than divorce), economic hardship and strained social bonds are undoubtedly not beneficial for social integration (Grover, 2008). When the 2003 White Paper on Crime declares that 'the majority of inmates in juvenile training schools have suffered bodily harm at home' (p. 403), and we are reminded that child abuse and domestic violence are recurrent topics in these documents (Chapter 3), it is reasonable to have 'changes in the family' on the aetiological agenda when studying *crime* (but without privatising or individualising the analysis). As documented in Chapter 6, the changing role of the family is probably *not* a main cause behind the *hikikomori* phenomenon (although it is not irrelevant), and the rapid increase in *suicides* is essentially related to economic rather than family problems.

While structural changes in the family institution and the labour market have weakened social bonds among people in Japan, I have found little support for arguments saying that structural changes within the *educational* institution can explain tendencies of social disruption. From my point of view, I would say that, to the extent that Japanese schools experience social problems (like bullying, absenteeism and violence), these problems can hardly have been caused by weakened formal or informal social control in schools (i.e. a *structural* explanation). As pointed out by Sugimoto (1997: 125) 'rigidity, stringency, and regimentation have *increasingly* dominated Japanese education since schools increased teacher control of pupils in the 1970s and 1980s' (italics added). The social control (formal and informal) that is built into an elaborate structure of primary groups within the school is as intact as ever (cf. Foljanty-Jost and Metzler, 2003).

Value systems

I maintain that Japanese society, especially since the economy went into a tailspin, has changed in an important way regarding some basic orienting values. By the expression 'orienting values' I think of the value system that has made people motivated to participate in and contribute to project 'Japan Inc.'. What I have in mind applies primarily to what I (in Chapter 1) have called the 'dominating values at the collective level', rather than the values transmitted through the process of socialisation (which still focus on 'traditional values', on 'moral education' and on 'community responsibility'). It is about a loss of hope for the future, a loss of commitment to project 'Japan Inc.' and a loss of confidence in the leaders' ability to find a way out of the abyss. The implications of the changes in the Japanese 'mentality structure' referred to have probably been most noticeable in relation to problems of *suicide* and *social withdrawal*. A feeling of resignation will certainly invite adaptations more in the direction of 'striking in' than 'striking out', as I elaborated on in Chapter 6.

In Japan, like in Western countries, climbing crime rates have been explained (especially in public debate) by referring to different expressions of 'moral decay' (i.e. expressing a change in value structure; cf. Chapter 1: 'values transmitted through the socialisation process'). For those focusing on the individual level when explaining crime, arguments about 'immediate gratification', 'low impulse control' and 'more hedonistic and self-actualising behaviour' have all been presented in the debate. To what extent do such perspectives have any relevance for understanding the new crime situation in Japan today? I think the assumption that increasing crime rates could be understood as a reflection of a 'new value structure' among Japanese people (especially *youth*) is hard to defend. Let me clarify this argument a bit further.

When the Ministry of Justice refers to 'juveniles with desolated mind', a 'hedonistic climate' and 'weakening cordiality among children' (WP 2003: 481), this could easily be read as expressing a 'mentality' among these youths. In this case, a loss of cordiality or too much hedonism is seen as expressions of more or less 'internalised' values. One gets the impression that what people do is a mirror of who they 'really' are and what they 'really' want. We know that this is often not the case. Even if one accepts the thesis that 'the criminal chooses crime' (Samenow, 2004), this is not synonymous with saying that the delinquent *expresses* his/her basic values through the criminal act. In general, criminals do *not* hold 'criminal values' (i.e. defending crime as justifiable behaviour). On the contrary, they are largely as 'straight' as the rest of us (for further details on this, see the 2003 White Paper on Crime: 326–28). Those who conclude that there has been a moral decay in Japan in recent years, and who use deviant behaviour as the proof of this, mix up what is cause and what is effect and end up in a cyclical argument, namely that 'Crime is increasing because of a moral decay. We know there is a moral decay because crime is increasing'. I say this to state clearly that I do not support those (Nobyuki, 2000) whose main approach to the new crime situation is to 'reinstate' traditional Japanese values. 'Moral education' is probably more focused than ever in the Japanese education system.

By saying this, I am not at a principal level excluding the independent relevance of 'changes in the belief system' as a part of our understanding of crime. What I wrote about *freeters, NEETs* and *parasite singles* (in Chapter 3) was that these phenomena could be explained partly structurally (the labour market) and partly as an expression of new value priorities among youth. One could not, *a priori*, reject an argument saying that 'value changes' are of no relevance when interpreting new patterns of crime. What I am saying, however, is that such changes (in Japan) are hard to identify at the level of the primary socialising agents, i.e. as a change in the values transmitted to the coming generation through family and school. The value structure of Japanese society is obviously changing as a result of economic recession and a stronger impact of global processes, but it is not changing as a result of, for example, a too lenient way of raising children.

From the above arguments, focusing on socio-structural parameters, it follows that one cannot expect that the type of social problems I have discussed in this book will disappear once the economic
wheels are back on track in Japan. Even though creating an inclusive
economic system (cf. giving people a stake in society) is fundamental for preventing social disruption, controlling crime is, as Garland
(2001: 194) points out, also about addressing 'a hedonistic consumer
culture', 'a pluralistic moral order', an increasingly 'incapable state'
and 'low levels of family cohesion and community solidarity'. Such
a statement seems to have validity in Japan, too, with the important
supplement that Japanese society is still quite a homogenous culture
(but clearly moving in a more pluralistic direction, see Eades et al.
2005). Japanese citizens, like citizens in most countries, will in
the coming years have to design their life trajectories within new
frames of risk and uncertainty. Changes in social structures (simply
put: from societies of relatively stable primary groups to societies of
changing secondary groups), as well as in cultural values (simply put:
from other-directed to inner-directed values), will influence the way
we live our lives. It is difficult to see that Japan could be isolated from
these processes, and it would be overly optimistic to disregard the
possible negative implications of this development for the type of
problems I have discussed in this book. From this summing up of the
main social problems Japan is facing at the turn of the century, let me
next make explicit my evaluation of the authoritative reactions to the
new social agenda in Japan.

Upholding a neo-liberal economy: Punishment and moral education

Two human essentials: 'to have' and 'to be'

I have maintained in this book that Japan still deserves its label as a low-
crime nation, but also that the crime situation *has* actually deteriorated.
Disregarding tendencies of moral panics and (from a Western perspective)
an exaggerated fear of crime (i.e. an imbalance between 'real danger' and
'perceived fear'), Japan is at the turn of the century less unique in a criminological sense than it used to be some 15 years ago, regarding not only
the total amount of crime, but also *reactions* to crime. In addition, I have
concluded that Japan has experienced a disturbing development in people
blaming themselves for their failure to compete. Being an 'all-or-nothing-
at-all' society (psychiatrist Setsuko, quoted in Tipton, 2002: 223), i.e. a
society where you have a role either as an insider or an outsider, processes

of marginalisation, exclusion and social withdrawal have escalated. In my judgement, the *political* reactions to the problems of both 'striking out' and 'striking in' have not shown Japan as a very caring country.

As a starting point for substantiating this assertion, let me quote an important statement made by Jock Young (1999: 156–57):

> There is a sense in which the conservatives are completely correct. If you wish to maintain an orderly society which is in essence unfair and inequitable you must train the individuals within it to accept the world as it is. Deterrence, obedience, respect for tradition, compliance with community norms must be drilled into the individuals from birth. Poor families must be the most disciplined because they have the greatest cross of inequities to bear.

I think Young's *principal* observation goes to the core of my argument about Japan. Creating an inclusive society implies (if we disregard deterrence and authoritarian strategies) safeguarding two human essentials: 'to have' (described as structural situatedness) and 'to be'[7] (a feeling of mental belonging). To my mind, Japan has fallen short on both these dimensions in recent years.

In a modern society, material 'necessities' ('to have') are not only about an income (be it wages or benefits) that safeguards essential minimums (food, housing, etc.). It is about a *fair share* of this income (cf. the discussion on *absolute* versus *relative* poverty) and about a *fair reward* between input and output[8]. People who feel deprived on the 'have' dimension will have to find new ways of surviving, whether by 'striking in' or 'striking out'. Emotional 'necessities' ('to be') concern social embeddedness, i.e. having a social network that gives people a *collective* identity as a member of a broader unity. This is about the certainty of being recognised by significant others as a significant *you* (cf. having a respected stake in society versus what Bauman, 2004: 13, calls 'social homelessness'). People who feel deprived in this regard, or have a feeling of redundancy, might either blame themselves or they might blame 'others'. If public reactions to loss of economic or social capital take the form of training individuals to accept the world as it is (deterrence, obedience and respect for traditions), these societies will indisputably end up with friendly, or even *un*friendly, authoritarian regimes. Let me elaborate the implications of the 'have' and the 'be' dimensions a bit further:

Re. 'to have'. In recent years Japan has taken a significant step in the direction of an economic liberalism that has challenged the 'have' dimension and the essential feeling of fairness. The reforms undertaken, especially during the Koizumi regime[9], had their focus on what was described as *economic* necessities. Quite independently of the economists' discussion on how *imperative* these necessities really were, in a Japanese safety- and consensus-seeking culture these reforms were perceived as deeply threatening. Compared to the safety net that citizens in the Nordic welfare regimes in particular experience, Japanese citizens during the 1990s detected that the so-called 'victimless capitalism' (McGregor, 1996: 36) of Japan was a myth. Even though the 25,000 (the official number; the real number is argued to be much larger, Kambayashi, 2004) declassed people living in cardboard boxes mirror the Japanese shame culture, this is most of all disclosing aspects of a 'sink or swim' society that few would connect with Japan. According to Vij (2007: 180), the shift from miracle to debacle has not resulted in improvements in unemployment benefits or in other forms of public assistance relief. It has been the other way around (a decline in both benefits and the total numbers of individuals in receipt of unemployment benefits). Japan has actually carried through a period of welfare state *retrenchment* (like in many Western countries) exactly when needs were escalating. The Japanese style of welfare regime provides a universal health care system and it provides relatively generous provisions for the elderly, but has comparatively little to offer when it comes to unemployment benefits, housing and poverty relief. In this regard, 'welfare' has not reached the status of 'entitlement', as a basic right guaranteed by the state (Esping-Andersen, 1990; Gould, 1993; Vij, 2006). This was perhaps not a pressing problem as long as the economy was expanding (cf. full employment) and the family institution could take care of basic security and safety. However, when these premises changed, a population socialised in the *amae* tradition faced new challenges. To whom could victims of exclusionary processes now turn? An increasing number of Japanese citizens joined the group of 'have nots' in the 1990s, and young people in particular have often been seriously marginalised.

It seems sustainable to argue that 'Japanese culture' did *not* stand the test as an inclusionary culture when the economy deteriorated. With the economic crackdown, Japanese society all of a sudden detected that the country was being split into 'winners' and 'losers', that those who did not succeed in being on the winning team were left behind and that society was divided in two: those *with,* and those *without* any, hope. The White Papers on Crime contain a lot of documentation about juveniles where parents have left their children to their own devices, about the majority of inmates in juvenile training schools suffering bodily harm at home, about large numbers of unemployed juveniles who cannot find their place in society, and so on. References to a significant deterioration of the environment surrounding juveniles are numerous in these documents. In a country famous for being a one where 'everybody' harboured a feeling of social inclusion, there appeared in the 1990s a debate about Japan's new misfits, about thousands of homeless people *and* about escalating crime, suicide and social withdrawal.

Re. 'to be'. As I elaborated in *Japan as a low-crime nation* (Leonardsen, 2004), Japanese culture is based on the principle that the individual is of little worth outside of the group. The individual attains social status primarily through the group of which he/she is a part. Living a complete life without belonging to a group is unthinkable. That is why so much endeavour is mobilised in order to avoid anybody leaving his or her group(s). However, when that occurs, life gets hard. To understand this, it is important to know about the distinction that Japanese practise regarding *uchi- soto,* or 'inside' versus 'outside'. Japanese can be repudiating or even hostile towards people who do not belong to their inner circle (their *uchi*). Iga (1986: 141) maintains that 'everything that goes beyond that small space around their own bodies is of no concern', and that Japanese are so afraid of involving themselves with other people that they even get hostile towards those who might need help. In a society where the nexus of morality, religion and law is as vague and weak as is the case in Japan, the 'marginalisation of misfits' might be the way this culture achieves social order (see Henshall, 1999: 163).

In a sense, one could say that Japanese group society operates by the principle of 'the inverted fridge': where the fridge creates warmth *outside* by creating cold *inside,* Japanese society is warm as long as you stay inside, but freezing cold for those who for different reasons cannot remain in the group (Stevens, 1997). Living a life outside a social network is difficult in individualistic Western countries, but almost impossible in collectivistic Japan. An increasing number of Japanese citizens experienced such isolation as the economic setback worsened.

Depression of mind through suppression of crime

When exclusionary processes escalated in Japanese society as a result of economic liberalisation during the 1990s, it appeared that it was the *disciplining* and *punitive* reactions in combination with *re-moralising* strategies that came to dominate. In Young's words above, people had to be trained to 'accept the world as it is', and this was to a large extent what happened. For sure, the strategies through which the citizens were governed were multifaceted, but they were more characterised by control and paternalism than by facilitation and empowerment. A condensed expression of what happened could be formulated like this:

> *While economic liberalism during the 1990s took a firmer hold in the 'base', social conservative ideals (discipline, perseverance) were reinforced in the 'superstructure'.*

This became particularly apparent through the revisions of the Juvenile Law in 2001. What started as a reform process with legitimate concerns about procedure (see Ryan, 2005: 157 ff.) ended in a punitive amendment that 'was coloured by political motives and a character easily understandable by voters, namely, tougher disposition' (op. cit.: 159). The fact that the voters also harboured quite punitive attitudes was disclosed in a survey showing that 91 per cent of the population supported the revisions of the Juvenile Law (op. cit.: 159). The ICVS study from 2000 revealed that Japanese citizens, even though they have a low victimisation rate, hold strongly punitive attitudes toward offenders.

In Japan, the importance of doing things the right way implies an element of discipline which is essential for understanding why social engineering strategies might have a stronger say in this country than in its Western counterparts. From a *bottom-up* perspective, acceptance of guidance from people in authoritative positions and a willingness to adapt to strict forms (whether language, dress or behavioural norms in general) contribute towards creating strong leads in the direction of submission rather than rebellion (cf. Bailey's, (1976) famous expression that 'Japanese people are policing themselves'). Since crime control practices embody a conception of the subjects they seek to govern (Garland, 1999: 23), one should notice that in Japan this conception takes as its starting point that different 'technologies of the self' are a part of the very soil from which crime prevention policies are to be implemented. From a *top-down* perspective (i.e. from the central state) the population is traditionally regarded almost as a malleable lump of clay that can be shaped and controlled (Ambaras, 2006)[10]. Furthermore, as Rohlen (1989: 38) has pointed out, 'the whole system ultimately rests on an assumption of human nature as embedded in social ties' and subordination to the group rather than standing up for what one might feel is 'the Japanese way'.

It is against this general cultural background that the present criminal justice policy should be analysed. In Japan, the 'cultural soil' is well prepared for top-down strategies by way of normative regulation. These strategies, which are continuously referred to in the White Papers on Crime, are what we within a Western terminology would define as a typically 'conservative', crime prevention ideology. As we know, criminal justice policy in many Western countries has been strongly influenced by this ideology since the early 1980s, and, accordingly, there is nothing sensational about the hardening of criminal justice policy in Japan in recent years. But due to the distinctive cultural characteristics of Japanese society, I am afraid that this strategy will affect the most vulnerable people in a particularly oppressive way. Formulated in a condensed way, there is reason to fear a situation described as:

the depression of mind through the suppression of crime.

By this formulation I want to draw attention to a danger that a deeper unrest in Japan will primarily be met with monitoring and disciplinary measures towards *a population that is socialised to endure.* The *intention* is certainly to create a law-abiding public by being 'tough on crime', and I would not deny that this, to some extent, might be attained (cf. a hierarchical society based on principles of obedience and shame). However, this way of thinking comes with a price, namely a further increase in the sort of retreatism I have discussed in this book.

To be fair, the harsh iron fist (*genbatsuka* policy) *has* been combined with a softer silk glove or what could be called the principle of 'educational guidance'. A more retributive way of thinking has gone hand in hand with a strong belief in the chances of correcting wayward people by way of education, encouragement and moral guiding, especially for juveniles. The White Paper on Crime (2003: 478) expresses this neatly when saying that 'juveniles are mentally immature and their moral awareness is weak. Although they sometimes commit serious offenses easily, it is possible, because of their flexibility, to prevent them from repeating offenses by taking prompt and proper measures'. The Ministry holds an optimistic view that by carrying out a proper investigation around each case (motives, background factors, modus operandi, accomplices and even the feelings of victims), the chances are improved of making 'juvenile offenders recognize the seriousness of the offenses that they have committed and become aware of themselves as members of the society, just like victims of their offenses, thereby increasing motivation for rehabilitation among them' (op. cit.). The links to Buddhism as well as Confucianism are evident in these prospects for changing track, and the implementation from words to practice is well documented in the White Papers. While for many years this broad belief in 'correctionalism' was also a part of a Western governmentalist style, gradually the strategies were changed (Garland, 2001; Hughes, 2007; Nutley and Loveday, 2005; Tilley, 2004). Not so in Japan. Punishment and moral guidance are still seen as two sides of the same coin in this country. However, this discussion touches upon a much broader philosophical debate involving two different cultural paradigms. At the bottom of the critique of the new punitivism (which concerns Western countries as much as Japan) lies a Rawls-inspired (1999) argument based on *moral individualism*. According to this way of thinking, it is only the interests of *individuals* that should be focused on when public policy is to be designed. From this perspective no claims are made on behalf of cultures' or groups' legitimate interests. As pointed out in this book, Japan is a *collectivist* culture, which in turn gives other leads to how one thinks about individual rights and individual considerations.

My *reservation* regarding a strategy of monitoring, paternalistic guidance and punishment as a way of curbing crime relates to an argument that delimits crime prevention to a question of 'what works' or not. Democratic societies are always obliged to legitimise their political agenda, and a reference to 'what works' could never be a sufficient green light for implementation. To the extent that repressive measures are efficient, one has to be aware of a parallel discussion on distributive justice. If unfair living conditions are taken as a given premise, then handling the negative implications of these living conditions by way of a regulatory regime is highly problematic. *Absolute* poverty and *physical* humiliation are 'easy' to identify and confront, especially if they take place in the Third World, while *relative* poverty and *structural* humiliation can be harder to recognise, even if they take place outside our own front door. This is exactly what the extensive literature on exclusion and humiliation in late modernity is about. 'Is there a role for me in this?' is the relevant question asked by those at the margins of society. Among those ending up with a negative answer to this question, some will act aggressively against others (crime), some will act aggressively against themselves (suicide) and some will 'suffer in silence' (*hikikomori*). It is especially the last type of reaction I fear most in the Japan of today. Consequently, I would like to state very explicitly that:

> *the more effective the re-moralising and punitive strategies function, the worse it is for the case in question.*

This expression is inspired by the philosopher Jon Hellesnes' (1975) principal critique of those who accept the use of natural science models (i.e. steering techniques) within the sphere of social life. As Hellesnes points out, natural science models certainly can be applied to human action, *and this is unfortunate, since society cannot be reduced to nature!* Transferred to my discussion, this perspective implies that re-moralising and punitive strategies are certainly applicable to solving social problems, and, especially in a consensus and apology oriented culture like Japan, such strategies are likely to have an effect. However, this effect will be controversial since it does not attack the fundamental challenges and it punishes those who already have been harmed.

Achieving an aim by 'unacceptable' means is not only problematic from an ethical perspective, but it is problematic because this strategy will represent nothing but a kind of window dressing that privatises what should be a political controversy.

In Japan today, the political reactions to increasing social unrest could to a large extent be described as: *'blaming the victim'* (criminal justice policy) and *'ignoring the victim'* (regarding suicide and social withdrawal). In the first case, it is about an active and open process of shaming. In the second case, it is about a more passive and hidden process of shaming. I asked in Chapter 1 if the collectivistic Japanese culture privatises or collectivises the solution to social problems. The answer is, especially related to problems of retreatism, that problems are to a large extent privatised. An ideology based on a genuine solidarity with the 'losers' is not very easy to identify. Accordingly, to describe Japan as a nurturant society would need some serious modifications.

Social inclusion: Not for the outsiders?

When Dore wrote about Japan in 1986, he declared that people in this country had understood that one would not get a decent moral society, or not even an efficient economy, by simply establishing a free market based on principles of self-interest. But *this* way of thinking is what has changed in Japan during the last 20 years. 'The power of culture to shape economic choices' (Fukuyama, 2000: 135) has deteriorated. Confucian values have apparently not had as much potential for solidaristic inclusion, as some would maintain, during the days of prosperity. When the days of decay arrived, it appeared that values like perseverance and obedience had a kind of 'contraction effect': people who were hit by the recession opted for different varieties of 'exit' rather than fighting the system or fighting injustice. *This* is actually what happens when superior and highly prized values (even in the West) like endurance and discipline become a given rather than a guiding star, and when the principle of mainstreaming people turns into something like a compulsory thought. In a critical analysis of Japanese culture, Dale (1986: 108) makes the important remark that it is easy to mix up watchfulness with sympathy and empathy. To *bother* about other people is not synonymous with *caring* about them, and it is probably in times of adversity that this distinction is easiest to observe.

The *un*friendly and exclusionary side of Japanese culture (i.e. for those who do not *want to* adapt or do not *succeed* in adapting) has been noted by many scholars (even in the years *before* 1990, cf. Chapter 6). Sugahara[11] (1994: 72) puts it bluntly by saying that 'Japanese society today not only excludes foreigners but continues to discriminate harshly against the disabled, Japanese who were raised and educated abroad, and others who in some way depart from the norm'. According to this observer, people have grown apathetic in the face of inequity and injustice (note: this was written as early as 1994). Zielenziger (2006: 124) adds to this description the generally negative attitude Japanese hold against homeless people or against people committing suicide in an 'irritating' way, and how stingy they are when it comes to charitable work. One-third of Henshall's (1999) book *Dimensions of Japanese society* is about living on the fringes of this society. Writing about ethnic minorities, foreigners or 'foreign-tainted' groups, day-labourers and vagrants, the diseased and the (physically as well as mentally) disabled, Henshall formulates as an understatement that (like many societies) Japan 'does not exactly embrace those who do not contribute to its prosperity and need to be supported' (p. 48). Finally, the phenomenon designated *oyako-shinju* gives a glimpse into a culture where the care-taking of children is strongly limited to the family. The term *Oyako-shinju* describes a parent's killing of a child before the parent takes his/her own life. Yamamura (1986: 34) explains the background for this type of murder in this way: 'When parents have formed an entirely private bond of identity with their child, there can be no hope that, after a parent's death, members of the community will take it upon themselves to look after the child's life and wellbeing. For such a parent, the only course remaining is to take the child's life as well'. If this is to be expressed in the language of extended solidarity, one could say with Fukuyama (1995) that in Japan the 'radius of trust' is quite short. Caretaking is not so much a communal concern as a 'privatised' one.

It follows from the above account that it is 'the significant other', not the 'generalised other' (Mead, 1934), who can derive advantage when in need. Benevolence is particularistic, not universal. 'The treatment of the outsider with a special sort of irritated contempt' is actually one of five criteria Conquest (quoted in Dale, 1986: 52) uses to define a system of totalitarian thought. This 'irritated contempt' is in some way built into Japanese culture, and it is still present in the Japan of today. A more punitive attitude towards offenders and irritation against people committing suicide are signs of this phenomenon. That these attitudes have become more pronounced in recent years is not so much a result of a sudden 'mentality change' among people, but rather an expression of a structural change that has altered the 'opportunity situation' for dissatisfaction. As a meritocracy one could argue that Japan should have a sensitive stethoscope towards those who do not 'merit'. However, neither the political system, nor the people in general, seems to be in a state of readiness to tackle the new social problems in Japan.

This is the rather gloomy story about some characteristics of Japanese culture; characteristics that have become more manifest during the recession. When Berger in 1987 was speculating about the most likely future of East Asian capitalism, he tentatively proposed that the values of individual autonomy would undermine East Asian communalism. If this was to happen, Berger foresaw that these societies would – sooner or later – 'face some of the current problems of Western societies' (p. 170). This book confirms Berger's prophecies, even though it was primarily the economic meltdown that made the 'non-communalistic' qualities of Japanese society so apparent. What is the most disturbing acknowledgement from my analysis is the recognition that far-reaching, silent suffering has not reached very high on the political agenda. It seems a paradox that an *individualistic* inspired saying that 'everybody is the architect of his/her own fortune' appears to be consistent with a *collectivist* culture like Japan to such an extent.

Japan – quo vadis?

Has Japan entered a stage of development with no return? Is the idea of 'modernisation without westernisation' a lost cause? Has Japan entered a new historical phase, where crime will reach the level of many Western nations? As we have seen, reported cases of crime reached a peak in 2002. Since then, figures shown a consecutive decrease until 2006 (the last year for which data are available), but are still at a high level compared with 1998. Regarding *suicide*, during the period 1997–2008 official figures exceeded 30,000 each year, and in spite of a governmental programme aimed at reducing the suicide rate by 20 per cent by 2016, the situation in 2009 indicates no turnaround trend (*Japan Times*, April 14, 2009). On the contrary, with the new financial crisis that entered the global scene in 2008 the prospects are poor. The head of a non-profit organisation that helps people in Akita Prefecture (which long had the nation's highest suicide rates) reported to *Japan Times* (op. cit.) that up to that time his group had helped three times more people than usual, and since there is a time lag between job loss and the deepest depression, suicides would most likely increase even more in the near future.

There are principally two different ways to confront the present situation of social unrest: an increase in *moral and disciplinary campaigns* and/or *structural intervention*. As I have underlined in this book, Japan is a society that is traditionally very receptive to all types of educational programmes. A fine balance between threat and persuasion, the sword and the chrysanthemum, has kept the Japanese in line throughout history. That is why Sugimoto (1999) has designated the 'Japanese way' as 'friendly authoritarianism'. Filial piety, concordance with neighbours, respect for seniors, responsibility of educating and disciplining oneself, contentment with the calling given and abstinence from villainy (Morishima, 2000: 227) are the Confucian values that have clearly moulded the Japanese people through centuries. The rewards have been evident in the past. Today, however, these rewards are volatile and uncertain, but educating the masses is an 'easy' and well tried strategy. One registers different symptoms and then acts upon these symptoms. New information, moral guidance and punishment are the 'inputs' supposed to expand the agency and thereby the freedom to choose differently.

To what extent the government will put the centre of gravity at the punitive or at the educational end of the scale remains to be seen. However, because a variety of educational programmes have better odds for success in Japan than in most of its Western counterparts I have found it pertinent to raise some sceptical remarks to *both* the moral *and* disciplinary strategies. To the extent that the socio-material conditions are in a sound condition, i.e. to the extent that these conditions give options for poor as well as for rich, for females as well as for males, for immigrants as well as for those with Japanese citizenship, etc., 'education' and 'punishment' could equally be said to represent legitimate strategies for a government. However, the more the 'facticity' surrounding the citizens represents a *common barrier*, the more one should refrain from the temptation to show strength by using these types of measures to keep people in check. Extensive changes in the socio-material environment in Japan in the last 20 years, not least among young people, have created a situation of more closed doors to potential life chances[12]. These closed doors are partly, but not only, of material character at the structural level (labour market), and partly of normative character at the individual level (belief and trust systems of society). While such a perspective accordingly does *not* imply a structural determinism that obviates the relevance of (for example) 'educating the heart' (which is as much an Aristotelian as a Buddhist rule of conduct), it directs us not to commit the fallacy of operating at the wrong level: 'systemic deficiencies' should primarily be attacked at the systemic level. If the problem is systemic, it is not only inefficient, but even *unjust* (against the 'have nots') to direct one's efforts towards the individual level by way of strategies of normative regulation. In the sphere of *techne*, this is quite evident when we apply the *wrong* technology to solve a problem; one does not use a hammer to cut wood. In the *socio-cultural* world, what is the 'correct tool' is far less obvious. But that makes this discussion even more important.

From these premises I infer that what should be given priority in present-day Japan is 'structural interventions'. Being aware of the complexity of these topics, let me nevertheless suggest some perspectives that I think should be given due attention in a debate regarding structural interventions:

- *Safeguarding the material subsistence level.* Poverty has once again become a pressing problem in Japan. The present situation for day-labourers, people living in cardboard boxes, the growing group of working poor, lone mothers and older people who do not want to be a burden on their children, *dignity* should be safeguarded by safeguarding *individual rights.* This is first of all a challenge to the Japanese welfare regime.
- *A concern about socio-economic divisions.* A main challenge with the 'moral education' approach lies in the two questions: 'whose moral values?' and 'who is the targeted group?'. As Yoder's (2004) research indicates, a more merciless expression of conformity and control[13] is at play in Japan today, and it is the typical conservative, middle class perspectives that distinguish the educational reforms. While in Chapter 5 I showed that the Ministry of Justice analysed the asserted new crime situation from a moral *as well as* a structural perspective, the educational reforms indicate that 'normative talk' has gained the upper hand in the educational system. The call for a re-socialisation of adolescents at home[14] and at school is explicit. There is a certain danger that it is most of all the 'friendly authoritarian' face of Japan that shows its face in these reforms, and that it is the 'have nots' who will be the primary target for the moral campaigns.

In Japan, the myth about one homogenous nation has been cultivated and most politicians barely have a language for talking about
class divisions, not least in the White Papers on Crime. Today, such
a language and such a perspective are badly needed. What Grover
(2008: xi) observes for Britain should be repeated for Japan as well:
'There is, then, a need to re-emphasise the fact that crime is structured through social status; it is something that disproportionately
affects poor people'.

- *A gender perspective.* Modern Japan is still a strongly gendered society (Burns, 2005; Goodman, ed., 2002; Miller and Kanazawa, 2000;
Tipton, 2002). Neither when it comes to labour market policy, nor
when it comes to welfare policy, could Japan be said to give full attention to female interests. I cannot enter this complex debate on what
'women's interests' exactly should imply, but the living conditions of
single mothers are but one illustration of flaws in the present welfare
regime. Cash handouts paid to the nominal leader of the household
(i.e. the husband) in cases of abuse (instead of to the victim of the
abuse) are another illustration of how poor economic conditions can
linger on.

- *The role of civil society.* Welfare in Japan has primarily been based
on an interplay between work and family. The employer has had
an extended responsibility for the employees compared to a typical
Western model, and the family (i.e. the female part of it) has been
expected to have a strong responsibility for the youngest and oldest
members. Both these arenas have had their caring capacity reduced
during the last 20 years. In this situation different scholars (Hirata,
2002; Kingston, 2004; Vij, 2007) have pointed out the transformation that has gradually taken place in Japan in the direction of an
extended role for civil society and for volunteering. 'Japan's quiet
transformation' (Kingston, op. cit.) is essentially a story of a gradual
reinvigoration of civil society. If financial and normative support
is given to the idea of developing Japanese civil society, interesting
perspectives open regarding both caring potentialities and meaningful tasks for vacant hands. The discussion in the wake of Putnam's
bestselling book *Bowling alone* should give plenty of inspiration for a
corresponding debate in Japan. However, without linking this debate
to my preceding remarks on gender politics, invigorating civil society might be synonymous with reversing gender equality politics.
Also, one should be aware that in a statist and hierarchical culture
like Japan, including civil society in social problem solving could
easily be absorbed within a *state corporatist* rather than a *corporate*

pluralistic framework. The Japanese state's historical role in 'moulding the Japanese mind' (Garon, 1997) should remind us that civil society and its organisations have to be independent of central government, not a part of the state apparatus, to fulfil an autonomous role based on some kind of bottom-up engagement.

• *A new political agenda.* Due attention should be paid to the agenda that is as relevant in Japan as in other rich countries: which goals do we aim for in countries characterised by a surplus of goods and a shortage of environmental resources, and how do we organise these societies in a way that includes people other than the most efficient, healthy and resourceful? As Bauman (2004: 15) observes, 'however adept we may be in the arts of crisis management, we do not really know how to tackle this trouble [of redundancy]. We lack perhaps even the tools to think about reasonable ways of tackling it'. Therefore, today's troubles are *goal-related* rather than *means-bound*. The tendencies of retreatism that I have discussed in this book are most likely an expression of a deeper change of values. However, a discussion on *goals* should pay due attention to Young's (2007) observation that the organic community of the past is in terminal decline (also in Japan) and that nostalgic dreams about the happy 1950s and 1960s will remain in the utopian sphere. Young warns against how in postmodern society disembeddedness and insecure identities might trigger essentialism (as a fake sense of solidarity) and dehumanisation of others. These perspectives certainly also have relevance for Japan. The capacity for 'othering' (at a national level) is hopefully a story of the past. But with the Japanese tradition of making a clear distinction between *uchi* (inside) and *soto* (outside), one cannot take it for granted that solidarity and nurturance vis-à-vis the most vulnerable citizens will be the outcome of the present social unrest.

In sum, my story about present-day Japan indicates that 'paradise' actually *is* lost. However, this conclusion applies to what I would describe as a deep 'existential confusion' among people rather than to a deteriorating crime situation. This existential confusion has been brilliantly described by Kisala and Mullins (2001) in their interpretation of the sarin gas attack at a Tokyo subway station. According to these authors, this act of terrorism brought into focus a profound inner emptiness among people who were obviously longing for deeper meaning in life. Too little thought had been given to basic moral questions of what kind of society Japan should be heading for. Perhaps then, it was a telling sign that, in connection with the New Year celebration in 2009 a record high of 99 million people were praying in the temples for the New Year (*Japan Times*, January 10, 2009).

In accordance with these perspectives, perhaps Japanese politicians should listen to the message sent by Layard (2005: 4) and his colleagues in the UK, when appealing to each government 'to reappraise its objectives, and everyone of us to rethink our goals'. It might seem that quite a few Japanese people have already started this process, while the government still is riding the two horses of economic liberalism and social conservatism. From a criminological point of view, I think Japan now has to restate the meaning of the old slogan about 'Japan Inc.'. The abbreviation should stand for 'inclusive' rather than 'incorporated'. To me, this calls for the best in a Keynesian demand side economy (i.e. a welfare state based on principles of solidarity) in combination with a Buddhist, compassionate philosophy. While the Government for some years now has been fighting to regain Japan's status as 'the safest country in the world', they should perhaps extend their endeavours to regain their lost paradise, not as a means-bound, but as a goal-related project.

Notes

1 Japan – Quo Vadis?

1. Mouer and Sugimoto (1986) confine themselves to presenting only *two* conflicting perspectives, namely a consensus versus a conflict perspective. Clammer (2000: 203) confirms the ambiguity in describing Japanese society by saying that 'there is little consensus among those who make it their business to understand Japan about the fundamental principles of interpretation that might be applied to this society'. Smith (1994: 4) comments on the same topic: 'There are many views of Japan and many bitter disputes about the true character of that society, which is, after all, a very complex one'. Even within a specified field as the role of the prosecutor in the Japanese criminal process diametrically opposing viewpoints exist. Accordingly, Johnson (2002: 7) maintains that, 'analysts agree that prosecutors play a pivotal role in Japan's criminal process, but advance sharply divergent views about the aims and effects of prosecutorial power ... is it "number one" or does it routinely trample human rights'?

2. As Tilley (2005: 271) remarks in his evaluation of the British Crime Reduction Programme (1999–2002), 'the triumphs were few and the failures many'.

3. In the case of Japan, this perspective has been clearly expressed by Miller and Kanazawa (2000: 50): 'Social order in Japan is not primarily maintained through the enactment of laws, the presence of police, the actions of politicians or even the internalisation of prosocial morals and values; rather, it is the by-product of a web of social networks and small groups, each maintaining order in pursuit of its own long-term objectives. In this regard, education and employment are the social institutions most responsible for order'. Hsu (1975) has elaborated how the unique social structure based on the principle of *iemoto* contributes to social order in Japan. The essence of the *iemoto* is the master-disciple relationship marked by mutual dependence. The relation between master and disciple is defined in a kind of pseudo-kinship term. 'From this point of view each *iemoto* is a giant kinship establishment, with the characteristic closeness and inclusiveness of interpersonal links, but without kinship limitations on its size' (ibid. p. 152). This means that whatever turbulent processes the individual experiences (cf. geographic and social mobility), on most occasions the individual will be linked to supportive and caring personal relations. 'The all-inclusive, interlinking mutual dependence among members of any two levels in a large hierarchical organisation has the effect of extending the feeling of intimacy beyond those situated in the closest proximity' (ibid. p. 152).

4. For important reservations to this statement, see Leonardsen (2004: 150).

5. In *The Spirit of Community*, Etzioni (1994) refers to a survey where people were asked what was special about the United States. Young people typically responded 'individualism', that 'you can do whatever you want' and that 'we really don't have any limits'.

6. The Japanese word for 'the public' (*hitome*) directly translated means 'people's eyes'.

7. Cf. the title of Fukuyama's (2000) book *The Great Disruption*, with the subtitle *Human Nature and the Reconstitution of Social Order*.

8. This is, of course, a very rough statement. Modern welfare states are characterised exactly by their ability to de-commodify the status of its citizens (Esping-Andersen, 1990). However, this does not imply (not even in the case of the generous Nordic welfare states) that the normative imperative for standing on one's own feet is abolished. Especially during the last ten years the pressure for each citizen to provide for him- or herself has increased significantly.

9. 'Moral panic' could be defined as a situation where types of action and groups of people become defined as a threat to societal values and interest, but where this reaction actually could be described as overheated and exaggerated. See Cohen (1967) or Goode and Ben-Yehuda (1999).

10. For a broader discussion on the importance of ideology (Kingston, 2004: 25, uses the phrase 'national psyche'); for the development in the Japanese economy, see Morishima, 2000.

11. In Leonardsen (2004) I elaborated this topic further under the headline 'A theoretical comment on comparative analysis. On emic and etic concepts and the social construction of crime'. The following quote from that book could represent my main argument on this complicated topic: 'Within an anthropological frame of reference one would define the term "individual rights" as an *emic* concept, meaning a concept that is "specific and peculiar to a particular culture, and meaningful only to its members" (Sugimoto, 1997, p. 20). Concepts that are more universally applicable, transcending national and ethnic boundaries are called *etic*. These terms are derived from linguistics where phon*etic*s refers to universal sounds found in languages all over the world, while phon*emic*s refers to sounds peculiar to a given language. This distinction has later been brought over from linguistics to the social sciences and made us aware of the danger of ethnocentrism. During the last 10–20 years it has become more and more apparent that Western social sciences have undertaken comparative studies where they have assumed to use etic concepts, but where it could be argued that their concepts are emic, based on a Western cultural model' (Leonardsen, 2004: pp. 24–25).

2 Reacting to and tackling social problems: moral panic and perseverance

1. I immediately rush with a short note regarding 'cultural characteristics', since this is a much-contested area. The so-called *nihonjinron* debate concerns questions about how peculiar and unique Japanese culture actually is. The debate has bordered on sensible topics like national identity, ethnicity, race, and biological commonality (see Dale, 1986; Henshall, 1999: 170). I will not enter this debate, but want to draw a clear line of demarcation between a very ideological debate on cultural and genetically uniqueness and an anthropological debate related to 'not-so-contested' documentation about Japanese culture. My principal argument in the present chapter can be regarded as an illustration of Cohen's (1989) thesis in *The

Symbolic Construction of Community, where he stresses the importance of analysing how external impacts are adapted and revised in local cultures.

2. Toyama-Bialke (2003: 43) expresses this perspective by saying that 'because of these strong norms shared by adults, Japanese society is also more likely to cause "moral panic"'.

3. As Levine (1985: 2) points out the ascetic attitude among Puritans could even be traced within their language: 'Ascetic Puritanism tended to promote an aseptic use of language, as in the famous "plain style" sermons of the New England divines. The idea of sincerity came to replace a courtly ideal of grace and charm with a call for plain and direct speaking'.

4. From another point of departure, Feeley (2007) comes to an opposite conclusion regarding Japan.

5. The following presentation does not pretend to be a complete description of Japanese society, but focus is put only on those aspects that are relevant to my discussion of interpretations of social change. Important sources have been: Ben-Ari, Moeran and Valentine (eds.) (1990), Dale (1986), Doi (1976; 1985), Goldman (1994), Henshall (1996, 1999), Hendry (1993, 1999), Henshall (1996; 1999), Smith (1994), Sugimoto (1997), Takahashi (1991), and van Wolferen (1989).

6. Confucius said this about the importance of reciprocity: 'There has never been a case where a man who did not understand reciprocity was able to communicate to others whatever treasures he might have had stored in himself' (McNaughton, cited in Goldman, 1994: 32).

7. Actually, to regard obedience as an expression only of vertical structures is a bit misleading since the vertical dimension is rapidly transformed into a horizontal peer pressure in Japan. Since loyalty to the group represents a dominating value, the strongest impulse for conformist behaviour comes from the equals. Takeuchi (1984: 1) illustrates this in his article on 'Peer Pressure in Japanese Organisations': 'In all Japanese organisations the unwritten laws have more power to control behaviour than do formal regulations. These unwritten rules are supported by peer group gossip and the peer pressure based on it'. He continues: 'The distinctive feature of Japan's controlled society is that everybody is everybody else's overseer, and at the same time, everybody is overseen by everybody else' (p. 2). This peer pressure is not the least highly developed in children's peer groups, something that contributes to explain why bullying is a big problem in Japanese schools.

8. Fenwick (1985: 73) adds to this description: 'As Becker (1984: 4) suggests, while entire families are not banished or exterminated for serious wrong doings of its members, the concept of collective responsibility, developed in the sixteenth century system of *gonin gumi*, is still relevant in present-day Japan'. See also Becker (1988).

9. The principle of verticality is also clearly expressed in what is called the *iemoto* system, cf. footnote 3 in Chapter 1.

10. Foljanty-Jost and Metzler (2003: 8) present the 'School Regulations of Aka Junior high School in Niigata Prefecture', which includes: 'Breaks between the classes should be used for preparation for the next class', 'dying and perming hair are forbidden', 'boys should have their hair shorter than the eyebrows and the ears', 'girls should bind their hair if longer than the

shoulders', and (outside school), 'it is forbidden to watch movies without parents with the exception of movies that are approved by the school', and 'it is forbidden to enter game centres'.

11. An interesting illustration of the omnipresence of *kata* in Japan can be seen among the homeless living in cardboard boxes with blue plastic sheeting to put up over their heads. Buruma (2009: 33) comments that civil niceties can still be observed among these people. With 'shoes fastidiously placed outside the tents, laundry flapping from taut lines, garbage put out in neat little piles'.

12. De Mente (1992: 6) elaborates on this: 'Learning how to draw the thousands of Kanji characters also imbued the Japanese with a highly developed sense of harmony, form, and style that combined to give them a deep understanding and appreciation of aesthetics, making each of them something of an artist. Training in writing Kanji thus became a mould that shaped the Japanese physically, emotionally, and intellectually, homogenising them and binding them into their culture'.

13. Dale (1986: 22) expresses the same viewpoint by saying that 'every inch of autonomous self-assertion by the individual is contested as threatening the hegemonic reach and authority of the corporate, national ideal. While intent on projecting an image of Japan's national uniqueness abroad, the *nihonjinron* vigorously deny the very possibility of individual, uniquely personal identity within itself'.

3   Economic, social, and cultural changes 1990–2005

1. McCormack (1996: 10) reports that the Japanese authorities' reaction to the earthquake was 'cold and more concerned with the preservation of its own control, or of the national "face"', rather than focusing on emergency relief. The confidence between politicians and citizens became heavily strained when people experienced that the outer world showed a stronger interest in helping than their own politicians.

2. Cf. Zielenziger's (2006: 262) characterisation: 'In the last years of the twentieth century, an acid joke began circulating among Japan's intelligentsia; how, after years of being hectored by foreign competitors, most notably the United States, over its mercantilist trade policies and insular structure, "Japan bashing" had evolved into "Japan passing" and then into "Japan nothing". The joke insinuated that, while the attention of the Western world was turned elsewhere, especially toward China, the Persian Gulf, and the Middle East, Japan's prestige and global influence continued to wither away' (Zielenziger, 2006: 262).

3. I am thinking about the classical criminological perspective as expressed in the title of Jock Young's (1999) book *The Exclusive Society*, i.e. a perspective that draws an explicit causal link between economic and social exclusion and increasing crime. See Chapter 5 for further elaboration.

4. Of course, this perspective excludes white-collar crime, violence in the private sphere, special law offenses, and crimes committed by states (to mention the most typical exceptions). I will comment on this question later on.

5. Cf. Murray (1984, 1990), Wilson (1985, 1993), and Charles Murray (1985, 1990); all authors who stress moral and cultural variables to explain rising crime and social problems.

6. Interview with the *Asahi Shimbun*, October 12, 2002.

7. Cf. Tipton (2002: 214): 'Japan's economy is still heavily regulated compared to other industrialised economies and is likely to remain so in the coming decades'. Vogel (1999: 19) is much of the same opinion, arguing that 'Japan is not likely to converge on the Anglo-American liberal market model', and he finds that 'the dramatic reform of the 1990s – like those of the late 1940s and the 1970s – end up being more momentous in form than in substance, as earlier institutions and practices reassert themselves in new forms'. Schoppa (2006) argues that the *resistance* against reform has been remarkable in Japan. The system has changed but has not been transformed, is his conclusion. Genda Yuji (2005) criticises the government for its failing ability to challenge established structures of power, which most of all hit young people.

8. Data from: http://www.stat.go.jp/english/index/official/203.htm#1. Visited August 26, 2009.

9. According to *Business Week* (August 17, 1998) anyone who works more than one hour in the last week of a month is regarded by the Japanese government to have a job. Furthermore, 'the official unemployment statistics don't reflect the throngs of housewives too discouraged even to try to return to the workforce, college graduates waiting at home with their parents for the economy to improve, and middle-aged workers "temporarily" laid off until their companies recover' (pp. 27 –28).

10. Toshikiko Ueno reports in an interesting article in *Japan Times* (June 21, 2007) that *freeters* 'are increasingly standing in open rebellion against the wide-spread claim in the "self-responsibility" debate that the youth of today prefer an unsettled life'. In May this year some 100 young people (organised by 'The Freeter Union of Fukuoka') demonstrated for improvements in working conditions for *freeters*. One of the demonstrators launched a critique that 'corporations cajoled young people into working for them for low pay. Businesses tossed them aside after getting all they could out of them'. The leader of the *freeter* organisation declared that 'it is not fair that corporations have a glut of money while *freeters* and temp staff cannot even earn enough to scrape together a living'. In 2005 an organisation called 'Union Botiboti' was set up to support non-irregular workers. The leader of this organisation said that the largest number of telephone calls they received had been from people who had been abruptly fired. Many of these had joined the group of homeless people (thus, the concept of 'working poor' has become well known in Japan).

11. According to Wikipedia there were between 2 and 4 million *freeters* in Japan in 2001/2002, and these numbers are expected to increase to 10 million in 2014. *Japan Times* reported on June 21, 2007 that *freeters* and irregular contract employees accounted for some 17 million in 2006.

12. Honda (2004: 105) describes the old system in this way: 'Almost all school-leavers and university graduates find their future posts before graduation in March, usually with the help of teachers handling offers from employers, in order to begin work the following year on 1 April. This "periodical blanket

recruitment" dates from the late Meiji era (Takeuchi, 1995). However, before the 1960s, it was mostly limited to white-collar workers in large companies. This practice also can be observed among white-collar workers in other countries. This distinctiveness of the Japanese case is that it expanded to blue-collar workers in large companies during the high economic growth of the 1960s.'

13. This conclusion does not exclude a perspective arguing that a significant group of young people, especially students, actually prefer the type of 'atypical' employment defined as 'side-jobs'. For this group the labour market adaptation could reasonably be described as a source of flexible employment that corresponds to their total life style preferences (Sato, 2001).

14. In Bauman's (2001: 11) words, 'inside the "warm circle" they won't have to prove anything, and whatever they do they may expect sympathy and help'.

15. This statement should be read *descriptively*, not *normatively*. In my earlier book I comment on the different aspects of repression that are built into the Japanese group structure. Group belongingness has a high price with regarding to individual freedom and autonomy. Also, one should also be aware (for example as Miyanaga, 1991: 126, points out) that members of one group can behave indifferently and even quite hostilely towards outside people. On the group level, Japanese society is rather pluralistic. To countervail this pluralism and safeguard the general social integration the Japanese government has tried to establish a set of united group values within the school system and the family (under the headline 'national spirit'). According to Miyanaga, this took place towards the end of the 1980s.

16. Cf. White and LeVine (1986: 56): 'The most highly valued qualities make a child *ningen-rashii*, or "human-like" (Shigaki, p. 15), that is, able to maintain harmony in human relationships. Performance qualities are important but are only the visible demonstrations of deeper abilities to be a good (social) person'.

17. According to McCargo (2004: 75), 'some Japanese marriages are little more than conveniences, maintained for pragmatic reasons by couples who would separate or divorce in other societies'.

18. In Japan, the family is an integral part of the so-called *ie* institution and ideology. Included in this is an elaborate system of registration (*koseki*) which, according to Sugimoto (1997: 136), 'penetrates into the life of every Japanese and controls it in a fundamental way'. One important implication of this system is that 'the *koseki* scheme deters women from divorcing, preserves the male advantages of the patriarchal order, and protects the *ie* system in a fundamental way' (p. 138).

19. http://www.stat.go.jp/english/data/handbook/c02cont.htm#cha2_4.Visited May 13, 2009.

20. http://www.glocom.org/special_topics/social.trends/20040210_trends_s69/index.html. Visited December 8, 2005).

21. 'The lack of welfare services in Japan discourages women from seeking full-time jobs, increases wives' dependence on their husbands, and further deters women from divorce. Less support for the welfare of single mothers in particular may explain the lower incidence of one-parent families in Japan relative to the countries of Scandinavia' (Ono, 2006: 13).

22. Surveys show that people have become more tolerant of divorce during the last 25 years, but still Japanese citizens are less tolerant of divorce than their Western counterparts (Ono, 2006: 6).

23. In the original *ie* system, the children were considered the responsibility of *all* adult members in the household rather than just their parents. In the same way, each *ie* was an integral part of the community. From this follows that each child was traditionally regarded as a member of the community rather than as the child of their parents (see Yamamura, 1986: 33).

24. According to *Mainichi Shimbun* (August 01, 2002) 'Japanese family law has no provision for visitation rights. No legal regulations exist for determining the rights of the parent without custody to meet their children. Nor does Japanese family law provide any framework or definition of joint custody once parents are divorced. In 2001, a major Japanese newspaper reported that some divorced fathers were seeking to change the law to allow for visitation and even joint custody, but that has not occurred'.

25. The strong link that exists between mother and child in Japan is illustrated in a phenomenon called *oyako-shinju* (a parent's killing of the child before the parent' s own suicide). Since the bond between mother and child is very strong in Japan, parents do not expect that their child will be properly cared for if they die. Consequently, parents who opt for suicide will often kill their offspring as well (Yamammura, 1986. Cf. Chapter 6).

26. This was explicitly expressed at a Tokyo rally July 1, 2007: 'When we take a day off or when we are sick, we are not paid. We feel uncertain about income. People working in spot-basis temp jobs always have such apprehensions' (*Japan Times*, July 7, 2007).

27. According to *Japan Times* (November 29, 2007) the Diet recently enacted two new laws that aim to set basic labour rules and raise the minimum wage. The first of these laws set rules for companies to better cope with diverse work styles (part-time, etc.), while the other law decides that the lowest accepted wage has to be above the levels of public assistance for low-income earners. The Minimum Wage Law is planned to come into effect within a year.

28. Cf. Curtin (2005: 1): 'Over the past decade, low wages for women, a non-functional child support payment system, an inadequate social welfare policy, and a weakening of traditional family support networks all have contributed to redrawing the Japanese poverty map. Previously, elderly households constituted the bulk of the poor, but today the balance has firmly shifted to mother-headed families'.

29. Later on the government has launched a state-sponsored programme to subsidise companies promoting single mothers who work as part-timers to full-time status, but according to the Health, Labour and Welfare Ministry's 2007 fiscal White Paper on single-mother households, only 26 per cent of local governments have implemented this programme. However, from April 2008 the government will cut part of its child-care allowances for single-mother households due to fiscal strains (*Japan Times*, June 2, 2007), and this happened after the government in August 2002 lowered the Dependent-child Allowance (Curtin, 2003a: 2).

30. A survey from 1990 documented that 30 per cent of fathers spent under 15 minutes a day on weekdays playing with or talking to their children, and

only 50 per cent spent more than 30 minutes (Goodman, 2002: 148). A statistical survey from 1987 disclosed that the average Japanese father spent only one hour and 32 minutes a week with his children (McCargo, 2004: 80). According to Azuma (1986: 8) the Jung-inspired psychologist Kawai, suggests that Japanese culture is basically matriarchic, and, according to a clinical psychologist called Sasaki, there is not, and there has never been, a substantial father figure in the Japanese family.

31. Curtin (2005: 2) reports: 'One recent case was reported at the beginning of February 2005 when a 27-year-old mother and her three-year-old son were found starved to death in their apartment in Saitama Prefecture near Tokyo. Police reported that there was no food in the apartment and the woman only had eight yen (\$ 0,07) in her purse'. Curtin continues with a story about an unmarried woman living on a very low income in a snowy northern part of Japan: 'It is hardest to manage in winter because of heating costs, especially this year. I try to stay at work for as long as possible because it's warm there and my son is in a well-heated day-care centre. For mothers like me day-care is free, so it is best he is there for as long as possible. At home, we stay in one room and wear blankets to keep warm'. *Japan Times* October 14, 2007, reports that 'there has been a series of starvation deaths in Japan as struggling regional cities are being forced to tighten welfare eligibility standards'.

32. Azuma (1986: 4) explains how this *amae* mechanism functions in a very concrete way: 'The assertion, "You don't have to obey me", was actually a very powerful threat. One mother said that it always worked. It carried the message: "We have been close together. But now that you want to have your own way, I will untie the bond between us. I will not care what you do. You are not a part of me any longer". This message was effective because the child had assimilated the *amae* culture in which interpersonal dependence is the key'.

33. This argument is very well documented by Gold (1982: 355–356) in his critique of social impact assessment analysis of American boomtowns. Arguing from an anthropological, 'bottom up' point of view, Gold makes his point clear: 'Don't fool with that bullshit data, fellows. Get out there and develop relationships of mutual trust and respect with other people in boomtowns, especially those who are up to their ears in value-related and other sociologically significant social problems, and find out what the people whose scene it is have to report about what is going on and what it all means to them and their community. Make an intelligent effort to study community structure directly, in depth, and over time, instead of preoccupying yourself with such hobgoblins as divorce statistics, which, by their very nature, tell precious little about impingements of natural resource development projects on the structure and functioning of the communities in question. To learn about the latter, there simply is no substitute for asking community members to inform you about what's happening, trying to make both folk and sociological sense out of this information, and then validating and reporting it as described above'.

34. Kyvsgaard (1992: 92) turns the argument this way: 'Instead of saying that divorces are of importance for the likelihood that children will commit crime, it is more correct to say that stability at home is of importance for

getting very law-abiding children' (my translation). For other discussions regarding the relevance of the changing family institution to crime, see Garland (2001: 82), Lea (2002: 22).

35. It should be added here that these seemingly contradictory ideologies regarding socialisation in the family and in pre-schools, in Japan are regarded rather as complementary and the result of intention. The official view is that children should be in the home with their mother until the age of three. During these years the child is supposed to receive a lot of physical and mental stimulation from the mother, and this is regarded as a prerequisite for normal development. As Ben-Ari (1997: 16) points out, 'so crucial are these conditions for "natural" development, it is held, that their lack is seen to eventuate in pathologies like juvenile delinquency later on in life'.

36. Smith's (1997: 155) assertion that 'there is little doubt that the family in contemporary Japan remains the source of moral order' could obviously be contested. The moral order that relates to *collective values* is mainly transferred via the school system rather than the family.

37. This is why Ben-Ari (1997: 7), on the basis of only one case study, maintains that his findings 'are representative of most day-care centres and may be suggestive of Japanese pre-schools in general'.

38. In my presentation it is not necessary to go into details regarding different types of pre-school institutions. However, for a more nuanced discussion one should be aware of the difference between kindergartens (*yoochien*) and day-care centres (*hoikuen*), between public and private pre-schools, and between licensed and un-licensed pre-schools (see Ben-Ari, 1997; Bookock, 1989, Ben-Ari, 1997). Today, pre-school is nearly a universal experience for Japanese children.

39. Hood (2001: 80) maintains that 'with the rise of juvenile delinquency, the traditionalists pointed to the inordinate amount of freedom and independence that Japanese children enjoyed and argued that they were neglecting their social responsibilities'.

40. This is not contradictory to the fact that the Japan Teachers' Union for a long period after the Second World War was in strong opposition to the Ministry, not least due to the ideological content of the education.

41. However, it should be added that towards the end of the 1980s more attention was given to the *individual* and the importance of expressing *personal* thoughts and feelings (Cave, 2001). Many teachers reacted negatively to these changes, arguing that too much freedom in loosely structured pre-schools was the main cause of the so-called 'collapsed classrooms' (*gakkyu hokai*) (Holloway, 2000: 8). Unruly children were seen as the logical consequence of an influence of more liberal, 'Western' values influence. This indicates that, even if I conclude that 'traditional values' for the most part have been preserved in Japan in recent years, one could argue that a general pressure in the direction of more flexibility and more focus on self-expression and creativity has made Japan a little bit less monolithic than it used to be. Less monolithic should not be read as less disciplinary. Yamamura (1986: 36) underlines that the asserted rise in juvenile delinquency in the 1980s 'resulted in a new emphasis on the disciplinary aspects of education during the early years'. In other words, the situation has to be described in

ambiguous words: Certain tendencies of liberalisation seem to have gone in tandem with an increased focus on discipline and moral guidance.

42. Although Japan also was extensively involved in the international economy also before the 1990s, a new phase started when the country became a member of the World Trade Organization, in January 1995.

43. The impact of globalisation is ubiquitous in Japan's political, economic, and cultural spheres, and in each of these spheres the fundamental crisis of the Japanese developmental state is visible (Hirata, 2002: 4).

44. At this point it should also be added that, while *my* focus here has been on *negative* implications of the economic crisis, *others* have pointed to more optimistic options and traits in this situation (see Hirata, 2002; Kingston, 2004; Hirata, 2002, Miyanaga, 1991). As an illustration, Kingston refers to political reforms, the reinvigoration of civil society, expanding volunteering, and greater acceptance of diversity and individuality, as political fields that give reason for optimism.

45. As Schoppa (2006: 199) comments: 'Is Japan changing....or not? Every author and commentator covering Japan's political economy has taken a stand on this question, and their answers have been all over the map'. Schoppa then diplomatically adds that the reality is a mix of two different views, and that 'what you "see" depends on which part of the elephant you're feeling'.

46. During recent years, it has been hotly debated if whether school children (as part of the curriculum) should take part in obligatory 'community service'. The appearance of this is a reaction to the mentioned (and asserted) 'classroom collapse' (unruly students), absenteeism, bullying, increasing crime, and loss of general commitment among young people (*Japan Times*, August 1, 2000; September 23, 2000; December 23, 2000; January 4, 2001; *Mainichi Daily News*, July 23, 2000; September 24, 2000; February 14, 2001). Three education reform bills passed the Diet in June 2000, aiming among other things at 'upgrading social education, starting at home' and to 'bolster discipline and "protect the right to learn"' (*Japan Times*, June 30, 2001).

4   Crime in Japan 1990–mid-2000s

I use the term 'mid-2000s' since my statistical data will vary a bit concerning the most recent data. My primary interest lies in finding out the realities behind the *upward* trend in reported crimes from the mid-1990s until 2002, rather than analysing explanations for the decrease in the following years (which represent a new research project in itself). It is the negative deviations away from the peaceful years that will be the focus. The mentioned period under discussion, which in time coincides with the economic decline, is (according to the figures) the most crime turbulent period as regards crime in Japan since the years immediately after the Second World War. The latest available edition of the White Paper on Crime is at the present moment the one covering 2006. However, the statistical presentation and analysis in the 2005 White Paper on Crime gives the most illustrative presentation over some time, and this is the reason why I use some of the data from this edition. Also, some of my statistical presentation will start *before* 1990 when such a broader overview seems relevant for the discussion.

1. Goto (2004: 25) expresses this view in this way: 'Strictly speaking, recognised crime cases and the number of arrests are simply the statistical byproducts of the way law enforcement organisations deal with crime, and they are not mirroring reflections of actual conditions'. Be that as it may, they are still the most useful barometers of criminal trends.

2. To the extent that 'fear' is related to identifiable and real external threats we should probably talk about increasing anxiety rather than increasing fear in Japan. Fear should be distinguished from anxiety, which typically occurs without any external threat. Additionally, fear is related to the specific behaviour of escape and avoidance, whereas anxiety is the result of threats which are perceived to be uncontrollable or unavoidable. "http://en.wikipedia.org/wiki/Anxiety" \o "Anxiety" "http://en.wikipedia.org/wiki/Fear" \l "cite_note-0#cite_note-0" \o ""

3. Japan is not unique in this regard. According to Shaftoe (2004: 38), fear of crime has increased in the Netherlands during a period when crime rates have stabilised or fallen.

4. Cf. the White Paper on Crime 2005: 471: 'Last year's 2004 White Paper on crime pointed out that, in many ways, the crime deterrent function inherent in society itself is decreasing, and that over the last 30 years Japanese society has greatly changed from the "peaceful days" in the past to the present "crime frequency society"....'.

5. Cf. the following statement from a TV news director in 2008: The job of commercial broadcasters is to 'describe human drama that viewers can appreciate' (referred cited in Hamai and Ellis, 2008b: 81). On the other hand, this perspective can easily be exaggerated. As Sparks (2001) shows in his chapter on 'Populism, media coverage and the dynamics of locality and globality in the politics of crime control', even though media plays a vital role in the social construction of crime, it is too simplistic to lapse into deterministic accounts of this role.

6. It should be added that increasing fear of crime in Japan to a certain extent might have a *demographic* explanation. Research tells us (Best, 1999: xi) that older people (and women, i.e. those who are relatively less likely to be victimised) are those who fear crime the most. Since the Japanese population is aging at a very high speed, fear will, *ceteris paribus,* increase.

7. Cf. Tanaka (2006: 10): 'As the numbers of crimes reflected in crime statistics is too diverse, it goes beyond my ability to comprehensively and individually analyze it'.

8. For further details about categorisation of homicides in Japan, see Finch (2001: 221).

9. The first two episodes are referred to in Akane, (2002: 5–6), the next is reported in Seto (1999), the third bullet point is taken from Smith and Sueda (2008), while the last two episodes are referred to in the 2005 White Paper on Crime (page pp. 388–390).

10. Homicide statistics are considered to be less affected by under-reporting than other crimes (Finch, 2001: 220).

11. The acquaintance rate for the nine violent offences referred to earlier shifted from the mid-1990s from a downward to an upward trend for all of these offences except for robbery. The WP 2002: 286 comments: 'There seems to be a tendency that offences of a violent nature are committed towards those who are closely acquainted with the perpetrators'.

12. The last part of this conclusion ('random killing') is most certainly cor-
    rect, but the assertion about 'clear personal motive' could easily be misun-
    derstood as meaning that most murders are strategically well prepared and
    committed in cold blood. This is hardly the case. Even though the argument
    of 'clear personal motive' behind the homicides is undocumented, one *could*
    put forward the hypothesis that some homicides in Japan are committed
    because of what is usually regarded as the most important crime preventive
    mechanism in Japan, namely *shame*. Crimes that 'start out' as types of lar-
    ceny, robbery or sexual assaults, might more easily develop into desperate
    murders in a shame culture than in more Western style cultures. As was dis-
    closed in a murder of two children, a boy (whose intention was to steal some
    money) killed because he thought that the children had recognised him.
    Since he himself lived only two doors away from the scene of the crime he
    hoped to avoid the shame when he failed to steal the money by killing the
    children. Also, mechanisms of group pressure, which is well known also in
    Western countries, are probably much stronger in a collectivistic culture
    like Japan, and this will probably easily transform minor offences into more
    grave ones. The observation that mechanisms contributing to *hampering*
    crime under given circumstances might have the opposite effect, is well
    documented by Miller and Kanazawa (2000) when it comes to white-collar
    crimes. They observe that 'the same processes that serve to discourage one
    type of crime might actually foster another type' (p. 91). Strong emphasis
    on group affiliation and group pressure certainly has a preventive effect on
    some types of crime, but 'it likely encourages certain types of white-collar
    crimes, particularly crimes committed in the course of one's work to benefit
    one's company' (p. 92).
13. According to Kopel (1993: 26) 'gun control in Japan is the most stringent
    in the democratic world' and this strict control became even stricter from
    2009. A law revision to the country's 'Swords and Firearms Control Law'
    bans the possession of double-edged knives and tightens gun-ownership
    rules. This revision was a response to a series of brutal crimes that took place
    in 2008, including a shooting spree and a mass stabbing attack that killed
    seven people.
14. According to the 'Japan Vending Machine Manufacturers Association',
    Japan has one vending machine per an estimated 23 people, which implies
    that Japan has one of the world's highest vending machine densities.
    However, more important than the number of vending machines is the fact
    that many of these machines sell alcoholic beverages (even hard liquor) and
    cigarettes.
15. In a policy document concerning 'Comprehensive Measures for Juvenile
    Protection and Delinquency Protection', the National Police Agency Deputy
    Commissioner General declared that 'the current juvenile delinquency
    problem is very severe' (PPRC/NPAJ 2004).
16. The Kobe murder in 1997, where the severed head of an 11-year boy was
    found at the gate of a junior high school, created a lot of fear and media
    attention. In the mouth of the victim was a message threatening further
    killings. Later on a 14-year-old boy was arrested for this killing and even
    confessed another killing (a 10ten-year-old girl). For a further analysis of this
    case, see Smith and Sueda (2008). Another shocking incident that triggered

public fear was the kidnapping and murder of a four4-year-old pre-schooler who was killed by a 12-year-old boy. This case prompted the establishment of a task force on juvenile delinquency. This report concluded that 'increasingly grievous crimes were committed by younger offenders and strongly appealed for measures to deal harshly with young criminals in response to growing concerns about the deterioration in public safety' (quoted in Goto, 2004: 24).

17. See http://www.npa.go.jp/english/seisaku5/20081008.pdf, p. 8.

18. As an illustration *Japan Times*, August 15, 2001, reports 'Decline in busts belies wide-spread drug use: NPA.' While the data reports fewer people violating the Stimulants Control Law, 'authorities believe drug abuse is on the increase', the newspaper reports. This is due to more sophisticated drug-smuggling and possession techniques. Also, in addition, a professional Japan expert on Japan like Henshall (1999: 211, fn. 40) gives the impression that 'drug and alcohol abuse among teenagers is increasing'.

19. Estimates for unreported crimes vary. Finch (2000: 246) suggests that for Japan 'over 60 per cent of certain crimes may go unreported to the police'. The 1993 Australia-wide Crime and Safety Survey produced the following figures: 94 per cent of robbery victims, 32 per cent of both assault and attempted breaking and entry victims, but only 25 per cent of sexual assault victims reported the incidents to the police (referred to in Anleu 1999: 133). Dahrendorf (1985: 16) maintains that some 80--85 per cent of all crimes go unreported.

20. As Curtin (2004) maintains, some mechanisms might also work in the opposite direction. Cases have been revealed where the police, in order to enhance performance ratings, have falsified investigation documents over several years. An 'easy' way to improve clearance rates is, of course, to shrink the number of reported crimes.

21. The debate on rising crime rates in Japan has, like in many Western countries, been marked by the traditional conflict related to the blaming of immigrants. Not least the White Papers on Crime argue that visiting foreigners are overrepresented in the crime statistics, a perspective that has been refuted by different commentators. Methodologically, this is a complex topic and I do not have the relevant data to enter this debate. However, the fact that many illegal foreign workers were among the first to lose their jobs when recession hit Japan, might of course (as McCargo, 2004: 85 argues) have generated incentives to turn to crime among some of these people.

22. The basic outline was: 1) reinforce the ability within the police administration to ensure transparency, 2) establish 'police for the people', 3) create a police force that can respond to the needs of a new generation, and 4) reinforce the human infrastructure that supports police activities (White Paper on Police 2006: 132). For further details, see 'Guidelines of police policy in Japan' (Police Policy Research Center/National Police Academy of Japan. Alumni Association for National Police Academy (undated). This is a compilation of 11 different outlines of measures for reform (except for two of these outlines, all are dated between 2000 and 2004).

23. Masahide Maeda (quoted in Miyazawa, 2008: 54), who is a well-known professor of criminal law at Tokyo Metropolitan University, argues that 'the increase in juvenile crime in general, and heinous crime in particular, is

real: that the situation is worse than reported in the news; that the decline in apprehension rates masks the real increase in juvenile crime; and that *genbatsuka* of juvenile crime in the USA has contributed to a decrease in juvenile crime'. Park (2006), who has written extensively on crime in Japan until 1988, supports (in the preface of his book) the argument that crime has increased during the 1990s, an argument that about which Johnson (2007, referring to Kawai) is more doubtful about ('there is reason to wonder whether the officially reported increases are more apparent than real').

24. As the Ministry of Justice reports in its own study on spousal violence (Research Department Report no. 24, 2003: 10) 'domestic violence is also believed to occur because of the inequality between men and women (according to gender)'.

25. The Ministry of Justice in Japan has the following comments on these data: 'The scope of what is considered a crime and the constituent elements of a crime (factors and conditions of which an act is judged as applicable to a specific offence) differs and methods of gathering statistics are not the same among these countries. Furthermore, it is not appropriate to judge the crime trends based only on the trends in the number of reported cases of specific offences. However, it is still considered beneficial to grasp the outline of the crime trends in each country by comparing the statistical figures in Japan with those in [the] other four countries, in the analysis of the crime trends in Japan from the international perspective' (WP 2006: 42).

26. Curtin (2004) reports in *Asia Times,* August 28, that 'while nearly all OECD countries recorded declines in criminality [during the1990s], in Japan the rates soared. This gave the country one of the most rapid increases in crime levels ever witnessed among the OECD countries'.

27. It should be added here that the claim about a general increase in punitivism among Western countries has been contested. In a report on the determinants of punishment policy it is concluded that 'many of the generalisations bandied about in discussions of penal policy in Western countries are not true... Penal policies are not becoming harsher everywhere' (Tonry, referred cited in Johnson, 2008: 20).

5   The authoritative interpretation of the crime situation

1. Simplified, there are two main positions; one arguing, like Felson (2002: 12), that 'in general, it is a mistake to assume that crime is part of a larger set of social evils, such as unemployment, poverty, social injustice, or human suffering. I call this the *welfare-state fallacy'* (cf. Fukuyama, 2000: 67). The other stand is presented in the text in this section, and is further elaborated by scholars like Grover (2008), Anleu (1999), Braithwaite (1991), Grover (2008), Muncie (1999) Taylor (1990, 1998), and Muncie, (1999). In the case of Japan, Evans concluded in 1977 that the declining crime rate in Japan after the Second World War could be attributed to the favourable labour market situation. Masahiro (1996), studying the impact of poverty, economic inequality, and unemployment, on homicide, robbery, and theft rates among the 47 prefectures in Japan, concludes that there is a significant positive relationship between unemployment rates and homicide and

robbery, and between the degree of economic inequality and property crime. Writing in 1996, Masahiro laid out a prospect against this background of a deterioration of the crime situation in Japan as the economic instability increased. Park (2006), studied factors that affected the longitudinal patterns of crime rates (five types of crime) during the period 1954–1988. He found that 'economic conditions characterised by the economic affluence along with the economic equality, and certainty of punishment as measured by clearance and conviction rates seem to be decisive factors of crime patterns in post-war Japan' (p. 161).

2. Young (1999: 5–6) clarifies this point by saying: 'I do not think that "unemployment" causes (*sic*) "crime" in some mechanical and deterministic fashion. What I *do* want to argue, however, is that there has been an absolutely fundamental transformation in the organisation of economic life in most Western societies over the last quarter-century (very often summarised as the move from economies organised around production to economies organised around consumption) and that this transformation has had absolutely fundamental effects on the forms and the substances of social life'.

3. Yonekawa (2003) underlines that poverty, lack of one parent, or the low educational background of the father does not directly lead to juvenile delinquency, but due to the *implications* such characteristics have for raising children (e.g. lacking the inability to invest in socialisation of their children, lack of communication between parents and children, etc.) the final result may be delinquency. Especially in an academically oriented society like Japan, juveniles who do not have the motivation for entering university, are easily defined as dropouts or even as 'dead pigeons', which, of course, implies a heavy psychological strain.

4. Let me bring this economic perspective down to earth by presenting a narrative referred cited by *Business Report* (February 9, 2008). After the Japanese government started implementing its de-regulation of the labour market, different staff replacement recruitment companies took over what used to be the work of the mafia in recruiting job seekers for construction and other menial work, characterised by instability, low wages and risk. The aggregate effect of this policy was said to be the creation of a new urban underclass which quickly developed a feeling of disrespect and injustice. The rest of the reportage is about a 29-year-old unemployed man who applied for help from a Tokyo charity: 'Togashi graduated from high school in the northern island of Hokkaido and then took odd jobs, delivering newspapers and working at a convenience store and a comic café. None of the jobs provided security, let alone professional satisfaction. It did not take long for him to fall into dire poverty with no safety net. One middle-aged woman tried to recruit him, offering what seemed to be an attractive job at a company. After he was asked to fabricate a document, he discovered it was a scheme for him to take out loans on behalf of her firm. "I got sick of everything in life, thinking that that was the only offer I was worth after being an unstable worker for so long", he said. With no support from family, Togashi asked for help from the Moyai charity, which supports poor people looking for a way out. With only about 1,000 yen (nine dollars) in his pocket, he took a ferry from Hokkaido to just north of Tokyo, from where he embarked on his 10-day, 100 kilometre (60 mile) walk to Moyai's office. He soon settled at a Tokyo homeless shelter,

eventually going to work for the charity. "I had no idea at the time how to get out of my situation", he said. "I would often ponder the best way to become happy, but couldn't find an answer". The Japanese government reported in April that some 18,500 homeless people were living on the streets across the country. But Makoto Yuasa, director of Moyai, the charity which helped Togashi, said that far more people were on society's fringes, staying quietly in all-night cafes, hospitals, rehabilitation clinics, or elsewhere'.

5. Cf. Felson (2002: 168), writing under the headline 'Findings that shook tradition', arguing that 'traditional crime theories assumed that offenders are low in income; yet self-report studies showed youths at all income levels committing a lot of crime'.

6. In connection with the debate leading to the revisions of the Juvenile Act (effective from April 2001) it was argued 'that juveniles were *deliberately* taking advantage of their rights to commit crimes without fear of sanction' (Ryan, 2005: 175). Ryan refers to a report in 1999 to the Prime Minister from the Juvenile Problem Legislative Advisory Committee that stated: 'One of the causes of the increase in problem behaviour amongst juveniles is that only the perspective of the freedom and rights of the juveniles has been emphasised, and adults don't even have the confidence to deny it' (op. cit.: 175).

7. Such a strategy as an important approach to prevent crime is typical within control theory, as explicated by Gottfredson and Hirschi (1990: 272–273): 'Apart from the limited benefits that can be achieved by making specific criminal acts more difficult, policies directed toward enhancement of the ability of familial institutions to socialize children are the only realistic long-term state policies with potential for substantial crime reduction'.

8. MM refers to 'Ministerial Meeting Concerning Measures against Crime', edited by the Police Policy Research Center and the National Police Academy of Japan, December 2003.

9. An intensification of the fight against juvenile delinquency was particularly visible in 1997–1998 when several expert committees were established: 1) In August 1997, the police formulated the 'Essentials of Promotion of Comprehensive Countermeasures Against Juvenile Delinquency', where the philosophy was to be based on 'strong and kind hearted' juvenile police operations (Sano and Kittaka, 2006: 4). When registered crime increased in 1997, the police implemented 'all counter-measures conceivable' (op. cit.) to cope with the new situation. 2) A new report which took a more long-term view was presented in 1998 ('Aiming to Protect Children from Delinquency – Present-day Problems of Juvenile Delinquency and Activities Implemented by Police'). Four pillars were mentioned in this report that should be addressed by the police: a) establishment of 'Juvenile Support Centers' with juvenile probation officers as the cores; b) strengthening of capabilities to investigate juvenile cases; c) enrichment of information transmission; and d) promotion of juvenile protection measures – 'meeting the trend of the times', as it was expressed in the report (op. cit.: 5). 3) In 1998 another committee ('The Expert Committee for Deliberation on Juveniles Playing Important Roles in Next Generation') was established under the Prime Minister. This committee indicated that it would be necessary for the entire government to deal with juvenile issues and it gave recommendations on specific studies to be done. These included 'strengthening of recognition/handling functions regarding

problem behaviour of juveniles', 'strengthening of case solving functions', 'strengthening of functions of transmitting information for forming model awareness and for arousing common problem awareness of society regarding the actual situation of juvenile delinquency', and 'strengthening of functions of purifying social environments surrounding juveniles' (op. cit.: 3).

10. According to Johnson (2008) Japan's imprisonment rate has risen 75 percent since 1992. In his article 'Japanese Punishment in Comparative Perspective' Johnson focuses on the increasing use of capital punishment in Japan, and from this perspective Japan has undoubtedly become more punitive.

11. Only once have I found a comment referring to increasing crime as a result of reporting routines. The 2002 White Paper on Crime maintains that the increase in reported and cleared cases for intimidation 'may be due to the hidden cases started being reported' (p. 287).

12. When discussing countermeasures and challenges regarding punishment the following declaration is given in the 2003 White Paper on Crime: 'When dealing with offenses that are malicious and serious in terms of various aspects such as the level of damage and social unrest that they cause, it is necessary to impose severe punishments for them while giving due consideration to feelings of victims. In particular, it is needless to say that offenses that might be easily imitated, such as serial robbery, robbery through causing unconsciousness by using sleep-inducing medicine and other drugs, and serial rape should be punished severely for the purpose of preventing the public from imitating such offenses. With respect to cases of heinous offenses committed by juveniles, efforts should be made to deal with such cases in accordance with the revised Juvenile Law, and for the purpose of nipping crimes in the bud, it is important to endeavour to take appropriate measures even for cases that have not resulted in serious cases, because juvenile offenders in these cases might commit more serious offenses if no measures were taken' (p. 479–480).

13. For a critical discussion of the argument of increased punitivsm as a *general* trend, see Tonry (2007).

14. A close up reading of the White Papers on Crime from the period 1999 to 2006 refers to a *nominal* world. Through text analysis I have been able to present an 'armchair' report of how the Ministry of Justice interprets the world of crimes and transgressions. It goes without saying that such a presentation says precious little about what is implemented in practical life. Of course, these documents can report on actual implementation of new laws and regulations, and they can give empirical data on registered crimes, sentences and so on. However, as is well known within political science, the sphere of ideologies, political declarations and policy formulations, is something very different from the sphere of implemented realities. I underline this methodological reminder to make it clear that by analysing crime policy I am talking about a rhetorical world. In this world tactical and idealistic formulations are mingled together without much chance for the critical reader to decipher what is what. However, when crime policy (i.e. *ideas* and *ideals*) is on the agenda this is where we have to start.

15. Due to limited space, it is not possible to give complete fairness to the full range of arguments in the White Papers regarding ways of understanding

crime increases. However, one more perspective, falling outside the analytical categories above, should be mentioned, namely *demographic* arguments. This relates to changes in age cohorts, to immigrants' 'contribution' to crime, and to the effects of a shrinking family.

16. Each year the White Papers on Crime have a special chapter on the 'Treatment of offenders' that gives detailed information on this subject.

17. In their analyses of 'The Killing of Children by Children', Smith and Sueda (2008) evaluate the authoritative authorities' reaction towards juvenile murderers with the conception 'modernist welfare approach', which implies a more positive judgement of Japanese criminal justice policy than the other scholars to whom I have referred to.

6   Social disruption? Self destruction and social phobia in modern-day Japan

1. I have to underline that these distinctions between active and passive responses to stress are primarily made for analytical reasons. Concepts like 'action' and 'reaction' are only seemingly diametrical opposite terms. If we move from a nominal to the factual world these terms are different 'values' on a floating continuum.

2. Cf. Kudo (quoted in Krysinska, 2006: 49): 'You can't pinpoint the reasons [of *hikikomori*] but you can pinpoint the context: it's Japan. Here, you have to be like other people, and if you aren't, you have a sense of loss, of shame. So you withdraw'.

3. According to Borovoy, (2008) the tendency for mainstreaming is evident in Japan from the earliest stages of education and socialisation. A main measure is to educate everyone *equally* through the years of compulsory education. 'Teachers and counsellors shy away from public discussions of innate, differing abilities of each student, and IQ tests were abandoned in the 1960s' (p. 559).

4. Krysinska (2006: 8) reports: 'Sometimes, parents ignore the problem as well. They hope their child will grow out of it or do not want to attract neighbours' attention by creating any form of commotion around their family. This may be related to the social stigma attached to shame in the Japanese society'.

5. Miyanaga (1991) writes about the concept of the 'New Men' that was commonly used in Japan from 1968. This concept did not originally have a negative connotation but gradually this changed, especially among older people. The argument was that this new generation was less group oriented than people used to be; its members were criticised for their 'relative' values, for giving priority to freedom instead of security, and for being too hedonistic.

6. A good illustration of this lament that children had changed in a worrying way was expressed in *Japan Echo* in 1998 (no. 3: 12–15), where 'Problems among Japan's young' were discussed. In an interview with five teachers representing 'The Group of Pro Teachers' the superior message was that 'we're seeing the emergence of a brand new personality type with which we don't know how to deal' (p. 12). According to this group of teachers (three

of them had written works on this topic) the most pressing problem (especial in high school) was not academic instruction but teaching children how to behave in school and society. It was teaching children about arriving on time, cooperating so that lessons could proceed normally, sitting in their assigned seats and not walking around during class. According to teacher Suwa, sometimes about 80 per cent of the teachers' energy was put into *guidance* of the children, and the emergence of what was called a 'modern ego' was used to describe the situation.

7. As early as in 1988 Chikio Hayashi announced the coming of a 'new breed' of Japanese. In an article in *Japan Echo* (vol. 15, p. 7) he declared: 'I believe that in the twenty-first century the nation will be reshaped by a new breed of Japanese. The change I envision is not simply a process of increasing westernisation, internationalisation, and sophistication. It is the emergence of a race of people unknown in Japan or in any other country heretofore. While sharing many traits with their predecessors, the members of the coming generation will exhibit radically different value systems and sensitivities'. The reason why Hayashi meant he was able to foretell this development was that this new breed had already come into view already in the mid-1970s and had been proliferating rapidly ever since. Based on longitudinal survey data, Hayashi presented a rather optimistic prophecy, describing the future Japanese individual as one who was able to *combine* traditional and modern values.

8. Watabe is a Professor of Social Networks, Faculty of Education and Human Sciences, Yokohama National University, and specialises in the sociological examination of youth problems, juvenile crime, youth culture, and educational issues. He is author of a number of books (in Japanese) about youth.

9. *Otaku* was originally a polite second-person pronoun used to address a non-acquainted person.

10. Cf. Watabe (2001: 4): 'There is good reason to believe that the mass media are searching industriously for behavioural problems among children. Classroom disruption is an example of finding what you expect to find'.

11. 'Estimates of the numbers of *hikikomoris* vary widely and existing statistical sources are, at best, wanting' (Furlong, 2008: 311).

12. Some scholars place age limitations to the phenomenon, most usually to the age group 15–34 years of age (see Dziesinsky, 2003; Krysinska, 2006; Dziesinsky, 2003).

13. At the same time, the government maintains that the causes of *hikikomori* are too diverse to identify (Hattori, 2005: 183).

14. Ogino (2004: 122) refers to a report (based on questionnaires) from health centres throughout prefectures and communities in Japan in 2003 where only 27 per cent of the *hikikomori* respondents could not leave their living spaces.

15. Tim Larimer (2000) reports: 'Some of those accused in the crime spree – including the bus hijacker and a man who kidnapped a girl and held her captive for 10 years – have been identified as *hikikomoris*...Fear of them has suffused the headlines. In a bizarre twist two months ago, a father and mother confessed to strangling their son because, the parents told police, the teenager had terrorised the family for the past year. Says psychiatrist Takeshi Tamura: "Parents are now afraid of their kids"'.

16. Cf. Ogino (2004: 121): 'They [*hikikomori*] have been usually described as being mild, serious, shy and so on'.

17. The perspective of spoiled children was clearly expressed in the referred interview (cf. footnote 6) with five teachers representing the so-called 'group of Pro Teachers': 'The kids are no longer willing to adjust their behaviour and attitude to fit various situations and relationships. I think the reason is that parents, by continually asking their children "Which do you want?" and "Do you want to do this or not?" have unconsciously conveyed to them the message that they're already equipped to deal with the world as fully formed, complete individuals' (p. 13). Teacher Kawakami expressed in the same interview that 'many times I've wanted to say, "Show some respect"', while teacher Suwa declared: 'Why is the school so timid and weak-willed? I think it's because society as a whole has an overprotective orientation and insists on the same from us' (*Japan Echo*, 1998, no. 3: p. 15).

18. I should add that this perspective is at best only half the story about growing up in modern society. As Currie (2004) shows in *The Road to Whatever*, one could as well bring forth the opposite story, about a generation growing up in an extremely demanding society where significant relatives are absent. Broad, generalising descriptions will always run the risk of leaving out contradictory elements. Often, parallel realities exist side-by-side in society.

19. Tamaki Saito is also referring to *amae* relations when explaining *hikikomori*. In an interview with BBC News he points to the relationship between mothers and their sons, describing it as 'a symbiotic, co-dependent relationship. Mothers will care for their sons until they become 30 or 40 years old' (http://news.bbc.co.uk/2/hi/programmes/correspondent72334893.stm).

20. It has to be added that The Ministry of Education has changed the definition of 'school refusal' from a student missing 50 plus days to 30 plus.

21. This is the main perspective in Ketano's (2006) analysis of the *hikikomori* phenomenon ('Japan's "socially withdrawn youths" and time constraints in Japanese society: management and conceptualisation of time in a support group for "hikikomori"'. *Hikikomori*, Ketano argues, 'may be understood as a kind of reaction to time pressure and role performances in Japanese society' (p. 233). Consequently, 'it may be said that the existence of *hikikomori* threatens the Japanese temporal framework – based on punctuality, deep refusal of wasting time, accelerated rhythms and so on – or more broadly, the mainstream social norms in Japanese society' (p. 246).

22. For a discussion on this, see West (2005: 221–223). West refers to Seward's work *Hara-Kiri*, Pinguet's *Voluntary Death in Japan*, and Iga's *The Thorn in the Chrysanthemum*, as illustrations of scholars who relate suicide in Japan to peculiarly Japanese, cultural values (Buddhistic fatalistic acceptance of death, Shintoistic animism, an historical warrior ethic, a general tradition of sacrifice, and value orientations like monism, groupism, accommodationism and authoritarian familism, that produce unrealistically high aspirations). Pinguet (1993: 2–3) has no reservations when he claims that 'the essential point is that in Japan, there was never any objection in principle to the free choice of death'. However, West is convincingly clear in pointing out that the referred 'factors' too easily become stereotypes rather

than causes. To West, the most important dimension is related to economic conditions.

23. When a cabinet minister hanged himself hours before facing a bribery probe, the Tokyo governor designated the dead man 'a real samurai' (Petrun, *CBS News*, July 2007). To what extent one should define these actions as suicide or as 'authorised murder' is debated, but since these actions in reality were *obligatory* deaths one might dispute using the term suicide.

24. The actual numbers will vary from source to source. *The Japan Times* (April 8, 2000) reports that a study conducted by the police showed that in more than 80 per cent of the cases, those who killed themselves left suicide notes.

25. Japan's most popular religions – Shinto and Buddhism – do not (like Christianity, Judaism and Islam) proscribe suicide (McCurry, 2008). However, critics of this theory point to China's significantly lower suicide rate as evidence that religious differences are hardly a relevant argument (Beam: 2007).

26. Holloway (2000: 9) maintains that there is too much focus on suicide among youths. In Japan, articles on this topic often 'go overboard in portraying Japan as a nation of groupthink, where individual rights count for little. One-dimensional contrasts – depicting the US as individualistic and Japan as collectivistic – are increasingly found in the academic literature as well'.

27. It is important to forget the demographic dimension when discussing suicide in Japan. As I already have noted, Japan has one of the world's longest average life expectancies, and it is highly relevant to include this information as a background for understanding the complex pattern of suicide in this country. With 20 per cent of the population over the age of 65 this age group will statistically also have relatively high suicide rates. Today, the suicide rate among elderly people is actually lower than it was in the 1970s, but because this group of people is a larger percentage of the population, the overall national suicide rate has increased.

28. It is noticeable that the Nordic Welfare State Model (in the table represented by Norway) seems to have as many suicides as the Minimum Welfare State Model of the US. Finland has a particularly high rate of suicides (31.1 for men and 9.6 for women in 2006), Denmark scores 19.2/8.1 (2001), Sweden 19.5/7.1 (2002), and Iceland 16.2/6.1 (2005).

29. Before discussing this any further, the massive agreement regarding the situational description should warn us against simplified conclusions. As Durkheim pointed out, increases in suicide can be triggered by economic bust but also by economic boom. Furthermore, an eventual statistical co-variation is not the same as a causal relationship. Linking data regarding economic upturns/downturns with rates of suicide does not permit any simple conclusions. This observation represents nothing more than a warning against jumping to conclusions when we register co-variations that 'fit' with our theory.

30. Even though some 60 per cent of females are working today, and even though unemployment rates have been rising for both sexes, the psychological impact of being fired is more stressful for men than for women. This is first of all due to the still very traditional gender roles present in Japan where the husband is supposed to be the natural bread winner.

31. The National Police Agency operates with the following eight categories: Family problems, health, economic hardship, job stress, male-female relationships, school, alcoholism and mental illness, and 'other'. According to West (2005: 223), Japan is one of the few countries to maintain such specified data.

32. Compare this with Henshall (2004: 189), who ends up his book on *A history of Japan from stone age to superpower*, by saying: 'As Japan moves on in the new millennium, it is vital that it revives a sense of purpose, and taps once again into appropriate traditional strengths such as its people's ability to achieve and willingness to learn'.

33. Another way the story about Japan as 'the land of the lonely' found its expression was in a report in *Japan Times* on June 24, 2008. The editorial reported that four governmental bodies (the Internal Affairs Ministry, the Health and Welfare Ministry, the National Police Agency, and the Infrastructure and Transport Ministry) had set up a panel of experts to discuss the issue of *dying alone*. According to this article, in Tokyo city almost 5,000 people died alone in 2005, which was an increase of 1000 in three years. As a reaction, the panel called for 'reviving the sense of community among people in general and helping elderly people feel that they have a role to play in the community' (op. cit.).

7   Depression of mind through suppression of crime?

1. In *many* regards the topic I am addressing represents a challenge common to most modern societies. Young (2007: 35) has labelled it 'the chaos of identity' syndrome. This is about ontological insecurity in times of rapid social change, it is about disembeddedness (Giddens, 1991), it is about adapting to a society of 'role making' instead of 'role taking' (Young, 1999), it is about liquid modernity and liquid lives (Bauman, 2000, 2004), it is about respect in a world of inequality (Sennett, 2004). As I have tried to uncover in earlier chapters, events like the Kobe earthquake and the Aum attack, together with disillusionments with the government's ability to safeguard people's basic economic and social security, all add up to a situation of confusion and pessimism. This situation is most certainly not unique to Japan, but, due to reasons I have discussed throughout this book, I do think that Japanese society is particularly hard hit. Loss of hope and confidence for the future, in combination with expectations about perseverance and not bothering other people, represents a very unhealthy cocktail.

2. This does not mean that the 'anti-modernisation' debate was unknown in Japan. In 1970, the *Asahi Shimbun* published a series of articles under the headline 'Down with GNP', which disclosed an interest in discussing social and environmental costs related to the rapid industrial growth. Japan experienced some of the student activism in the late 1960s that Western countries did (opposition to the Vietnam War, renewal of the Japanese-American Security Treaty, and radical students occupying university buildings). Also, in the late 1960s there was a wave of what Tipton (2002: 184) calls 'my home-ism', which emphasised 'more attention to family life as well as buying or remodelling a house' (op. cit.). However, it was only some 20 years

later that 'alternative values' became influential outside very minor groups of people.
3. One group of teachers, in particular, represented for a short period a critical opposition to nationalistic and disciplinary aspects of educational policy in Japan. Also, Japan had its version of student revolt towards the end of the 1970s. However, in spite of these alternative and quite distinct voices, during the last four decades Japanese society has not experienced much critical discussion in the public sphere.
4. Toyama-Bialke (2003: 40), when taking an 'insider perspective' (i.e. the motive) of crime, differentiates between a) the attraction of the deviant action in itself, b) the role the deviant action plays in the adolescent search for identity, and c) the deviant action as a result of dynamics in peer groups.
5. As a further nuancing of this complex topic, it should be noted that in the Ministry's own surveys (WP 2005: 244–249) undertaken among juvenile delinquents, the data show that the self-identification of juvenile delinquents has changed in a positive direction between 1990 and 2005 (they are 'more absorbed in something', and fewer have 'a feeling that they are disliked' or that they 'seldom experience heart-warming moments'). Also, these surveys report that the juvenile delinquents are more satisfied with their friends (between 1990 and 2005), they are more satisfied with their family life, and the rate of juveniles who feel that 'my parents don't care about me' and 'my parents are moody', has been on a slightly declining trend. Only some 8 per cent of these delinquents blame their family for their transgressions, while 53 per cent blame themselves (and 33 per cent blame their friends).
6. In this regard, my argument goes contrary to Roberts and LaFree (2001). In an article entitled 'The role of declining economic stress in explaining Japan's remarkable post-war crime decreases, 1951 to 1997', these scholars maintain that even though 'culture' may be important to understanding the general low crime rate, it is *declining economic stress* (low unemployment rates, income equality, and little poverty) that best explains *decreasing* crime in Japan. Since rapid urbanisation, increasing divorce rates, and increasing female labour force participation (these three dimensions are used as operationalisations of 'culture') have been dominating features in Japanese society in the post-war period, these authors give favourable *economic conditions* as the main role in explaining decreasing crime. In Leonardsen (2003) I have questioned the way these scholars operationalise negative social change measures, especially the use of 'female labour force participation' as an indicator that should predict more crime. Also, I am doubtful of the strong influence Roberts and LaFree assign to economic variables. Other countries (for example Norway) have had a comparatively more positive economic development than Japan, while having a more generous welfare benefit system than this country, but nevertheless have an increasing crime problem. The way I look at it, it is the unique cultural characteristics *in interaction* with a solid economic foundation that have brought crime down in Japan and have made this country unique.
7. Using these two concepts represents a simplification of Allardt's (1975) famous three partite distinction between 'to have', 'to be', and 'to love'.
8. A main argument in Young's (1999) book *The Exclusive Society* is that modern market societies are characterised by being 'palpably unmeritocratic'. Instead of a consistent and predictable relation between input and output, people

experience 'a chaos of reward, where wealth is seemingly distributed willy-nilly without rhyme or reason' (p. 152). As long as people experience injustice in the distribution of rewards and as long as they feel that endurance and good will are not enough to succeed, it is difficult to create a tranquil social order. Yuji' s (2006) *A Nagging Sense of Insecurity* contains much of the same message concerning the Japan of today, especially in relation to how young people's problems regarding employment are overlooked.

9. Vij (2007: 171) says: 'It is under the Koizumi leadership (2001–2006), however, that some of the more publicised attempts at reform and de-regulation have gained ground, leading some critics (Dore 2000; 2001; Itoh 2001) to vigorously denounce the "Americanisation" of the Japanese corporate system and the impending shift from welfare capitalism to "stock exchange capitalism" (Dore 2000) advocated by the reform lobby in Japan as unnecessary, indeed potentially disastrous, for the Japanese economy'. Even though Vij argues that the de-regulation of the labour market is 'by no means as wide-spread as popular perceptions would have it' (p. 188), this de-regulation, he argues, signals an emerging repudiation of Japan's commitment to placing social limits on the market.

10. An illustration of this 'forming of people' is tellingly expressed by Ambaras (2006: 6): 'Social workers, juvenile court officers, and educators also endeavoured to turn homes (*katei*) into "a type of reformatory" by eliminating aspects of family life deemed conducive to delinquency and inculcating new forms of domesticity that responded to the demands of the capitalist economy and the imperial nation-state. "Vocational guidance" experts attempted to manage working-class children's transition from elementary school to the workforce, thereby overcoming what they saw as parents' incompetence, employers' abusive practices, and the dangers that these portended. And as we have seen, the police and other reformers launched repeated campaigns to suppress autonomous youth cultures and restrict young people's access to the rapidly expanding site of commercial pleasure, in the process treating virtually any unauthorised or unsupervised use of free time by young people as a transgressive act in need of correction'.

11. Sugahara has for many years worked for the government on issues relating to young people, and he has been the head of the Statistical Information Division of the Management and Coordination Agency's Statistics Bureau.

12. *Japan Times* reported on May 1, 2009, that more than 2000 new graduates had their job offers cancelled. This was nearly double the previous record of 1077 marked in 1998.

13. Kawai (a clinical psychologist) uses the terrible Kobe murder case (a middle school student killing an elementary school student) as the starting point for a strong critique of the Japanese 'guidance society'. The inability of adults to supervise children's lives was by many taken as one cause of the Kobe murder. To prevent such incidents in the future, measures to keep children from being able to hide from adults were implemented, for example by cutting down thickly growing trees (a strategy Kawai describes as 'truly idiotic'). Kawai comments: 'If you consider matters from the children's point of view, the problem is quite the opposite. Today's Japanese children suffer from too much adult supervision and control, preventing them from developing and branching out freely and playing as children are supposed

to. Cutting down concealing vegetation is a symbolic act that ignores the real problem, which is that children are already pushed to reveal every part of their lives' (Kawai, 1998, p. 10).

14. In the Ministry's reform measures it is formulated that 'we will provide families more opportunities to learn home discipline and to share experience, and promote measures to support and encourage fathers' participation in home discipline' (Kreitz-Sandberg, quoted in Yoder, 2004: 167).

References

ABC News (2009) 'Japan Suicide Hotline Struggling to Cope', 7 January.

Ackermann, P. (2004) 'How Japanese Teenagers Cope: Social Pressures and Personal Responses', in G. Mathews and B. White (eds) *Japan's Changing Generations: Are Young People Creating a New Society?* Abingdon: Routledge.

Adler, F. (1983) *Nations Not Obsessed with Crime,* Littleton: Rothman & Co.

Akane, T. (2002) 'A View of Crime Trends and Victims in Japan', Paper, UNAFEI, 21 May.

Akira, S. (2004) 'An Introduction to This Issue's Special Topic: "Atypical" and "Irregular" Labour in Contemporary Japan', *Social Science Japan Journal,* October, no. 4: 159–160.

Ambaras, D. R. (2006) *Bad Boys,* Berkeley: University of California Press.

Anderson, S. (1996) 'Japan's Welfare Policies on Trial: Cracks in the System?' NIRA Review, http://www.nira.go.jp/publ/review/96spring/ander.html, accessed 28 September.

Anleu, S. L. R. (1999) *Deviance, Conformity and Control,* Melbourne: Longman.

Aoki, H. (2006) *Japan's Underclass: Day Labourers and the Homeless,* Melbourne: Trans Pacific Press.

Asahi Shimbum (2000) 24 August.

Asia Times (2004) 28 August.

Azuma, H. (1986) 'Why Study Child Development in Japan?', in H. Stevenson, H. Azuma, and K. Hakuta (eds) *Child Development and Education in Japan.* N. Y.: W H Freeman and Company.

Balvig, F. (1995) *Kontrollbilleder* [Pictures of Control], Holte: SocPol.

Balvig, F. (1996) *Kriminalitet og social kontroll* [Crime and Social Control], Copenhagen: Columbus.

Balvig, F. and Kyvsgaard, B. (1986) *Kriminalitet og ungdom* [Crime and Youth], Copenhagen: Borgen.

Balvig, F., Homberg, L., and Sørensen, A.-S. (2005) *Ringstedforsøget* [The Ringsted Experiment], Copenhagen: Jurist- og økonomiforbundets forlag.

Barr, C. W. (2000) 'Young Japanese Retreat to Life of Seclusion', *Christian Science Monitor,* vol. 92, no. 186.

Barry, M. (2006) *Youth Offending in Transition: The Search for Social Recognition,* Abingdon: Routledge.

Bauman, Z. (2000) *Liquid Modernity,* Cambridge: Polity Press.

Bauman, Z. (2001) *Community: Seeking Safety in an Insecure World,* Cambridge: Polity Press.

Bauman, Z. (2004) *Wasted Lives: Modernity and Its Outcasts,* Cambridge: Polity Press.

Bauman, Z. (2005) *Liquid Life,* Cambridge: Polity Press.

Bauman, Z. (2006) *Liquid Fear,* Cambridge: Polity Press.

Bayley, D. H. (1991) *Forces of Order. Policing Modern Japan,* Berkeley: University of California Press.

Beam, C. (2007) 'Why So Many Suicides in Japan?' *Slate*, 31 May, http://www.slate.com/toolbar.aspx?action=print&id=2167295, accessed 17 March 2009.

Beauchamp, E. (1991) *Windows on Japanese Education*, Westport: Greenwood Press.

Beck, U. (1986) *Risk Society: Towards a New Modernity*, London: Sage Publications.

Becker, C. B. (1988) 'Report from Japan: Causes and Controls of Crime in Japan', *Journal of Criminal Justice*, vol. 16: 425–435.

Becker, H. S. (1963) *Outsiders: Studies in the Sociology of Deviance*. N.Y.: The Free Press.

Becker, H. S. (1967) 'Whose Side Are We On?' *Social Problems*, vol. 14, no. 3: 239–247.

Bellah, R. N. (2003) *Imagining Japan: The Japanese Tradition and Its Modern Interpretation*, Berkeley: University of California Press.

Ben-Ari, E. (1997) *Japanese Childcare:. An Interpretative Study of Culture and Organization*, London: Kegan Paul.

Ben-Ari, E., Moeran, B., and Valentine, J. (eds) (1990) *Unwrapping Japan*. Manchester: Manchester University Press.

Benedict, R. (1967) *The Chrysanthemum and the Sword*, London: Routledge & Kegan Paul.

Berger, P. L. (1987) *The Capitalist Revolution: Fifty Propositions about Prosperity, Equality, and Liberty*, Aldershot: Gower.

Best, J. (1999) *Random Violence: How We Talk About New Crimes and New Victims*, Berkeley: University of California Press.

Bigsten, A. (2004) 'Can Japan Make a Comeback?', Paper, Department of Economics, Gøteborg University, 8 August.

Bookock, S. (1989) 'Controlled Diversity: An Overview of the Japanese Preschool System', *Journal of Japanese Studies*, vol. 15, no. 1: 41–68.

Borovoy, A. (2008) 'Japan's Hidden Youths: Mainstreaming the Emotionally Distressed in Japan', *Culture, Medicine and Psychiatry*, vol. 32, no. 4: 552–576.

Braithwaite, J. (1989) *Crime, Shame and Re-integration*, Cambridge: Cambridge University Press.

Braithwaite, J. (1991) 'Poverty, Power, White-Collar Crime and the Paradoxes of Criminological Theory', *The Australian and New Zealand Journal of Criminology*, no. 24, vol. 91: 40–58.

Braithwaite, J. (1993) 'Shame and Modernity', *The British Journal of Criminology*, vol. 33, no. 1: 1–18.

Braun, S. (2008) 'Feature. Open House', http://metropolis.co.jp/tokyofeaturesstories/386/tokyofeaturestoriesinc.htm, accessed 15 April 2008.

Bremner, B. (2002) 'Business Suicides: Japan's Death Trap', *Business Week Online*, http://www.businessweek.com/magazinw/content/02_22/b3785141.htm?%24se, accessed 16 March 2004.

Brunelli, C. R. (2003) 'Heaven for a Cop? Policing a High(er) Crime Society', Paper, Department of Government, Harvard University, Comparative Politics Research Workshop, 8 October.

Burns, C. (2005) *Sexual Violence and the Law in Japan*, London: RoutledgeCurzon.

Buruma, I. (2009) 'Escape in Japan', *The New York Review*, 11 June.

Business Report (2008), 9 February.

Business Week (1998), 17 August.

Business Week Online (2002), 3 June.

Caranci, J. (2007) 'Divorce, Japanese Style', *Japan Zone*, http://www.japan-zone. com/features/007_divorce_japanese_style_1.shtlml, accessed 11 December 2007.

Cave, P. (2001) 'Educational Reform in Japan in the 1990s: "Individuality" and Other Uncertainties', *Comparative Education*, vol. 37, no. 2: 173–191.

Chen, J., Choi, Y. J., and Sawada, Y. (2009) 'How is Suicide Different in Japan'? *Japan and the World Economy*, no. 21: 140–150.

Chiavacci, D. (2005) 'Transition from University to Work under Transformation: The Changing Role of Institutional and Alumni Networks in Contemporary Japan', *Social Science Japan Journal*, vol. 8, no. 1: 19–41.

Christie, N. (2004) *A Suitable Amount of Crime*, London: Routledge.

Clammer, J. (2000) 'Received Dreams: Consumer Capitalism, Social Process, and the Management of the Emotions in Contemporary Japan', in J. S. Eades, T. Gill, and H. Befu (eds) *Globalization and Social Change in Contemporary Japan*, Melbourne: Trans Pacific Press.

Clarke-Stewart, A. and Brentano, C. (2006) *Divorce: Causes and Consequences*, New Haven: Yale University Press.

Cohen, A. K. (1955) *Delinquent Boys: The Culture of the Gang*, N. Y.: The Free Press.

Cohen, A. P. (1989) *The Symbolic Construction of Community*, London: Routledge.

Cohen, S. (1967) 'Mods, Rockers, and the Rest: Community Reactions to Juvenile Delinquency', *Howard Journal*, vol. 12, no. 2: 121–130.

Cohen, S. (1973) *Folk Devils and Moral Panics*, St Albans: Paladin.

Cooley, C. H. (1964) *Human Nature and the Social Order*, N.Y.: Schocken Books.

Cooley, C. H. (1983) *Social Organization: a Study of the Larger Mind*, New Brunswick, N. J.: Transaction Books.

Currie, E. (1998) 'Crime and Market Society: Lessons From the United States', in P. Walton and J. Young (eds) *The New Criminology Revisited*, Basingstoke: MacMillan Press.

Currie, E. (2004) *The Road to Whatever*, N.Y.: Metropolitan Books.

Curtin, J. S. (2002) *'The Current State of Divorce in Japan: A Record Number of Marital Dissolutions in 2001'*, 7 October, http://www.glocom.org/special_topics/social_ trends/20021007_trends_s10/index.html, accessed 11 January, 2009.

Curtin, J. S. (2003a) *'Family Trends: Part Two – Poor Families Suffer As the Japanese Economy Continues to Deteriorate'*, 24 March, *http://www.glocom.org/special_ topics/social_trends/20030324_trends_s30/index.html*, accessed 11 January 2009.

Curtin, J. S. (2003b) 'Suicide in Japan: Part One – the Suicide Crisis Amongst Middle-Aged Men', 10 february, *http://www.glocom.org/special_topics/social_ trends/20030324_trends_s30/index.html*, accessed 13 May, 2008.

Curtin, J. S. (2004a) 'Suicide in Japan: Part Nine – Suicides Reach Record High in 2003', 5 August, http://www.glocom.org/special_topics/social_ trends/20040210_trends_s69/index.html, accessed 1 November 2009

Curtin, J. S. (2004b) 'Suicide in Japan: Part 10 – Youth Rural Suicides on the Rise', 13 august. http://www.glocom.org/special_topics/social_trends/20040210_ trends_s69/index.html, accessed 1 November 2009.

Curtin, J. S. (2004c) 'Suicide in Japan: Part 12 – Factors Influencing the Increasing Suicide Rate', 20 August. http://www.glocom.org/special_topics/social_trends/20040820_trends_s80/index.html, accessed 1 November 2009.

Curtin, J. S. (2004d) 'Suicide in Japan: Part 15 – An introduction to Internet Suicide', 20 October, http://www.glocom.org/special_topics/social_trends/20041020_trends_s69/index.html, accessed 13 May 2008.

Curtin, J. S. (2004e) 'Attitudes towards the Police in Contemporary Japan – Part Three: Scandals Undermine Public Confidence in the Police'. September 21, http://www.glocom.org/special_topics/social_trends/20040921_trends_s86/index.html, accessed December 8, 2005.

Curtin, J. S. (2005) 'Poor Families in Today's Japan: Part Six – Surge in the Number of Poor Japanese Families'. 25 February http://www.glocom.org/special_topics/social_trends/20050225_trends_s99/index.html, accessed 3 September 2007.

Dahrendorf, R. (1985) *Law and Order,* London: Stevens & Sons.

Dale, P. N. (1986) *The Myth of Japanese Uniqueness*, London/Oxford: Croom Helm and Nissan Institute for Japanese Studies, University of Oxford.

Davidsen, T. H. (2006) 'Hikikomori', *Weekend avisen* [The Weekend Newspaper], June 16–22.

De Mente, B. (1992) *Discovering Cultural Japan. A Guide to Appreciating and Experiencing the Real Japan,* Lincolnwood: Passport Books.

Desapriya, E. B. R. and Nobutada, I. (2002) 'Stigma of Mental Illness in Japan', *The Lancet,* vol. 359, page 1866 25 May.

Doi, T. (1976) *The Anatomy of Dependence*, Tokyo: Kodansha International.

Doi, T. (1985) *The Anatomy of Self,* Tokyo: Kodansha International.

Dore, R. (1986) *Flexible Rigidities: Industrial Policy and Structural Adjustment in the Japanese Economy 1970–80,* London: The Athlone Press.

Dore, R. (1987) *Taking Japan Seriously: A Confucian Perspective on Leading Economic Issues,* London: The Athlone Press.

Durkheim, E. (1952) *Suicide: A Study in Sociology*, London: Routledge & Kegan Paul.

Durkheim, E. (1982) *The Rules of Sociological Method: And Selected Texts on Sociology and Its Method,* London: Macmillan.

Dziesinski, M. J. (2003) *'Hikikomori,* Investigations into the Phenomenon of Acute Social Withdrawal in Contemporary Japan', Paper: University of Hawai'I Manoa. Honolulu: Spring.

Eades, J. (2005) 'Introduction: Globalization and Social Change in Contemporary Japan', in J. Eades,T. Gill, and H. Befu (eds) *Globalization and Social Change in Contemporary Japan*. Melbourne: Trans Pacific Press.

Eades, J. S., Gill, T., and Harumi, B. (eds) (2005) *Globalization and Social change in Contemporary Japan,* Melbourne: Trans Pacific Press.

EAMM (1996) *The Japanese Experience in Social Security,* East Asian Ministerial Meeting on Caring Societies, 5 December.

Economic and Research Council (undated) 'Youth, Citizenship and Social Change'. Research Program, http://www.tsa.uk.com/research/projects_completed/esrc.html, accessed 12 April 2006.

Erbe, A. (2003) 'Youth in Crisis: Public Perceptions and Discourse on Deviance and Juvenile Problem Behavior in Japan', in G. Foljanty-Jost (ed.) *Juvenile Delinquency in Japan: Reconsidering the 'Crisis'*, Leiden: Brill.

Erikson, K. (1966) *Wayward Puritans: A Study in the Sociology of Deviance*. N.Y.: Macmillan.

Esping-Andersen, G. (1990) *The Three Worlds of Welfare Capitalism*, Cambridge: Polity Press.

Esping-Andersen, G. (1997) 'Hybrid or Unique? The Japanese Welfare State Between Europe and America', *Journal of European Social Policy*, vol. 7, no 3: 179–189.

Etzioni, A. (1994) *The Spirit of Community*, N. Y.: Touchstone.

Evans, R. (1977) 'Changing Labour Markets and Criminal Behaviour in Japan', *Journal of Asian Studies*, vol. 36, no. 3: 477–489.

Feeley, M. M. (2007) 'Three Hypothesis about Crime Developments in Japan and the West', Paper presented at the Second Anglo-Japanese Symposium on Criminal Justice and Corrections (March 3 and 4), Ryokoku University, Kyoto.

Felson, M. (2002) *Crime and Everyday Life*, Thousand Oakes, California: Sage.

Fenwick, C. R. (1985) 'Culture, Philosophy and Crime: The Japanese Experience', *International Journal of Comparative and Applied Criminal Justice*, vol. 9, no. 1: 67–81.

Fenwick, C. R. (2005) 'Youth Crime and Crime Control in Contemporary Japan', in C. Summer (ed.) *The Blackwell Companion to Criminology*, Malden: Blackwell Publishing Ltd.

Field, N (1996) 'Foreword'. in McCormack, G (1996) *The Emptiness of Japanese Affluence*, N. Y.: M E Sharp.

Finch, A. (2000) 'Criminal Statistics in Japan: The White Paper on Crime, Hanzai Hakusho and Hanzai Tokeisho', *Social Science Japan Journal*, vol. 3, no. 2: 237–249.

Finch, A. (2001) 'Homicide in Contemporary Japan', *British Journal of Criminology*, vol. 41, no. 2: 219–235.

Foljanty-Jost, G. (ed.) (2003) *Juvenile Delinquency in Japan: Reconsidering the 'Crisis'*, Leiden: Brill.

Foljanty-Jost, G. (ed.) (2004) *Japan in the 1990s: Crisis as an Impetus for Change*, Münster: LIT Verlag.

Foljanty-Jost, G. and Metzler, M. (2003) 'Juvenile Delinquency in Japan: A Self-preventing Prophecy', *Social Science Japan*, February, no. 25: 39–43.

Foote, D. H. (1992) 'The Benevolent Paternalism of Japanese Criminal Justice', *California Law Review*, vol. 80, no. 2: 317–390.

Foster, J. (2002) '"People Pieces": The Neglected but Essential Elements of Community Crime Prevention', in G. Hughes and A. Edwards (eds) *Crime Control and Community. The New Politics of Public Safety*, Cullompton, Devon: Willan Publishing.

Fujita, H. (2003) 'The Reform of the Japanese Education System as an Answer to Delinquency', in G. Foljanty-Jost (ed.) *Juvenile Delinquency in Japan: Reconsidering the 'Crisis'*, Leiden: Brill

Fujita, Y., Inoue, K., and Tanii, H. (2008) 'Present and Future Subjects of Suicide-related Reports in Japan', *West Indian Medical Journal*, vol. 57, no. 2: 184.

Fukue, N. (2009) 'Single moms fight for kids' futures', *Japan Times*, July 2.

Fukuyama, F. (1995) *Trust*, N. Y.: The Free Press.

Fukuyama, F. (2000) *The Great Disruption*, London: Profile books.

Furlong, A. (2008) 'The Japanese Hikikomori Phenomenon', *The Sociological Review*, vol. 56, no. 2: 309–325.

Fushimi, M., Sugawara, J., and Saito, S. (2006) 'Comparison of Completed and Attempted Suicide in Akita, Japan'. *Psychiatry and Clinical Neurosciences,* June, vol. 60, no. 3: 289–295.

Garland, D. (1999) '"Governmentality" and the Problem of Crime', in R. Smandych (ed.) *Governable Places, Readings on Governmentality and Crime Control,* Aldershot: Ashgate.

Garland, D. (2001) *The Culture of Control: Crime and Social Order in Contemporary Society,* Chicago: The University of Chicago Press.

Garon, S. (1997) *Moulding Japanese Minds: The State in Everyday Life,* Princeton: Princeton University Press.

Genda, Y. (2000) 'Don't Blame the Unmarried Breed', *Japan Echo,* vol. 27, no. 3: 54–56.

Genda, Y. (2005) *A Nagging Sense of Job Insecurity: The New Reality Facing Japanese Youth,* Tokyo: I-House Press.

Gibran, K. (1996) *The Prophet,* Hertfordshire: Wordsworth Editions Ltd.

Giddens, A. (1991) *Modernity and Self-Identity: Self and Society in the Late Modern Age,* Cambridge: Polity Press.

Goffman, E. (1959) *The Presentation of Self in Everyday Life,* N.Y.: Doubleday Anchor Books.

Gold, R. L. (1982) 'Commentary', *Pacific Sociological Review,* vol. 25, no. 3: 349–357.

Goldman, A. (1994) 'The Centrality of Ningensei to Japanese Negotiating and Interpersonal Relationships: Implications for U.S.- Japanese Communication', *International Journal of Intercultural Relations,* vol. 18, no. 1: 29–54.

Goode, E. and Ben-Yehuda, N. (1999) Moral Panics. The Social Construction of Deviance (in italics). Oxford: Blackwell.

Goodman, R. (1998) 'The "Japanese-Style Welfare State" and the Delivery of Personal Social Services', in R. Goodman, G. White, and H. Kwon (eds) *The East Asian Welfare Model: Welfare Orientalism and the State,* London: Routledge.

Goodman, R. (2000) *Children of the Japanese State: The Changing Role of Child Protection Institutions in Contemporary Japan,* Oxford: Oxford University Press.

Goodman, R. (ed.) (2002) *Family and Social Policy in Japan: Anthropological Approaches,* Cambridge: Cambridge University Press.

Goto, H. (2004) 'Crime Anxieties Bred by Neglect', *Japan Echo,* vol. 31, no. 4: 24–28.

Gottfredson, M. R. and Hirschi, T. (1990) *A General Theory of Crime,* Stanford, CA: Stanford University Press.

Gould, A. (1993) *Capitalist Welfare Systems: A Comparison of Japan, Britain and Sweden,* London: Longman.

Grover, C. (2008) *Crime and Inequality,* Cullompton, Devon: Willan Publishing.

Haley, J. (1998) 'Apology and Pardon: Learning from Japan', *American Behavioral Scientist,* vol. 41, no. 6: 842–867.

Hamai, K., Ellis, T., Lewis, C. and Williamson, T. (2003) 'Rising Crime in Japan? Moral Panic and Getting Tough Policy', Paper presented at ASC annual Meeting in Denver, November 18–22.

Hamai, K. and Ellis, T. (2006) 'Crime and Criminal Justice in Modern Japan', *International Journal of the Sociology of Law,* vol. 34, no. 3: 157–178.

Hamai, K. and Ellis, T. (2008a) 'Genbatsuka: Growing Penal Populism and the Changing Role of Public Prosecutors in Japan', *Japanese Journal of Sociological Criminology,* no. 33: 67–91.

Hamai, K. and Ellis, T. (2008b) 'Japanese Criminal Justice: Was Re-integrative Shaming a Chimera?', *Punishment and Society*, vol. 10, no. 1: 25–46.

Hattori, Y. (2005) 'Social Withdrawal in Japanese Youth: A Case Study of Thirty-Five Hikikomori Clients', *Journal of Trauma Practice*, vol. 4, no. 3–4: 181–201.

Hayashi, C. (1988) 'The National Character in Transition', *Japan Echo*, vol. 15, Special Issue: 7–11.

Hellesnes, J. (1975) *Sosialisering og kontroll* [Socialisation and Control], Oslo: Gyldendal Norsk Forlag.

Hendry, J. (1986) 'Kindergartens and the Transition from Home to School Education', *Comparative Education*, vol. 22, no. 1: 53–58.

Hendry, J. (1993) *Wrapping Culture: Politeness, Presentation and Power in Japan and Other Societies*. Oxford: Clarendon Press.

Hendry, J. (1999) *An Anthropologist in Japan*, London: Routledge.

Henshall, K. G. (1996) *A History of Japan from Stone Age to Superpower*, Basingstoke: Palgrave Macmillan.

Henshall, K. G. (1999) *Dimensions of Japanese Society*, Basingstoke: MacMillan Press.

Herbert, W. (2005) 'The Yakuza and the Law', in J. Eades, T. Gill, and H. Befu (eds) *Globalization and Social Change in Contemporary Japan*, Melbourne: Trans Pacific Press.

Hirata, K. (2002) *Civil Society in Japan: The Growing Role of NGOs in Tokyo's Aid and Development Policy*, Basingstoke: Palgrave Macmillan.

Holloway, S. D. (2000) *Contested Childhood: Diversity and Change in Japanese Preschools*, N.Y.: Routledge.

Honda, Y. (2004) 'The Formation and Transformation of the Japanese System of Transition from School to Work', *Social Science Japan Journal*, vol. 7, no. 1: 103–115.

Honda, Y. (2006) 'The Transformation of the Youth Labour Market and the Reemergence of the Issue of Educational Credentials', *Social Science Japan*, October, no. 35: 3–6.

Hood, C. P. (2001) *Japanese Education Reform: Nakasone's Legacy*, London: Routledge.

Hook, G. and Hiroko, T. (2007) ' "Self-responsibility" and the Nature of the Postwar Japanese State: Risk Through the Looking Glass', *Journal of Japanese Studies*, vol. 33, no. 1: 93–123.

Hosoi, Y. and Nishimura, H. (1999) 'The Role of Apology in the Japanese Criminal Justice System', *Conference Paper*, Tokyo University/Kokushikan University.

Hougaard, B. (2005) *Curlingforeldre og servicebarn: en handbok i barneoppdragelse* [Curling Parents and Service Children: A Handbook in Raising Children], Oslo: Gyldendal Akademisk.

Hsu F. L. K. (1975) *Iemoto: The Heart of Japan*, N. Y.: Halsted Press.

Hughes, G. (1996) 'Communitarism and Law and Order', *Critical Social Policy*, vol. 16, no. 4: 17–41.

Hughes, G. (2007) *The Politics of Crime and Community*. Basingstoke: Palgrave MacMillan.

Hughes, G. and Edwards, A. (ed.) (2002) *Crime Control and Community. The New Politics of Public Safety*, Cullompton, Devon: Willan Publishing

Huus, K. (2003) 'Japan's Chilling Internet Suicide Pacts. New Trend Highlights Social Problems, Mental Health Crisis' '. *MSNBC.com*. http://www.msnbc.msn,.com/id/33404456/, accessed 17 March 2009.

Iga, M. (1986) *The Thorn in the Chrysanthemum: Suicide and Economic Success in Modern Japan,* Berkeley: University of California Press.

Inoue, K., Hisahis, T., Hisanobu, K., Masayuki, N., Yuji, O., and Tatsushige, F. (2008) 'Suicide among Younger Age Groups in Japan', *The American Journal of Forensic Medicine and Pathology,* vol. 29, no. 4: 384–385.

Ishida, H. (2006) 'The Persistence of Social Inequality in Postwar Japan'. *Social Science Japan,* vol. 35, October.

Ishikida, M. Y. (2005) *Japanese Education in the 21st Century,* N. Y.: iUniverse.

Ituralde, M. (2007) 'Punishment and Authoritarian Liberalism: The Politics of Emergency Criminal Justice in Colombia'. Paper presented at the annual meeting of the Law and Society Association, TBA, Germany, http://www.allacademic.com/meta/p_mla_apa_research_citation/1/7/6/8/3/p176834_insex.html, accessed 22 August 2009.

Ives, C. (2005) 'What's Compassion Got to Do with It? Determinants of Zen Social Ethics in Japan', *Journal of Buddhist Ethics,* vol. 2: 37–61.

Iwao, S. (2004) 'Law Enforcement on Trial', *Japan Echo,* vol. 31, no. 4: 12–13.

Japan Echo (1998) 'Crisis in the Schools: A Colloquium of the Group of Pro Teachers', vol. 25, no. 3, June.

Japan Echo (2005) 'Japan's New Misfits', vol. 32, no. 1, February.

Japan Insight 'Being Young. Drugs', http://jin.jcic.0r.jp/insight/html/focus07/being_young/drugs.html, accessed 25 February 2003.

Johnson, D. T. (2002) *The Japanese Way of Justice: Prosecuting Crime in Japan.* Oxford: Oxford University Press.

Johnson, D. T. (2003) 'Above the Law? Police Integrity in Japan', *Social Science Japan Journal,* vol. 6, no. 1: 19–37.

Johnson, D. T. (2006) 'The Vanishing Killer: Japan's Postwar Homicide Decline', *Social Science Japan Journal,* vol. 9, no. 1: 73–90.

Johnson, D. T. (2007) 'Trends in Crimes Rates in Postwar Japan', Book review, *International Criminal Justice Law,* no. 17: 153.

Johnson, D. T. (2008) 'Japanese Punishment in Comparative Perspective', *Japanese Journal of Sociological Criminology,* no. 33: 20–39.

Johnson, E. H. (1996) *Japanese Corrections: Managing Convicted Offenders in an Orderly Society,* Carbondale: Southern Illinois University Press.

Jolivet, M. (1993) *Japan: The Childless Society? The Crisis of Motherhood,* London: Routledge.

Kadowaki, A. (2003) 'Changes in Values and Life Orientation among Japanese Youth', in G. Foljanty-Jost (ed.) *Juvenile Delinquency in Japan: Reconsidering the 'Crisis',* Leiden: Brill.

Kageyama, J. (2000) 'Juvenile Crime and Its Psychology', Tokyo Institute of Technology, http://www.fpcj.jp/e/gyouji/br/2000/000614.html, accessed 20 November 2006.

Kageyama, Y. (2003a) 'Loan Sharks Feasting on Ballooning Number of People Deep in Debt', *The Japan Times,* February 14.

Kageyama, Y. (2003b) 'Debts, Loan Sharks and Culture of Shame a Recipe for Suicide', *Japan Times,* March 13.

Kaji, N. (2000) 'Call for a Return to Popular Morality', *Japan Echo,* vol. 27, no. 3: 57–59.

Kalland, A. (1986) *Japan bak fasaden* [Japan behind the Facade], Oslo: Cappelen.

Kambayashi, T. (2004) 'Japan's Homeless Face Ageism', *The Christian Science Monitor,* 18 October.

Kaneko, S (2006) 'Japan's "Socially Withdrawn Youths" and Time Constraints in Japanese Society: Management and Conceptualization of Time in a Support Group for "Hikikomori"', *Time and Society*, vol. 15, no. 2/3: 233–249.

Kaplan, M., Kusano, A., Tsuji, I., and Hisamichi, S. (1998) *Intergenerational Programs: Support for Children, Youth, and Elders in Japan*, Albany: State University of New York Press.

Kawai, H. (1998) 'Charged-up Children: What Can We Do?', *Japan Echo*, vol. 25, no. 3.

Kawakami, R. (1998) 'A Teacher's Diary', *Japan Echo*, vol. 25, no. 1: 48–53.

Kawanishi, Y. (2006) 'On Karo-Jisatsu (Suicide by Overwork): Why Do Japanese Workers Work Themselves to Death?', http://www.allacademic.com/meta/p102860_index.html, accessed 13 December 2007.

Kerr, A. (2001) *Dogs and Demons: The Fall of Modern Japan*, London: Penguin Books.

Ketano, S. (2006) 'Japan's "Socially Withdrawn Youths" and Time Constraints in Japanese Society', *Time and Society*, vol. 15, no. 2–3: 233–249.

Kingston, J. (2004) *Japan's Quiet Transformation: Social Change and Civil Society in the Twenty-First Century*, London: RoutledgeCurzon.

Kisala, R. J. and Mullins, M. R. (eds) (2001) *Religion and Social Crisis in Japan: Understanding Japanese Society Through the Aum Affair*. Basingstoke: Palgrave.

Kopel, D. B. (1993) 'Japanese Gun Control', *Asia Pacific Law Review*: 26–52, http://www.guncite.com/journals/dkjgc.html, accessed 10 December 2003.

Kotani, S. (2004) 'Why are Japanese Youth So Passive?', in G. Mathews and B. White (eds) *Japan's Changing Generations: Are Young People Creating a New Society?* Abingdon: Routledge.

Krysinska, D. (2006) ' "Hikikomori" in Japan: Discourses of Media and Scholars: Multicausal Explanations of the Phenomenon'. Thesis, submitted to the Graduate Faculty of Arts and Sciences, University of Pittsburg.

Kyvsgaard, B. (1992) *Ny ungdom? Om familie, skole, fritid, lovlydighed og kriminalitet* [A New Youth Generation? On Family, School, Leisure Time, Law-Abidingness and Crime], Copenhagen: Jurist- og Økonomforbundets Forlag.

Larimer, T. (2000) 'Natural-Born Killers?', *Time*, August 28.

Lasch, C. (1979a) *The Culture of Narcissism – American Life in an Age of Diminishing Expectations*. N. Y.: Warner.

Lasch, C. (1979b) *Haven in a Heartless World: The Family Besieged*, N.Y.: Basic Books.

Layard, R. (2005) *Happiness: Lessons from a New Science*, N.Y.: Penguin Press.

Lea, J. (2002) *Crime and Modernity*, London: Sage Publications.

Lea, J. (2003) *Crime and Modernity. Continuities in Left Realist Criminology*, London: Sage Publications.

Leonardsen, D. (1993) *Rammer for velferdspolitikken* [Restrictions for welfare politics], Skrifter, ODH, No. 79.

Leonardsen, D. (2002) 'The Impossible Case of Japan', *Australian and New Zealand Journal of Criminology*, vol. 35, no. 2: 203–229.

Leonardsen, D. (2003) 'Declining Crime in Post-War Japan: Cultural or Economic Explanations?'. Unpublished paper.

Leonardsen, D. (2004) *Japan as a Low-Crime Nation,* Basingstoke: Palgrave Macmillan.

Leonardsen, D. (2006) 'Crime in Japan: Paradise Lost?' *Journal of Scandinavian Studies in Criminology and Crime Prevention,* vol. 7: 185–210.

LeTendre, G. K. (2000) *Learning to be Adolescent. Growing up in US and Japanese Middle Schools,* London: Yale University Press.

Levine, D. N. (1985) *The Flight From Ambiguity: Essays in Social and Cultural Theory,* Chicago: University of Chicago Press

Levitas, R. (1986) 'Competition and Compliance: The Utopias of the New Right', in R. Levitas (ed.) *The Ideology of the New Right.* Cambridge: Polity Press.

MacIntyre, A. (1984) *After Virtue: A Study in Moral Theory,* Notre Dame: University of Notre Dame Press.

Mainichi Daily News, 7 July 2000, 24 September 2000, 25 July 2003.

Mainichi Shimbun (2002), August 1.

Marr, M. (2003) 'The Homeless, Contemporary Society, and the Welfare State', Book review, *Social Science Japan Journal,* vol. 6, no. 2: 300–304.

Masahiro, T. (1996) 'Economic Structure and Crime: The Case of Japan', *Journal of Socio-Economics,* vol. 25, no. 4: 497–515.

Mathews, G. (2004) 'Seeking a Career, Finding a Job. How Young People Enter and Resist the Japanese World of Work', in G. Mathews and B. White (eds) *Japan's Changing Generations: Are Young People Creating a New Society?* Abingdon: Routledge.

Mathews, J. (2008) 'Suicide and the Japanese Media', Discussion Paper 7, http://www.japanesestudies.org.uk/discussionpapers/2008/Mathews.html, accessed 17 March , 2009.

Mathews, G. and White, B. (2004) 'Introduction: Changing Generation in Japan Today', in G. Mathews and B. White (eds) *Japan's Changing Generations: Are Young People Creating a New Society?* Abingdon: Routledge.

McCargo, D. (2004) *Contemporary Japan,* Basingstoke: Palgrave Macmillan.

McCormack, G. (1996) *The Emptiness of Japanese Affluence,* N. Y.: M E Sharpe.

McCurry, J. (2003) 'Loan Sharks Fuel Japan's Suicide Rise', *The Observer,* August, 2003.

McCurry, J. (2008) 'Japan to Rethink Suicide-prevention Policies', *The Lancet,* vol. 371, June 21: 2071.

McGregor, R. (1996) *Japan Swings,* St Leonards: Allen & Unwin.

McVeigh, B. J. (1997) *Life in a Japanese Women's College,* London: Routledge.

McVeigh, B. J. (2000) *Wearing Ideology: State, Schooling and Self-Preservation in Japan,* Oxford: Berg.

McVeigh, B. J. (2004) ' "Guiding" Japan's University Students through the Generation Gap', in G. Mathews and B. White (eds) *Japan's Changing Generations: Are Young People Creating a New Society?* Abingdon: Routledge.

Mead, G. H. (1934) *Mind, Self and Society: From the Standpoint of a Social Behaviorist,* Chicago: Chicago University Press.

Merton, R. K. (1968) *Social Theory and Social Structure,* N.Y.: The Free Press.

Mieko, Y. (1999) 'Domestic Violence: Japan's "Hidden Crime" ', *Japan Quarterly,* vol. 46, no. 3: 76–82.

Miller, A. S. and Kanazawa, S. (2000) *Order by Accident: The Origins and Consequences of Conformity in Contemporary Japan,* Boulder: Westview Press.

Mills, C. W. (1970) *The Sociological Imagination*, Harmondsworth: Penguin Books.

Miyanaga, K. (1991) *The Creative Edge: Emerging Individualism in Japan*, New Brunswick: Transaction Publishers.

Miyazawa, S. (2008) 'The Politics of Increasing Punitiveness and the Rising Populism in Japanese Criminal Justice Policy', *Punishment and Society*, vol. 10, no. 47: 47–77.

Möhwald, U. (2005) 'Trends in Value Change in Contemporary Japan', in J. S. Eades, T. Gill, and H. Befu (eds) *Globalization and Social Change in Contemporary Japan*. Melbourne: Trans Pacific Press.

Morioka, K. (1986) 'Privatization of Family Life in Japan', in H. Stevenson, H. Azuma, and K. Hakuta *Child Development and Education in Japan*, N.Y.: W. H. Freeman and Company.

Morishima, M. (2000) *Japan at a Deadlock*, Basingstoke: Macmillan Press/ St. Martin's Press.

Moss, G. (1997) 'Explaining the Absence of Violent Crime among the Semai of Malaysia: Is Criminological Theory up to the Task?', *Journal of Criminal Justice*, vol. 25, no. 3: 177–194.

Mouer, R. E. and Sugimoto, Y. (1986) *Images of Japanese Society: A Study in the Social Construction of Reality*, London: Kegan Paul International.

Muncie, E. (1999) *Youth and Crime: A Critical Perspective*, London: Sage.

Murray, C. (1984) *Losing Ground*, N. Y.: Basic Books.

Murray, C. (1990) *The Emerging British Underclass*, London: Institute of Economic Affairs.

Nakagawa, J. (1999) 'An Introduction to This Issue's Special Topic: Deregulation and the Japanese Economy', *Social Science Japan Journal*, vol. 2, no. 1: 1–2.

Nakane, C. (1970) *Japanese Society*, Berkeley: University of California Press.

Nakao, N. and Takeuchi, T. (2006) 'The Suicide Epidemic in Japan and Strategies of Depression Screening for its Prevention', *Bulletin of the World Health Organization*, June, vol. 86, no. 6: 492–493.

National Police Academy (undated) (ed.) *Crimes in Japan in 2006*, Alumni Association for National Police Academy, Tokyo.

National Police Agency (undated) *White Paper on Police 2005*, Tokyo.

National Police Agency (2007) 'Situation of Juvenile Delinquency in Japan in 2006', Unpublished note, March.

Nesse, R. M. (1999) 'The Evolution of Hope and Despair', *Social Research*, vol. 66, no. 2: 429–469.

Nobuyuki, K. (2000) 'Call for a Return to Popular Morality', *Japan Echo*, vol. 27. no. 3: 57–59.

Nutley, S. and Loveday, B. (2005) 'Criminal Justice – Tensions and Challenges', *Public Money and Management*, vol. 25, no. 5: 263–265.

Ogino,T. (2004) 'Managing Categorization and Social Withdrawal in Japan: Rehabilitation Process in a Private Support Group for Hikikomorians', *International Journal of Japanese Sociology*, no. 13: 120–133.

Okano, K. and Tsuchiya, M. (1999) *Education in Contemporary Japan: Inequality and Diversity*, Cambridge: Cambridge University Press.

Ono, H. (2006) 'Divorce in Japan: Why It Happens, Why It Doesn't', *EIJS Working Paper Series*, no. 201.

Ono, Y., Tanaka, E. and Sakamato, S. (2002) 'A New Psychological Approach for Dealing with Major Depressive Disorder in Japan: Preventing Suicide Through

Psychoeducation and Psychotherapy', in T. Okuma, S. Kanba, and Y. Inoue (eds) *Recent Advances in the Research of Affective Disorder in Japan*, Amsterdam: Elsevier.

Osawa, M. (2001) 'People in Irregular Modes of Employment: Are They Really Not Subject to Discrimination?', *Social Science Japan Journal*, vol. 4, no. 2: 183–199.

Ôta, T. (2004) 'Public Safety in Today's Japan', *Japan Echo*, no. 4, vol. 31: 20–23.

Ozawa-de Silva, C. (2008) 'Too Lonely to Die Alone: Internet Suicide Pacts and Existential Suffering in Japan', *Culture, Medicine and Psychiatry*, vol. 32, no. 4: 516–551.

Park, W. K. (2006) *Trends in Crime Rates in Postwar Japan: A Structural Perspective*, Law and Political Science Series of the University of Kitakyushu, 20, Shinzansha.

Petrun, E. (2007) *CBS News*, 12 July.

Pinguet, M. (1993) *Voluntary Death in Japan*, Cambridge: Polity Press.

Piven, F. F. and Cloward, R. A. (1993) *Regulating the Poor: The Functions of Public Welfare*, N. Y.: Vintage Books.

Police Policy Research Center/National Police Academy of Japan (eds) (2003) 'Action Plan to Create A Crime-Resistant Society: To Re-Establish Japan as "The Safest Country in the World"', Ministerial Meeting Concerning Measures against Crime, December.

Police Policy Research Center/National Police Academy of Japan (ed.) (undated) *Guidelines of Police Policy in Japan*, Alumni Association for National Police Academy.

Pontell, H. N. and Geis, G. (2007) 'Black Mist and White Collars: Economic Crime in the United States and Japan', *Asian Criminology*, vol. 2, no. 2: 111–126.

Pratt, J. (2007) *Penal Populism*, London: Routledge.

Prideaux, E. (2007) 'World's Suicide Capital – Tough Image to Shake', *The Japan Times*, 20 November.

Putnam, R. D. (2001) *Bowling Alone: The Collapse and Revival of American Community*, N.Y: Simon and Schuster.

Rawls, J. (1973) *A Theory of Justice*, Oxford: Oxford University Press.

Rees, P. (2002) 'Japan: The Missing Million', *BBC News*, October 20.

Research and Training Institute (2000) *Summary of the White Paper on Crime 1999*, Tokyo: Ministry of Justice.

Research and Training Institute (2001) *Summary of the White Paper on Crime 2000*, Tokyo: Ministry of Justice.

Research and Training Institute (2002) *Summary of the White Paper on Crime 2000*, Tokyo: Ministry of Justice.

Research and Training Institute (2003) *Summary of the White Paper on Crime 2002*, Tokyo: Ministry of Justice.

Research and Training Institute (2003) 'Research Department Report 24', *Study Concerning Perpetrators of Domestic Violence (DV)'*. Tokyo: Ministry of Justice.

Research and Training Institute (2004) *Summary of the White Paper on Crime 2003*, Tokyo: Ministry of Justice.

Research and Training Institute (2005) *Summary of the White Paper on Crime 2004*, Tokyo: Ministry of Justice.

Research and Training Institute (2006) *Summary of the White Paper on Crime 2005*, Tokyo: Ministry of Justice.

Research and Training Institute (2007) *Summary of the White Paper on Crime 2006*, Tokyo: Ministry of Justice.

Roberts, A. and LaFree, G. (2001) 'The Role of Declining Stress in Explaining Japan's Remarkable Postwar Crime Decreases, 1951 to 1997', *Japanese Journal of Sociological Criminology*, no. 26: 11– 33.

Roberts, G. S. (2002) 'Pinning Hopes on Angles: Reflections From an Aging Japan's Urban Landscape, in Goodman (ed.) *Family and Social Policy in Japan,* Cambridge: Cambridge University Press.

Rohlen, T. P. (1983) *Japan's High Schools,* L. A: University of California Press.

Rohlen, T. P. (1989) 'Order in Japanese Society: Attachment, Authority and Routine', *Journal of Japanese Studies,* vol. 15, no. 1: 5–40.

Ryan, T. (2005) 'Creating "Problem Kids": Juvenile Crime in Japan and Revisions to the Juvenile Act', *Journal of Japanese Law,* no. 19: 153–188.

Saito, T. and Genda, Y. (2005) 'NEETs: Young People Who Fear Society's Gaze', *Japan Echo,* vol. 32, no. 1: 14–17, February.

Sakurai, T. (2004) 'The Generation Gap in Japanese Society Since the 1960s', in G. Mathews and B. White (eds) *Japan's Changing Generations: Are Young People Creating a New Society?* Abingdon: Routledge.

Samenow, S. E. (2004) *Inside the Criminal Mind,* N.Y.: Crown Publishers.

Samuels, D. (2007) 'Let's Die Together', *The Atlantic Online,* May. http://www.theatlantic.com/doc/print/200705/group-suicide, accessed 17 March 2009.

Sano, Y. and Kittaka, K. (2006) 'Activities by Juvenile Support Centers for Protecting Juveniles', *Current Juvenile Police Policy in Japan,* Police Policy Research Center/National Police Academy of Japan, March.

Sato, H. (2001) 'Atypical Employment: A Source of Flexible Work Opportunities?,'*Social Science Japan Journal,* vol. 4, no. 2: 161–181.

Sato, H., Osawa, M., and Weathers, C. (2004) '"Atypical" and "Irregular" Labour in Contemporary Japan: The Authors Debate', *Social Science Japan Journal,* vol. 4, no. 2: 219–223.

Sato, H. (2001) 'Is Japan a "Classless" Society?, *Japan Quarterly,* vol. 48, no. 2: 25–31.

Sayer, R. A. (1992) *Method in Social Science: A Realist Approach,* London: Routledge.

Schad-Seifert, A. (2006) 'The Gap and the Media', *SSJ Forum Archive,* http://ssj.iss.u-tokyo.ac.jp/archives/2006/06/ssj_4091_re_the.html, accessed 14 November 2006.

Schoppa, L. J. (1991) 'Education Reform in Japan: Goals and Results of the Recent Reform Campaign', in E. Beauchamp (ed.) *Windows on Japanese Education,* Westport: Greenwood Press.

Schoppa, L. J. (2006) *Race for the Exits: The Unravelling of Japan's System of Social Protection,* N. Y: Cornell University Press.

Scraton, P. (2002) 'Defining "Power" and Challenging "Knowledge": Critical Analysis as Resistance in the UK', in K. Carrington and R. Hogg (eds) *Critical Criminology: Issues, Debates, Challenges,* Culllompton, Devon: Willan Publishing.

Sellek, Y. (2001) *Migrant Labour in Japan,* Basingstoke: Palgrave.

Sennett, R. (2004) *The Formation of Character in a World of Inequality,* London: Penguin.

Seto, J. (1999) 'Juvenile Crime. The Current Situation', *Foreign Press Center, Japan.* http://www.fpcj.jp/e/shiryo/jc/jc.html, accessed 30 January 2003.

Shaftoe, H. (2004) *Crime Prevention: Facts, Fallacies and the Future,* Basingstoke: Palgrave Macmillan.

Shimizu, K. and Nakamura, A. (2007) 'Is Help Really on Way for the Working Poor?' *Japan Times,* 7 April.

Smith, D. and Sueda, K. (2008) 'The Killing of Children as a Symptom of National Crisis: Reactions in Britain and Japan'. *Criminology and Criminal Justice, vol.* 8, no. 15: 5–25.

Smith, R. J. (1994) *Japanese Society: Tradition, Self, and the Social Order,* Cambridge: Cambridge University Press.

Smith, R. J. (1997) 'The Japanese (Confucian) Family: The Tradition From the Bottom Up', in T. Wei-Ming (ed.) *Confucian Traditions in East Asian Modernity: Moral Education and Economic Culture in Japan and the Four Mini-Dragons,* Cambridge: Harvard University Press.

Sparks, R. (2001) ' "Bringing it All Back Home": Populism, Media Coverage and the Dynamics of Locality and Globality in the Politics of Crime Control', in K. Stenson and R. R. Sullivan (eds) *Crime, Risk and Justice: The Politics of Crime Control in Liberal Democracies,* Cullompton, Devon: Willan.

Stenson, K. and Sullivan, R. R. (2001) *Crime, Risk and Justice: The Politics of Crime Control in Liberal Democracies.* Portland: Willan Publishing.

Stevens, C. S. (1997) *On the Margins of Japanese Society: Volunteers and the Welfare of the Urban Underclass,* London: Routledge.

Stevenson, H., Azuma, H., and Hakuta, K. (eds) (1986) *Child Development and Education in Japan.* N. Y.: W H Freeman.

Strecher, M. (2008) '(R)evolution in the Land of the Lonely: Murakami Ryu and the Project to Overcome Modernity', *Japanese Studies,* vol. 28, no. 3: 329–344.

Struck, D. and Sakamaki, S. (2003) 'Foreigners Find Divorce Means *Sayonara* to Kids', *Washington Post,* www.davidappleyard.com/japan/jp21.htm. Visited 12 November, 2007.

Suehiro, A. (1998) 'An Introduction to this Issue's Special Topic: Japanese Society and "Community"', *Social Science Japan Journal,* vol. 1, no. 2: 163–164.

Suehiro, A. (2001) 'An Introduction to this Issue's Special Topic: "Atypical" and "Irregular" Labour in contemporary Japan', *Social Science Japan Journal,* vol. 4, no. 2: 159–160.

Sugahara, M. (1994) 'Five Fatal Symptoms of the Japanese Disease', *Japan Echo,* vol. 21, no. 2: 68–74.

Sugimoto, Y. (1997) *An Introduction to Japanese Society,* Cambridge University Press.

Sugimoto, Y. and Mouer, R. (eds) *Constructs for Understanding Japan,* London.

Tachibanaki, T. (2005) *Confronting Income Inequality in Japan: A Comparative Analysis of Causes, Consequences, and Reform.* Cambridge: The MIT Press.

Takahashi, K. (1991) 'Structure of Submission to Authority in Japanese Society: The Interaction between Benevolence and Obedience under the Influence of Confucian Philosophy', Japan Centre for Economic Research, Tokyo, *JCER Discussion Paper,* no. 20.

Takeuchi, Y. (1984) 'Peer Pressure in Japanese Organizations', *Japan Echo,* vol. 11, no. 3: 53–59.

Taki, M. (2003) 'Changes in School Environment and Deviancy – A Survey Analysis and an Intervention Program for Schools', In Foljanty-Jost, G. (ed.) *Juvenile Delinquency in Japan: Reconsidering the 'Crisis'*, Leiden: Brill.

Tamura, M. (2004) 'Changing Japanese Attitudes toward Crime and Safety', *Japan Echo*, vol. 31, no. 4: 14–19.

Tanaka, N. (2006) *Changes in the Criminal Situation and Their Underlying Causes: A Study of Crime Control*, Tokyo: Police Policy Research Center, National Police Academy of Japan.

Tanikawa, M. (2002) 'Lack of Enforcement Weakens Effect of Japan's Divorce Provisions', *International Herald Tribune/The New York Times*, 2 February.

Taylor, I. (ed.) (1990) *The Social Effects of Free Market Policies*, N. Y.: Harvester Wheatsheaf.

Taylor, I. (ed.) (1998) *Crime and Political Economy*, Aldershot: Ashgate.

Taylor, I., Walton, P., and Young, J. (1973) *The New Criminology: For a Social Theory of Deviance*, London: Routledge and Kegan Paul.

The Associated Press (2007) 'Japan Targets High Suicide Rate', http://www.usatoday.printthis.clickability.com/pt/cpt?action=cpt&title=Japan+targets+high, accessed 17 March 2009.

The Economist (2005) October 6.

The Japan Times, 13 October 1997, 1 August 2000, 23 September 2000, 26 November 2000, 14 February 2001, 30 June 2001, 31 July 2001, 20 December 2001, 22 December, 2001, 7 March 2002, 7 February 2003, 13 March 2003, 15 June 2003, 14 September 2003, 7 July 2007, 14 October 2007, 29 November 2007, 24 June 2008, 16 October 2008, 10 January 2009, 07 March 2009, 12 March 2009, 25 March 2009, 14 April 2009, 1 May 2009.

Thornton, E. (1998) 'Japan: Invisible Jobless', *Business Week*, August 17: 27–29.

Tilley, N. (2005) 'Crime Reduction: A Quarter Century Review', *Public Money and Management*, vol. 25, no. 5: 267–274.

Tilley, T. (2002) 'The Rediscovery of Learning: Crime Prevention and Scientific Realism', in G. Hughes and A.Edwards (eds) *Crime Control and Community. The New Politics of Community*, Cullompton, Devon: Willan Publishing.

Time (2001), 26 January.

Times Online (2008), 19 June, http://www.timesonline.co.uk/tol/news/world/asia/article4170649ece#, accessed 12 February 2009.

Tipton, E. K. (2002) *Modern Japan: A Social and Political History*, London: Routledge.

Tokuoka, H. (2003) 'Repression of Deviancy as a Reason for Recent Deviancy', in G. Foljanty-Jost (ed.) *Juvenile Delinquency in Japan: Reconsidering the 'Crisis'*, Leiden: Brill.

Tonry, M. (2007) 'Determinants of Penal Policies', in M. Tonry (ed.) *Crime, Punishment, and Politics in Comparative Perspective*, Crime and Justice: A Review of Research, vol. 36: 1–48. Chicago: The University of Chicago Press.

Toyama-Bialke, C. (2003) 'The "Japanese Triangle" for Preventing Adolescent Delinquency – Strengths and Weaknesses of the Family-School Adolescent Relationship from a Comparative Perspective', in G. Foljanty-Jost (ed.) *Juvenile Delinquency in Japan: Reconsidering the 'Crisis'*, Leiden: Brill.

Traphagan, J. W. (2004) 'Interpretations of Elder Suicide, Stress, and Dependency among Rural Japanese', *Ethnology*, vol. 43, no. 4: 315–329.

Triandis, H. C. (1994) *Culture and Social Behavior,* N.Y.: McGraw Hill.

Triandis, H. C. (1995) *Individualism and Collectivism,* Boulder: Westview Press.

Tsuneyoshi, R. (2004) 'The New Japanese Educational Reforms and the Achievement "Crisis" Debate', *An Interdisciplinary Journal of Education Policy and Practice,* vol. 18, no. 2: 364–394.

Ueda, N. (2000) 'The Collapse of Human Relationships and the Middle Perspective', *Monthly Review,* March.

Ueno, K. (2005) 'Suicide as Japan's Major Export? A Note on Japanese Suicide Culture', *Revisita Espaco Acadêmico,* no. 44, January, http://www.espacoaca-demico.com.br/044/44eueno_ing.htm, accessed 17 March 2009.

Ueno, T. (2007) ' "Precariat" Workers Are Starting to Fight for a Little Stability', *Japan Times,* 21 June.

van Dijk, J., van Kesteren, J. N., and Smit, P. (2007) *Criminal Victimisation in International Perspective: Key Findings From the 2004–2005 ICVS and EU ICS,* http://english.wodc.nl/onderzoeksdatabase/icvs-2005-survey-aspx?cp=45&cs6796, accessed 26 May 2009.

van Kesteren, J. N., Mayhew, P., and Nieuwbeerta, P. (2000) 'Criminal Victimisation in Seventeen Industrialised Countries: Key-findings from the 2000 International Crime Victims Survey', The Hague: Ministry of Justice, WODC.

van Wolferen, K. (1989) *The Enigma of Japanese Power,* N.Y.: Alfred Knopf.

Vij, R. (2007) *Japanese Modernity and Welfare. State, Civil Society, and Self in Contemporary Japan,* Hampshire: Palgrave Macmillan.

Vogel, E. (1979) *Japan as no. 1: Lessons for America,* Harvard: Harvard University Press.

Vogel, S. (1999) 'Can Japan Disengage? Winners and Losers in Japan's Political Economy, and the Ties that Bind Them', *Social Science Japan Journal,* vol. 2, no. 1: 3–21.

Walton, P. and Young, J. (eds) (2002) *The New Criminology Revisited,* Basingstoke: Palgrave Macmillan.

Watabe, M. (2001) 'Youth Problems and Japanese Society', *The Japan Foundation Newsletter,* vol. 28, no. 3/4: 1–5/20.

Watts, J. (2002) 'Public Health Experts concerned about "Hikikomori" ', *The Lancet,* vol. 359, 30 March.

Watts, R. (1996) 'Unemployment, the Underclass and Crime in Australia: A Critique', *The Australian and New Zealand Journal of Criminology,* vol. 29, no. 1: 1–19.

Welsh, B. C. and Farrington, D. P. (2006) *Preventing Crime: What Works for Children, Offenders, Victims and Places,* N.Y.: Springer.

West, M. D. (2005) *Law in Everyday Japan,* Chicago: The University of Chicago Press.

Westerman, T. D. and Burfeind, J. W. (1991) *Crime and Justice in Two Societies. Japan and the United States,* Pacific Grove: Brooks/Cole.

White, M. I. and LeVine, R. A. (1986) 'What is an *Ii ko* (Good Child)?, in H. Stevenson et al. (eds) *Child Development and Education in Japan,* N. Y.: W.H. Freeman and Company.

White Paper on Police (2006). National Police Agency, Japan. Tokyo.

Wilson, J. Q. (1985) *Thinking About Crime,* N Y.: Vintage Books.

Wilson, J. Q. (1993) *The Moral Sense,* N. Y.: The Free Press.

Wilson, J. Q. and Kelling, G. (1982) 'Broken Windows', *Atlantic Monthly,* March: 29–38.

Wiseman, P. (2007) 'A Suicide Epidemic Grips Japan', http://usatoday.com/news/world/2008–07–20-japan-suicides_Nhtm, accessed 17 March 2009.

Wolferen, K. (1990) *The Enigma of Japanese Power: People and Politics in a Stateless Nation,* N. Y.: Vintage Books.

World Health Organization. www.who.int/mental_health/media/japa/pdf, accessed 30 March 2009.

World Health Organization. http://www.who.int/mental_health/prevention/suicide_rates/en, accessed 30 March 2009.

Yakushiji, S. (2003) 'Protecting Children: Keeping Kids Safe Nation's Newest Priority', Asahi.com.http://www.asahi.com/english/lifestye/TKY200310040113.html, accessed 5 March 2004.

Yamada, M. (2000) 'The Growing Crop of Spoiled Singles', *Japan Echo,* vol. 27, no. 3: 49–53.

Yamada, M. (2005) 'The Expectation Gap : Winners and Losers in the New Economy', *Japan Echo,* vol. 32, no. 1: 9–13.

Yamamura, Y. (1986) 'The Child in Japanese Society', in H. Stevenson et al. (eds) *Child Development and Education in Japan,* N. Y.: W H Freeman and Company.

Yamashita, S. H. (1997) 'Confucianism and the Japanese State, 1904–1945', in T. Wei-Ming, (ed.): *Confucian Traditions in East Asian Modernity: Moral Education and Economic Culture in Japan and the Four Mini-Dragons,* Cambridge: Harvard University Press.

Yamazaki, M. (1984) 'Signs of a New Individualism', *Japan Echo,* vol. 11, no. 1: 8–11.

Yoder, R. S. (2003) 'Youth Deviant Behaviour, Conflict, and Later Consequences: Comparison of Working and Middle Class Communities in Japan', in G. Foljanty-Jost (ed.) *Juvenile Delinquency in Japan: Reconsidering the 'Crisis',* Leiden: Brill.

Yoder, R. S. (2004) *Youth Deviance in Japan: Class Reproduction of Non-Conformity,* Rosanna: Trans Pacific Press.

Yonekawa, S. (2003) 'Inequality in Family Background as a Reason for Juvenile Delinquency', in G. Foljanty-Jost (ed.) *Juvenile Delinquency in Japan: Reconsidering the 'Crisis',* Leiden: Brill.

Yoneyama, S. (1999) *The Japanese High School: Silence and Resistance,* London: Routledge.

Yoshida, T. (2000) 'Confession, Apology, Repentance, and Settlement Out-of-Court in the Japanese Criminal Justice System: Is Japan a Model of "Restorative Justice?"', Conference paper.

Young, J. (1999) *The Exclusive Society,* London: Sage Publications.

Young, J. (2007) *The Vertigo of Late Modernity,* London: Sage.

Yuasa, T. (2004) 'Wage Cuts Must be Considered to Protect Jobs', *Asahi.com.* http://www.asahi.com/ebgkush/opinion/TKY200401160136.html, accessed 5 March 2004.

Zielenziger, M. (2002) 'Japan's Suicide Rate Highest among Industrialized Countries', *Knight Ridder Newspapers,* December 18.

Zielenziger, M. (2006) *Shutting Out the Sun: How Japan Created its Own Lost Generation,* London: Doubleday/Random House.

Zinsmeister, K. (1993) 'Japan's næringspolitikk virker ikke' [Japan's Policy On Trade and Industry Does Not Work], in *'Ideer om frihet'* [Ideas about Freedom'], http://www.ideeromfrihet.no/1993–6-zinsmeister.php, accessed 20 October 2005.

Index